CAD

Confessions of a Toxic Bachelor

RICK MARIN

CAD

Confessions of a Toxic Bachelor

HYPERION NEW YORK

Library of Congress Cataloging-in-Publication Data

Marin, Rick.
    Cad : confessions of a toxic bachelor / Rick Marin.—1st ed.
      p. cm
ISBN: 0-7868-6882-1 (alk. paper)
     1. Marin, Rick, 1962– 2. Marin, Rick, 1962—Relations with women. 3.
    Journalists—United States—Biography. I. Title
    PN4874.M4824 A3   2003
    070.92–dc21
    [B]   2002038799

Hyperion books are available for special promotions and premiums. For details contact Hyperion Special Markets, 77 West 66th Street, 11th floor, New York, New York 10023, or call 212-456-0133.

FIRST EDITION

10 9 8 7 6 5 4 3 2

For my parents,
who caused none of my problems

A Note to the Reader

With one notable exception, I have changed the names and identifying details of the women in this book, in the interest of not revealing anyone but myself.

Acknowledgments

Which always sound like a cross between Oscar speeches and high school yearbooks, but many thanks to:

My agents—David McCormick, Leslie Falk, Nina Collins—and editor, Leigh Haber.

My friends John Daly, Tad Low, John Podhoretz, David Eddie and A. J. Jacobs for letting me use their names and some of their jokes.

All readers of the manuscript, including John Capouya, Paul Tough, Ayala Cohen, Julie Mason, Debra Rosenzweig, Eleni Gage, T. D. Richardson and copy ace Frances Marin.

Spiritual advisors Ike ("It's all mental") Smith, Ted Barnett, Cynthia Rowley, Val Frankel, Mark Marvel,

Ellen Tien, Eric Kert, Mark Zimmerman and Marshall Sella (*Io non bev'*).

And last but first, the Cadette, who made it happen.

"The road of excess leads to the palace of wisdom."

—WILLIAM BLAKE

"The older I grew, the more what attached me to women was intelligence."

—GIACOMO CASANOVA

CAD

Confessions of a Toxic Bachelor

PART ONE

"People say, 'Dig deep into your emotions' and I find I don't have any depth or any particular emotions, so it's very tricky."

—HUGH GRANT

HOW DO *YOU* FEEL?

"Yeah, I don't really like to talk about it."

I peeled off my glasses and peered myopically in the general direction of the woman I was trying to impress.

"Talk about what?" asked Chloe, my elusive and enigmatic date, taking a moody swig of cognac.

I gazed deeply into what might have been her left ear and pulled out the only juicy detail on my emotional résumé.

"My marriage."

"Oh," she said, eyes widening.

It was almost three months since Elisabeth had left. Sex was a remote memory even then—and starting to seem like a remoter possibility now if I couldn't "close" tonight. An emergency situation, clearly, or I wouldn't have broken the glass on my fresh personal tragedy. Well, perhaps tragedy wasn't quite the right genre. At twenty-eight, I felt like one of those middle-aged swingers in a sixties sex farce. Peter Sellers chasing Goldie Hawn in *There's a Girl in My Soup*. I had the horn-rims, and Chloe had the gauzy peasant blouse, one that brought to mind the phrase "balloon smuggler." Odd that she'd chosen the same outfit I'd met her in at a party two nights ago. Were those *jodhpurs*? But then, she was a little odd.

A press screening of *The Doors*, the new Oliver Stone movie, had seemed like the perfect date for a chick who claimed Jim Morrison came to her in her dreams. So did Nell's, the ratty-chic club on Fourteenth Street where we were now swilling overpriced paint thinner in an ambience of demimonde decadence. I'd been marshaling all my journalist's powers of observation and interrogation to fill the yawning conversational maw that is a first date—and none of it was working. As we drifted onto the dance floor, Chloe jerked her arms and legs in a bizarre puppet choreography I hoped would translate into bizarre puppet sex later.

"*The CIA*," she shouted into my eardrum, as she hopped and flailed.

"Sorry?" I made a "loud-in-here" gesture and pointed us to the bar.

"They want me. The CIA. I've been told I would make an excellent *courier*."

She pronounced it "coo-re-*yay*," in French, and tipped her glass somberly.

A "Check, please!" moment if ever there was one. I waved to the bartender and said, "Another cognac for the lady."

That was when I peeled off my glasses. And Chloe said, in her enigmatic way, "You were married. Speak about this. . . ."

I had her.

"Three and a half years," I said, caressing the taut, forest green leather of my Conran's couch. "Sort of a . . . youthful, impetuous thing. We'd only known each other five months before the wedding."

"Children?" Chloe clasped her hands under her chin as if she was being told a bedtime story, which in a way this was.

"No kids, no cats," I said, stealing a line from *Sea of Love.*

"Was the breakup—how do you say?—amicable?"

Chloe was from Buffalo. Why did she talk like Catherine Deneuve? No, Kathleen Turner. Same throaty voice and sloppy sexuality.

"Oh, yeah," I said, prying the bottle of Tio Pepe from her hands and taking my own moody swig of dry Spanish sherry. "Totally mutual."

If you call moving in with another guy mutual.

Chloe put her hand on my arm. "Perhaps I have something to make you feel better?"

I leaned in.

She bent over and emptied her bag on the floor.

I pulled away just in time to avoid a head collision as she bobbed up again.

"My demo," she said, handing me an unmarked cassette. "From when they wanted to market me as the next Cyndi Lauper."

Wondering who "they" were, I put in the tape prepared for the worst. What I heard was powerful, raspy—punctuated by well-timed squeals and sighs.

"You sound just like—"

"*Shhh,*" she said, pressing two fingers against my lips. "That *is* Cyndi Lauper. Listen. . . ."

After a scratchy pause, out came another type of noise, this one more like a weasel in heat, or baby seals being clubbed to death— the soundtrack to some wildlife snuff film. I couldn't think of anything to say, so I took an emboldening gulp and went back in. She pulled away.

"You desire to kiss me?"

"Yes," I said, over the din of rabbits being gassed.

"Good. Please do so."

She had an enveloping, mouthy style, like she was trying to get my entire head in there.

I pressed on.

"We must go slow," she said, releasing the drawstring on her peasant blouse.

"Okay," I said, because I would have agreed to anything.

The gauze parted. The boys were out! Again, she pulled away.

"You are very special," she said, planting a beneficent kiss on my forehead on her way to the bathroom.

Coast clear, I turned off the floor lamp with a force that nearly knocked it over, then checked the bottle. I was already well over the legal Tio Pepe limit. Polishing it off, I heard a flush, fluffed my hair and assumed a posture of suave repose.

Chloe returned with the top few buttons on the side of her jodhpurs undone.

"How do I feel?" she said, descending upon me. "How do *you* feel?"

I wondered if she was angling for some dirty talk, some naughty *badinage*? Never my strong suit. Always seemed a bit . . . redundant. In search of a "line," I dusted off a chestnut from my bachelor days.

"I've wanted to do that for a long time," I said, while tugging off one, then the other, of what I now saw were actual riding boots.

I hadn't seen a getup like this since *Emmanuelle 3 in 3-D*.

"Don't speak!" she said. "I understand. . . . Your lady, she is still a part of you, yes?"

We relocated to my antique sleigh bed—another connubial holdover. I hoped I'd achieved critical alcohol mass, the precisely calibrated window between inebriated and insensate. Chloe was blurting words like *now* and *there* into my ear. Nothing bizarre or puppetlike was happening, but the wild ones, I recalled, never turned out to be.

It was still dark when I woke up, drunk. All quiet, except for the steady tick of my Braun alarm. 5:35 A.M. The sheet under me was damp and cold. What was that awful smell? Tea Rose! All of a sudden I became overwhelmingly tired of Chloe and everything to do with her, as desperate to exit this stranger from my bed as I had been to lure her into it. I rolled onto my back and surreptitiously slid on my boxers. Chloe propped herself up on one elbow.

"I think perhaps I am not just a rebound," she said. "I want only honesty."

Really?

"Shall we spend the day together?" she asked, letting the sheet fall off her and favoring me with a coquettish pose.

I caught a glimpse of nipple hair.

"I don't want to throw you off your schedule," I said.

"I'm not temping today," she said.

The message wasn't getting through.

"Do you have enough money for a cab?"

"And what if I did not?"

"We'd go to my cash machine and get some."

That worked.

"We did *not* make love," she said, pulling the sheet up. "We had *sex*."

I went into the bathroom and scrubbed my hands like Howard Hughes. Then, gripping a towel around my neck, locker-room style, I watched her gather her things, a trail of lacy breadcrumbs leading back to the couch. A poignant sight—for someone who cared. The bra and panties that had been such lust-triggers two hours ago had lost all their carnal power. On the floor by her boots was a pair of socks no man should be allowed to see.

"You don't *know* me," Chloe was saying. "I could make fifty thousand dollars in four weeks. . . ."

One advantage of realizing, or deciding, a chick is crazy: no guilt.

"Don't forget your shawl," I said, handing it off on her way out.

On the landing, she stopped to fumble in her bag.

"I can't leave until I have my . . ."

I prayed she wouldn't say "can of Mace."

". . . keys."

Would it kill me to let her stay? I thought. To walk her to a cab?

Then she said, "Please remember that I'm here as a human being."

I shut the door.

WE'VE GOT TO CUT THE CAKE!

In what passed for morning, I staggered into the bathroom and stared down the stranger in the mirror. Who was this *character*? Not me, surely. His jaw was slacker, tongue chalk-coated. He had less hair than I did and it was sticking straight up. He cocked his head one way, then the other, looking for his good side.

Maybe he had no good side.

Hot water bounced off my head as dialogue from the night before ricocheted around my brain. "Speak about this." The *CIA*. Did I really use my marriage as a pickup line? Painful though they were, these memories were untainted by moral qualms. Elisabeth had left me a wounded animal, quick to anger, eager to be left alone in my lair. *I* was the injured party. Besides, Chloe was nuts. Maybe all women were either too sane or too crazy. No, that couldn't be, any more than with men. But men like me are not drawn to Sweet Janes offering sensibly fleeced lives in the suburbs. We crave the unpredictable, the unstable, the Zeldas. Neck-snappingly beautiful or heartrendingly wan. Prone to poetry and drama. Instantly seductive, with a genius for X-rated eye contact and outrageous outbursts, shaming public scenes, cryptic disappearances. Wild and (so the fantasy goes) wild in bed. . . .

The phone interrupted my deep thoughts. I turned off the shower, wrapped a towel around my waist and pictured Chloe hunched over a nearby Bell Atlantic booth.

I screened the call.

"Hey. It's Daly. Calling from your homeland—the Great White Waste of Time. Hope I'm not waking you up. I'm sure you've been at your desk for hours firing off trenchant TV reviews for 'America's Newspaper.'"

Elisabeth, my estranged but not-yet-ex-wife, had always accused me of having superficial male friendships. But when she went back to D.C., John Daly—an old college-newspaper crony—had flown in from Toronto and stayed with me for two weeks, ostensibly to look up some local prospect, but really to make sure I was okay. A purely humanitarian mission, though he spared me the indignity of saying it. Elisabeth, meanwhile, didn't last two days at her best friend Janine's apartment during the worst of our troubles.

"America's Newspaper" was a sardonic allusion to the *Washington Times*—the right-wing Moonie organ. I was its television critic.

I picked up the receiver with a hungover hello.

"You sound bad," Daly said, when he'd finished laughing. "Lying on the couch staring at the ceiling again?"

"No." The leather seat cushions exhaled as I fell backwards into them. "Now I am."

Is this what therapy's like? I wouldn't know. Introspection was not my bag. But shallow men run deep. Underneath my layer of superficiality is a layer of depth, under which there's another layer of superficiality, but under *there* is a bedrock layer of depth. Or so I liked to think.

"How are you doing, really?" John asked, a note of concern slipping out.

"Great!" I said. "Never better. Full recovery. Ready for the next ex-Mrs. Richard T. Mar—oh, by the way, remember Chloe?"

"Who?"

"The chick we met at that party," I said.

"With the Jim Morrison fixation? I'd stay clear of that one."

"I was with her last night."

"I see. Did you 'close'?"

"Postmarital virginity lost, postmarital depression gone."

He paused. "That's very 'evolved' of you."

Daly was a master of invisible quotation marks. Not in the conventional usage of bracketing a cliché, but to convey his second-nature skepticism.

"I told her about Elisabeth."

Another skeptical pause, longer this time.

"You used Elisabeth as 'material'?"

Now I saw eyebrows shooting up into his high forehead.

"Worked like a charm," I said. "Then I kicked her out."

"Oh, no," Daly groaned. "Maybe I should come down there again."

"Nah. I'm fine. Really."

We hung up. I turned sideways on the couch, eye level with the white Ikea entertainment center I had assembled with a young husband's can-do industriousness. It held: my TV (a twenty-seven-inch JVC from Crazy Eddie), VCR, lots of lonely-guy music (Lyle Lovett, Richard Thompson) and lonely-girl music (Sarah McLachlan) to keep the self-pity flowing. On the wall above it was a poster I'd bought from a street vendor on St. Mark's Place for three dollars: a four-by-four, black-and-white photograph of a picador on a bull ranch in Spain. He's on his horse, his back to the camera, resting the tip of his long pic on the ground, bowing his bolero to the earth with a brooding melancholy that matched my own.

I'd dodged a bullet, a lifetime of bullets—that much I knew. And I got custody of this big two-bedroom on West Twenty-fifth Street, in the fashionable Sewing Machine Repair Shop District. The place had a big L-shaped living room, lots of windows, high ceilings and a skylight—the only advantage to being on the top floor of a fifth-floor walk-up. I never would have chosen such a palace for just me, with my income, but I was apartment-hunting for two then. . . .

I rolled off the couch and crawled to the VCR. Two TV movies awaited my critical verdict. Both reviews were due by four o'clock. They could wait. The tape I put in was an amateur production, a short feature shot by my best man at the Algonquin Hotel in the summer of '87. Prone again, remote in hand, I subjected myself, for the first time in three and a half years, to this grainy, hand-held documentary of my nuptials. As the jumpy video started, I remembered John Daly's description of that memorable Memorial Day:

"There was a sense of impending dread. The way Hitchcock would set a wedding for a marriage that would later have lots of dark elements. And the heat!"

The ceremony is a blur—literally. Off-screen, I can hear a couple of my high school friends coughing "green card!" into their hands, *Animal House*–style, at our Canadian-American union. The camera doesn't come back into focus until the reception. I'm surrounded by friends, laughing and talking, when Elisabeth appears in the frame. Her face is whiter than her dress—Kabuki white. And there's a knife in her hand.

"We've got to cut the cake!" she says.

Okay, a cake knife. But her tone has an edge beyond wedding day nerves. My smile goes from relaxed to tense, as I abandon my friends and follow her out of the frame. The video jumps to Elisabeth sticking her tongue out at me over the cake, with me recoiling in hysterical, nervous laughter.

Daly was wrong. Not Hitchcock—the *Zapruder*! Unlike that home movie of the Kennedy assassination, there was no actual blood spilled in my case. But it was a head wound, all right—even if I didn't know it at the time.

We met at *Harper's*. I was twenty-four, recently released into the world by Columbia's Graduate School of Journalism. Most hungry young J-school pups dream of rolling up their sleeves on the Metro desk of some big-city daily with a reputation for hard-nosed newspapering—the *Miami Herald*, the *Philadelphia Inquirer*. My dream job was at "America's oldest continuously published literary magazine."

I was hired as an assistant editor. A glorified intern, I considered myself lucky for the $14,000 stipend that went with the title. The magazine was on the eleventh floor of 666 Broadway, on the corner of Bond Street. I had a window office, with a Village view. Until the fact checker took it. She outranked me on the masthead. Everyone did, except the interns and Joe in the mailroom. I was relocated to a supply closet. I had to buy my own typewriter.

My closet was two doors down from the editor in chief—a dashing dinosaur from the days when cuff-linked intellectuals ruled Manhattan's publishing jungle. He spoke with a nicotined rasp and wore chalk-striped suits tailored before the fall of Saigon.

As an avid subscriber, I'd always marveled at this legendary Man of Letters' ability to begin each month's column with obscure aphorisms from Montaigne or Thomas De Quincey. So when I'd overhear him bellowing at his secretary, I expected it to be something along the lines of, "Where the hell's my copy of Seneca's *Epistulae Morales ad Lucilium*!" But usually it was more like, "Don't pay that American Express bill! I think we've got a few more days."

The aphorisms, I learned (the first time I stepped onto the creaking hardwood floor of his long, airy office), came not from his deep reading of the classics, but from books of quotations. His shelves were lined with them.

The magazine's young publisher also had the stuff of legend in his blood. He was a descendant of the great Chicago newspaperman who cowrote *The Front Page*. Whenever this affable Boy Millionaire poked his head in my door, I was ready to answer any tough journalistic query he wanted to throw at me. Then he'd ask, "Have you seen *Eight Million Ways to Die*? I was thinking of taking a date tonight." Or, "Do you have a paper clip?"

Disillusionment with the literary life, or my lowly station in it, was setting in fast. The new receptionist started just in time.

It was an icy December morning. I showed up at the crack of ten for another day of highbrow serfdom and there she was, behind the desk facing the elevator bank, with her porcelain-doll skin, long black hair and eyes—as Fred Flintstone once said of Wilma, "as black as frying pans."

"Hello," I said, in a low voice suggesting preoccupation with weighty literary matters.

"Hi," she said, with a shy, embarrassed smile.

I tried not to rubberneck as I checked the phone message cubby on the wall behind her—no calls—and made my way down the hall to my supply closet. I took off my heavy tweed overcoat (thrift shop, twenty-five dollars), sat at my desk and tried to contrive an excuse to go back out there. I checked my In box. Just a single fax, obviously several generations old, of blonde jokes.

> *Why do blondes wear panties?*
> *To keep their ankles warm.*

About twenty of those. I knew who'd left them for me. Sue in ad sales. I'd had the occasional impure thought about Sue's professional pumps and ad-gal suits, but she was "business side" and my dating preference was strictly editorial.

I took out a piece of memo paper, stapled it to the blonde jokes and addressed it to Fareed Zakaria. On the RE: line, I wrote "Readings?"

Fareed was one of the unpaid interns, a Yalie from India who affected the genius-on-deck gravitas of a guy who knew he was going to edit *Foreign Affairs* some day. The Readings section at the front of the magazine was made up of excerpts and short bits of information from other publications. I left the FROM: blank, so Fareed wouldn't know whether he had to take the memo seriously or not, and took my little interoffice gag to the reception area.

"Any messages?" I asked.

Her hair was pulled back. She wore a long plaid skirt and a beige sweater with her watch over the sleeve. I noted with approval this little style idiosyncrasy.

"Not since you came in five minutes ago."

"Just checking," I said. "Because I wrote this Op-Ed for *The Wall Street Journal* last week and—"

"You *did*? What on?"

"Colorization," I said.

"What's that?"

"Y'know, taking old black-and-white movies and coloring 'em up. It's got the fruity cineaste types up in arms."

I was sort of half sitting on the side of the reception desk.

"So you were writing about how terrible it is?"

"No, in favor," I said. "I'm a bit of a contrarian. Anyway, I thought some hate calls might have come in for me."

"Nope."

Was she impressed? Did she think I was a pretentious ass? The phone rang.

"Sorry," she said, picking up. "*Harper's* magazine—could you hold please?" And to me: "I better get back to work."

"Right," I said. "See that Fareed gets this. It's fairly urgent."

During another unnecessary and lingering visit (once to replenish her stapler from my stash), I got a name and vital statistics. Elisabeth—"with an *s*"—was twenty-two, freshly minted by Vassar, with a penchant for intrigue. This I learned because on my way out to lunch, she slipped me a *New Yorker* cartoon of a man telling a small boy, "Always exaggerate. It makes life more interesting." She laughed when she slipped it to me, covering her mouth.

"Funny," I said, not really thinking it was all that terrific, and handed it back.

"I cut it out of the office copy," she whispered. "Do you think I'll get in trouble?"

"I won't tell," I said.

What other mysteries lurked under that china-white exterior?

That afternoon, my boss, Terry Teachout, summoned me. Terry had hired me to work in the magazine's Forum section. We organized symposia on literary and political themes. A polymath with a photographic memory, he had me do his grunt work, but he could have done it faster and better himself. When he called me into his office, I think it was just to have someone to talk to.

"Whom do you look like?" he asked, from the floor behind his desk.

He often lay there like that, reading Chesterton. Lower back problems, he claimed.

"I don't know," I said, truthfully.

"Oh, come now. Everyone thinks they look like someone."

"A wasted fan at a Southside Johnny concert once mistook me for Bruce Springsteen," I said. "Now with the glasses, I get Elvis Costello. But if anybody says Woody Allen, I reach for my gub."

"You mean gun."

"No, gub. It's a line from *Take the Money and Run.*"

Crazed laughter from the floor, which stopped abruptly.

"Who's Southside Johnny?"

Terry wasn't Mr. Pop Culture, but I liked him.

"Forget it," I said. "Who do you look like?"

"A cross between Garrison Keillor and Roger Ebert," he said, with enviable self-knowledge.

Our colloquies could go on like that for some time. But now my mind was elsewhere. At the end of Elisabeth's first day, I waited for the elevator, in no hurry for it to arrive, but completely out of conversation. An awkward silence threatened to cancel all my hard work. She broke it with a giggle, mischievously covered with both hands.

"I've already written the first half of a new one-act," she said, lifting a pile of *Harper's* correspondence to flash me a few pages of dialogue underneath.

"Half a play, in one day?"

I was lucky if I produced half a book review during office hours. And I had nothing to do.

"Usually I do more," she said. "But the phones. . . ."

"Can I read them?" I asked.

"Oh, not yet. I don't know you well enough."

I became aware that Sue was standing in her coat, subtly tapping one pump. The elevator dinged. Sue and I got on. I waved to Elisabeth as the doors closed.

"So how's your switchboard sweetie?" Sue asked, taking out a compact and painting the contours of her generous lips.

"Jealous?" I said, as two people got on at six.

She pouted and smacked her lips at me.

Oh, these normal girls, with their makeup and heels, neatly organized wallets and saucy, boyish jokes—why couldn't I fall for one of them?

The doors opened. On Broadway, we stood for a second in the storefront fluorescence of Wings, a discount denim and sneaker emporium that occupied the ground floor of 666—the Building of the Beast.

"Just teasing," Sue said, giving me an over-the-shoulder hair toss. "I love those dark, intense eyes. I'm sure she's very . . . deep."

"She is!" I shouted, as Sue's heels clicked uptown.

I turned to walk home, down Broadway to Houston Street and west six blocks to my building, on the corner of Houston and Mac-Dougal.

"Great Champion!" Wally bellowed, as I walked in. "What happened?"

Wallace W. Poirier Jr., Allstate's top salesman under thirty in the tristate area, was my first roommate and landlord in New York. Wally was a tall, skinny, prematurely bald guy who sold insurance to used car dealers. Amazing salesman. He'd cold-call some angry used car huckster who was all pissed off about his premiums going up and by the end of the conversation would have sold him a new policy and some life insurance on the side. Pure *Glengarry Glen Ross*. "What happened?" was a rhetorical greeting. He didn't want an answer. He just liked looking around like he'd heard a gunshot while saying it.

"Nothing," I answered.

"How's the little woman? Still bustin' your balls?"

I realized he was talking into his headset.

I left him kneeling at his desk in his backless ergochair and shut the door of my room. Another supply closet. There was a bed on one wall and unpainted plywood shelving for my books and clothes on the other, with a built-in desk. But it had a window. I could lean out and look down at the old Italian ladies clinging to their rent-controlled tenements. My friend Dave Eddie once threw up out this window. Memories! That was in the dark days when none of us could get any girly action.

I'd like to blame my difficulties with girls in those months before I met Elisabeth on my sad bachelor pad. But I had a better excuse. No adult woman in her right mind, I reasoned, wants anything to do with an under-twenty-five male. Why would she? Either he's a deadbeat, a student or both. His career, no matter how "promising," is still pure speculation. America's oldest continuously published literary magazine wasn't exactly an aphrodisiac in clubland. Try going up to a chick at the Palladium or Save the Robots and saying, "I work at *Harper's*. No, not *Harper's Bazaar. . . .*"

I wouldn't have to explain to Elisabeth what *Harper's* was. But I couldn't get up the nerve to ask her out. She sent me into some kind of fugue state. In meetings, an editor whose claim to fame was that he once hugged Salman Rushdie would be droning on—"Some kind of *cognitive* thing happens in the writing that really gets at what he's *up to*"—while I stared at the dark down on Elisabeth's arms, fixated on what I imagined was her feral femininity.

Finally, after a couple of weeks of epic elevator bank conversations, she said she was going to a "spoken word" reading on the Lower East Side. Did I want to come?

I have nothing against poetry. In high school, I was already parsing the sonnets of Sir Thomas Wyatt (*"And wilt thou leave me thus/That hath loved thee so long"*—itals. mine). In university, I studied William Blake under Northrop Frye. I went so far as to write an incredibly boring master's thesis on Wordsworth. My academic specialty had always been Romantic poetry. Now, I was ready for the real thing. Romance, that is—not some goateed neo-beatnik pummeling bongos.

"Love to," I said.

That night, as Elisabeth drifted asleep in my cot-sized bed for the first time, I listened to her heart and mine and genuinely believed they were, like in the U2 song, beating as one. Corny? This was love. The real thing. It made all previous poetry seem like juvenilia.

With furtive urgency, we began trading risqué notes on *Harper's* stationery, maintaining the thrilling fiction that there was nothing between us. The office must not know! My apartment was close enough for lunch hours of dangerous passion, though the only real danger was finding Wally working the phone in his ergochair. I'd give him back his wink-and-gun salutation before shutting the door of my bedroom where Elisabeth could read me her plays-in-progress.

I wasn't sure why the daughter of a history professor and a nonprofit fund-raiser wrote in white trash, but it all seemed creative in a way I was not. Even her memos were little pictograms: a house instead of the word *house,* a bee for *be.* She was childlike, though a few dirty martinis made her wantonly grown-up. After work, we often hit Rudy's, a Hell's Kitchen dive, to get drunk and make out in the corner booth. On one visit, we came up for air to the sight of half a dozen grizzled barflies hovering over us, dropping coat hangers on our table—some kind of wino code for "get a room."

Our clandestine trysting had been going for three months when I announced that my student visa was about to expire. We were at the old Blue Bar at the Algonquin. I told Elisabeth that if I went to Canada for a weekend, U.S. Immigration might not let me back in.

"An F One visa is good for a year after graduation," I said. "But after that it's green card or go home."

"I'd marry you," she said. "To keep that from happening."

"Really?"

I pointed the remote at the VCR and pressed stop. That was enough. Shoving the wedding video behind the other tapes, I looked at the two women-in-jeopardy TV movies: *Hell Hath No Fury* and *Lies Before Kisses.*

Not yet.

Toss that Tio Pepe empty. Tilex the bathroom. Expunge all traces of last night. Some men sink into slobdom to soothe their morning-after malaise. I clean. Boiling the sheets in the laundry room downstairs, I resolved not to let another crazy woman into my life, knowing I almost certainly would.

GIVE ME A CALL

To structure my solitude, I'd joined the Y. I'd been hitting it every other morning at nine for the last three months—to drop some of the sedentary depression flab I'd put on in D.C., where my only exercise had been marriage anxiety. My ass was okay, but the gut needed work. It was still less of a six-pack than a keg.

High on Clorox and Fantastik fumes, I put on shorts and a T-shirt and clambered down my five flights to where Carlton the Crackhead was blocking my way out.

Carlton—I named him after the drunk doorman on *Rhoda*—often fed his habit in our phone booth-sized vestibule. "Suckin' on the glass dick!" he'd say, jubilantly. Or "Crack it up! Crack it up!" when he was selling. The remains of a ballpoint pen, its clear shaft blackened with smoke, were on the tiled floor, and the sweetish stench in the air told me Carlton had just finished suckin' on his glass Bic. He was probably harmless, but I stiffened as I squeezed by, or rather over, him then jogged under the Chalfin Thread sign—offering to ser-vice all my industrial-thread needs—and past Manex France Display, purveyors of pertly-nippled mannequins, where I reflexively glanced in the window. (Is it weird to get aroused by a mannequin?) I turned down Seventh Avenue and onto my stretch of Twenty-third Street, which I thought of as the Boulevard of Broken Dreams. There was the Chelsea Hotel, with its Sid Vicious memorial suite; the Associated Blind, whose Seeing Eye Dog poop on the sidewalk in front made you feel guilty for wishing the blind people could pick it up; and the McBurney YMCA, which looked more like the besieged seven-ties police station in *Fort Apache, the Bronx* than a "health club."

The McBurney clientele was mostly preening gay men and ex-cops. I hit the StairMaster, Gravitron, rowing machine—bachelor basic training—and listened to the Chelsea boys trade painful-sounding morning-after anecdotes. "So then *I* was in the sling and he was. . . ." In the mat room, where I did sit-ups, a few of New York's Former Finest—barrel-chested men with spindly legs—leaned on the old leather medicine balls reading the *Daily News*.

It was almost as depressing as the couch. But this is what a man does when a woman exits his life. He tries to restore order and logic, as if there ever had been any. He works out. He tries to come up with amusing nicknames for his surroundings.

Back from the gym, I took another shower and made my daily breakfast of Quaker Oats (regressing to the comfort gruel of my youth) and carbolic Cuban coffee. By 10:30, I was in my small "home office" obsessing over my To Do list.

Wednesday, March 27, 1991:

> WORK OUT
> GO TO A&P
> SUBSCRIBE TO *NYT*

GET LAUNDRY TOKENS
BUY TRASH CAN
MAIL STUFF
CALL ALISTAIR COOKE
REVIEW NBC MOVIES DUE TODAY
SKYRINK TO INVU MOIRA KELLY
WATCH *THE MARLA HANSON STORY*

This was a bad dream, the kind with random celebrities in it.

I wrote three, four, sometimes five pieces a week. Reviews and interviews. No A-listers—I didn't have the clout. I worked the margins. Up-and-comers and has-beens, children and half-wits. The kid who played Urkel, the supergeek on *Family Matters*? That was about my level.

Only one entry on my schedule did not fill me with career ennui: "Moira Kelly." Up-and-coming actresses. No male reporter is immune to them. He knows any starlet worth her salt rubs isn't going to fall for a lowly journalist. But every time he has one of these "dates," he secretly thinks she'll be the exception.

I put on a jacket, carefully knotted a tie, then carefully loosened it, and made sure I had a pen. On the way out, I checked my look in the mirror. A Springsteen line came into my head: *I wanna change my clothes, my hair, my face.*

No time. My date with Moira was at 11:00.

The Skyrink was a refrigerated rooftop way over on the West Side. I was here to observe my subject practice her form for a figure-skating movie. The first thing I observed was that her form was fantastic.

Nose pressed against the Plexiglas boards, I watched this callipygian beauty glide from blue line to blue line in black leggings and a light, tight blue sweater. I began to compose the story in my head.

Fair, with dark hair and
dark eyes, her black Irish
parentage shows . . .

Could I get away with *callipygian*?

Moira—we hadn't met but I was already on a first-name basis—shimmered over and said hello.

"You're younger than they usually are."

"So are you," I said.

Clouds of condensed breath evaporated between us. I followed as she tiptoed into the Skyrink Café—a forlorn arrangement of chipped Formica and ripped orange vinyl.

"Coffee?" I asked.

"I'd love a hot chocolate."

When I returned with our steaming Styrofoam, Moira was unlashing a white skate from her slender ankle.

"Looks like you're really getting into this part," I said, alluding to her upcoming ice-skating romance, *The Cutting Edge*.

"Yeah, but I'm only in character when they yell 'Shoot!' "

I continued composing:

For one so relatively
young, Ms. Kelly takes
a surprisingly old-fashioned
view of her trade. She's no
Method actress . . .

We covered her normal, stable family life on Long Island, her Irish immigrant parents and her acting debut as Yum Yum in a ninth-grade production of *The Mikado*.

"My mother was in *The Mikado*," I said. "In university."

"I *love* Gilbert and Sullivan," she said, spilling her hot chocolate in the heat of the moment. "Oops! Sorry."

"I'll get you another," I said—Sir Galahad, with seventy-five cents at the ready.

"That's okay. Doug always calls me a klutz."

> Too new at the game to be
> slick with the press, she is
> refreshingly nervous and
> without a trace of vanity . . .

"Is Doug your . . . boyfriend?"

"Coach," she said, cocking her head toward the rink. "I don't have a boyfriend. Are you in a relationship?"

I remembered the prime directive of celebrity journalism: *Never* talk about yourself, because they truly *don't care.*

"I was married," I said.

"You were?"

"Yeah," I said, glasses off, myopic gaze on stun. "I don't really like to talk about it."

I clenched my jaw stoically, to signal inner torment, but also to stop my teeth from chattering. It was nippy as hell in here.

"Really?" she said.

Were those Long Island-Irish eyes widening?

"Three years," I said. "Got married after three months. I was twenty-four, she was twenty-two. It was a . . ."—I tried to remember what I'd said to Chloe—". . . youthful, impetuous thing."

Dumb, would be another way to describe it. Warming Elisabeth's cold feet (and mine) with reassurances that we were the perfect couple. My friends were shocked. Mr. Deliberate marrying some chick he barely knew. But I was in love. With her or New York, or some heady combination of the two, I'm not so sure.

"I'm twenty-two!" Moira said.

"I know," I said, then, so I wouldn't sound like a stalker, added, "from the bio."

Looked like her, too: a more famous, slimmer-ankled version of Elisabeth.

"What happened?"

Good question. I wish I had the answer.

"I guess I didn't read the signs."

"Like what?"

"Well," I said. "About six months after we got married, I found all our wedding present thank-you notes hidden under the bed. She told me she'd mailed them."

"Wow."

"After we were married, she was still introducing me as her 'friend.'"

"No way."

"*Break's over, eh!*" shouted a deep, coarse voice.

On the rink, a guy in a Maple Leafs jacket pointed at his watch.

"Sorry. My coach is pretty strict. *Coming!* Hey, if you ever want to hang out or anything. . . ."

Hang out?

She took my pen and autographed her hot chocolate-stained napkin in a strong, feminine hand, then a phone number. I noted the area code.

"Five-one-six?" I said.

"I live with my parents."

With her hardworking, immigrant parents!

"*It's your nickel, princess!*" came the voice from the rink.

"I better go," she said. "Give me a call."

"I will," I said, as she floated out to center ice. "I will."

Walking across Thirty-third Street in the midday sun, another high school song popped into my head. Jethro Tull: "Skating Away on the Thin Ice of the New Day."

I turned down Eighth Avenue in the bright noonday sun. If I'd been a free man three years ago, who knows how much celeb action

I would have gotten? Why *didn't* I let Elisabeth off the hook when I had the chance? Or call it quits on the honeymoon, on one of our windy bike rides through the desolate dunes of Amagansett during a freak cold snap the week after Memorial Day. Impending dread indeed. The beaches were devoid of sunshine or human life. Elisabeth kept complaining that she had no job and no friends in Washington. (Except her best friend, who happened to be moving there, too, but I didn't argue the point.) She didn't want to leave New York, having just arrived. I didn't either. But it was a job, at double my *Harper's* salary. And I could finally put my misspent youth—an eight-hour-a-day TV habit—to good use. To lift her out of her funk, I posed for "wacky" pictures under a marriage counselor's shingle on Main Street. It didn't work.

Two days later, we moved into a light-filled two-bedroom in a cathedral-like prewar on the edge of Adams Morgan—the "funky" section of D.C. (Not until later would I discover that D.C. has no funky section.) The swampy summer heat was brutal. Someone told me the British foreign service considers Washington a hardship post, like Rangoon or Jakarta, because of its tropical swelter. Before we bought an air conditioner, Elisabeth sat in the apartment sweating like a malaria victim while I went off every day to a frostily climate-controlled newsroom with a forty-foot wall of glass facing the lush green of the Washington Arboretum.

The editors and reporters weren't Moonies (well, not many), but occasionally groups of mysterious Korean businessmen toured the newsroom, looking down from the mezzanine level at their ink-stained menagerie. The editor in chief was a perma-tanned former Vietnam correspondent who kept a cot in his office and a collection of uniforms in his closet in the event that he might suddenly be called away to cover some far-flung war zone. Occasionally, there was the embarrassment of a mass wedding.

In our newlywed nest, I tried to replicate the happy home of my youth. I feathered it with junk shop versions of my parents' antiques. I clipped coupons, paid bills on time. But Elisabeth wasn't buying into my domestic idyll. She landed a part-time gig as a researcher for a local talking head, but the hours weren't very demanding. When I called from the office at lunch, she'd just be getting up. She was sleeping later and later. When I put a calendar on the inside of our bedroom door (in my parents' house, there was a calendar in every room), Elisabeth made me take it down. She said she didn't want to know what month it was.

We had long talks about her addiction to the Tweeds catalog. If she wanted to wear long skirts and nubby sweaters and stare off into windswept fields, fine. But my Visa was maxed out, and I was still sponging off my parents. It was bad enough squandering their frugality on my excesses, but hers?

Even when she was home all day, I ended up cooking, squinting over my mother's recipe cards, a dishtowel on my shoulder, while Elisabeth played with her toy theater. On bad nights, I played with it, too.

Her behavior got more and more petulant and inscrutable. I kept up the role of relationship cheerleader. "Everything's going to be fine. . . . We'll work it out. . . . You're doing great."

One boiling, leaden-aired evening, I came home from work to bloodshot eyes and cigarette embers glowing at me from the darkened den. Elisabeth was sitting on the floor.

"What are you doing?" I asked, putting a hand on her shoulder.

"Thinking."

"About what?"

"Nothing," she said. "I can't talk about it."

"Why not?"

"Because."

"Fine."

"Close the door, please."

I made one of my roast chickens (stuffed with an onion and served with baked potatoes and frozen peas). An hour and a half later, I set the table and called, "Dinner!" She dragged herself to the table, ate for a while in silence, then let loose.

"*I* moved here for *you*," she said. "Would *you* go somewhere *I* wanted to live?"

"Like where?" I said.

"Rome," she said.

"Rome?" I asked.

"*Oklahoma.* Rome, Oklahoma."

The stultifying heat and torpor of the nation's capital in the Reagan-Bush years was getting to me, too. But we had different escape fantasies. Mine was New York. Hers was a dustbowl hamlet whose residents were in a constant emotive orgy of door-slamming and colorful Sam Shepard dialogue. She spent long hours on a play "about us" that I was never allowed to see but I imagined taking place in a trailer with tumbleweeds blowing by. I was starting to find her yen for life on the edge less endearing than I once did.

"What would we *do* there?" I asked.

"*Write.*"

"We can write here."

"Get our own trailer," she said, rising from the table and walking to the air conditioner. "Hang out at the Dairy Queen. Everyone in Rome goes to the DQ."

"How could I do what I do in a place where the 'DQ' is the center of intellectual life?"

"You want to stay here writing about . . . dumb TV shows?"

"That's a nice way to describe my career," I said.

True, I'd just finished a five-day series called "Hits from Hell," devoted to dissecting *Mr. Belvedere, Who's the Boss?* and *Matlock,* among other superdreck. But I was no snob. I loved TV. As a critic, I was a takedown artist, a master of finding fault. I was more *My Sister Sam* than Sam Shepard.

Elisabeth took her plate and dumped what was left on it in the trash. At least she was helping clean up.

"I don't plan to do it forever," I said.

She slept in the den that night. The dirty martini days were over.

I used to love her troubled energy. Now I dreaded ministering to her moods. I remember reading that Pierre Trudeau, Canada's playboy prime minister, had a quilt on the wall of the official residence in Ottawa embroidered with his motto, Reason Over Passion. When his young wife Margaret walked out of their marriage, she ripped the thing off the wall and threw it down the stairs. I thought my "reason" would rub off on Elisabeth, but I think it drove her even crazier.

To make up for Rome, we planned a trip across the Pond. My sister, Fran (half sister, really, from my father's first marriage), and her family lived in London. Elisabeth wanted to make a pilgrimage to the grave said to contain Thomas Hardy's heart. I thought it might cheer her up.

The night before our flight, I was busy organizing—my things and hers.

"Maybe you should take the big one," I said, pulling the larger of her two suitcases out of the closet.

"Whatever," Elisabeth said, coiled on the couch like a black cat.

I snapped open the bag and stared at what was inside.

"What's this?" I asked.

"Oh," Elisabeth said, with a challenging feline stare. "I cut my hair and put it in there."

She laughed mirthlessly and walked out of the room.

Cut her hair into a suitcase. Was this something out of *The Bell Jar*? I tried to think through my reaction. Scream for help? Act natural? Say I was going to the corner for milk and never come back?

I grabbed a couple of heavy wool sweaters and stacked them on the bed. *Frommer's* said it could get chilly on the moors this time of year.

"She was such a sweet girl," said my mother, sipping a glass of sangria.

This was a frequent refrain of hers, after the breakup, and she repeated it when they, Fran and Diego, came down from Toronto for my birthday a few days after *l'affaire* Chloe.

We were having dinner at El Quijote, an unreconstructed Spanish restaurant in the Chelsea Hotel. We only went to Spanish restaurants.

My father was exiled from his native land in 1939, after fighting on the Republican side in the Spanish civil war, but he never really left. As a professor (now emeritus) of Spanish at the University of Toronto, he devoted his life to his country's literature and language. All his friends were Spanish. So were all our plumbers and electricians. Everyone in his life was, except my mother. But she had taught high school Spanish and spoke it fluently.

"Who?" I asked her, knowing full well who.

"Elisabeth," she said, raising an eyebrow.

"Oh, right," I said.

"I remember when you called and said you were marrying someone we'd never met, I was worried I wouldn't like her," she said. "But I did. Her family was nice, too."

"Yeah, well," I said. "You didn't really know her."

Neither did I. She wore her makeup to bed every night.

"Where is she living now?" my father asked. "Still in the apartment?"

I didn't want to think about where she was living or what was going on there.

I fished some apple from the bottom of my sangria.

"I think she's staying with her friend Janine."

"Everything seemed fine when we were in Spain," he said. "You seemed to be getting on well."

Sure, when we weren't fighting over every missed train and cramped *pensión* we stayed at, we (or I) put on quite a show for my Spanish relatives.

"I got a letter from Laura," I said—the oldest of my father's three sisters. "She said she could tell I was more interested in Elisabeth than she was in me."

"How could she tell that?" asked my mother, sounding doubtful.

My Canadian half did not always agree with the Spanish half.

"Who knows?" I said. "But in those pictures from the trip I notice my arms are always around her, clutching tight. Never the other way around."

"Interesting," my mother said, still not totally buying it. "She just seemed young to me. Remember that year she came for Christmas and you sent me a list of foods she wouldn't eat? Omelets, boiled potatoes, ground beef, Jell-O—it really made me laugh, that list."

Remember? It was a page long. Who doesn't like Jell-O?

"Didn't that strike you as a little weird?" I said.

"Not really. I figured she'd grow out of it."

She didn't have to be so damned good-natured about it.

The waiter brought the paella, though the entree was really me, lightly grilled.

I hadn't expected this. After the breakup, my Uncle Don—my mother's brother—had sent the perfect letter of condolence: "Heard about Elisabeth. Sorry it didn't work out. Hope you're doing okay." Laconic, sincere, on to other matters. That was how we handled these things in my family.

"I think they're going to lower my rent," I said. "Mrs. Wedig, my chain-smoking German super, offered to knock a hundred bucks off when Elisabeth left. Can you believe it? I don't think that's ever happened in the history of Manhattan real estate."

"We can offer more financial assistance, remember," my father said. "If you need it."

His English, learned in England, was dictionary-perfect, but slightly formal sometimes.

"Thanks. I might take you up on that," I said, scrounging for more fruit in the bottom of my glass.

It was embarrassing, three days away from twenty-nine, still to be on the parental payroll. But at least we weren't talking about Elisabeth anymore.

"Were there . . . *sexual* problems?" my father asked.

I couldn't believe my ears. Maybe it was a function of having older parents (he'd just turned seventy-seven, she was ten years younger), or just the kind of parents I had, but sex was *not* discussed. Not by me anyway, with them.

"No-no-nothing like that," I said, as fast as possible and grabbing a passing waiter. *"¡Más sangría por favor!"*

"As long as you're convinced this is for the best," my father said. "We trust your good judgment."

"I always did," my mother said. "Even when you were little.

My friends were always worried about their children doing dangerous things. But you were such a cautious boy."

The Godfather was on when I got home. I never owned the tape, but if it came on TV, I couldn't not watch to the end. There is no better antidepressant when a man feels lost, in need of a code of conduct and masculine dialogue. We all have our key scenes. I came in on the movie just before mine. Michael is standing guard outside the hospital with Enzo the Baker, protecting his father. After the men sent to assassinate the Don pull away, Enzo's hands are still shaking so badly he can't light a cigarette. Michael lights it for him and, snapping the Zippo shut, notices his own hands are completely calm. That gesture marks his transformation from war hero to Godfather-in-waiting. Michael, the battered idealist, the ruined romantic. Cool, detached, untouchable. But the movie's palliative powers only last until the credits roll and the theme music stops. I tried to think of a line I could apply, like a balm, to my situation.

"She was beautiful! She was young. She was innocent. She was the greatest piece of ass I ever had, and I've had 'em all over the world!"

Not really.

"Tattaglia's a pimp."

Great, but. . . .

"Never tell anybody outside the family what you're thinking again."

No, I didn't even tell anybody *inside* the family what I was thinking.

If I'd given them an honest accounting of the marriage, what would I have said? Year one: *bad.* Year two: better. Almost happy, though I recall a pregnancy scare sending me into night sweats. (She wasn't too thrilled either—another sign both of us pretended to ignore.) Year three: even our goldfish were committing suicide. I found them on the floor halfway between the door and the window. Making a break for it, maybe. I didn't blame them.

We never bickered in front of friends, even though I remember disagreeing violently with almost everything she said. When we were alone, it wasn't so much the fighting as the cold acknowledgment of the other person. Excessive politeness. "Would you mind passing the . . . ?" "Thank you." "You're welcome." I went to movies every night to avoid going home. Elisabeth wanted us to try therapy. I refused. If anybody needed couch time, I argued, it wasn't me.

Why stick it out even three years? Because people say, "Marriage is hard. It takes work." Because I didn't want to go back on a promise. Because I didn't want to admit to the world at large that I'd made a terrible, silly mistake. *(Hey, everyone! That solemn, moving ceremony I asked you to travel hundreds of miles to witness and reward with gifts? I take it back.)* Because I'm Canadian, brainwashed to suffer in polite silence and to do the right thing. And because I still loved her.

In November 1990, she moved out, and in with a guy from her office. "Just a friend," she insisted, nothing more. "Drew." (I always thought of his name in quotation marks.) He'd been over for dinner a couple of times. Never my favorite person. A man doesn't go sniffing around other men's wives. I talked myself into believing her because I didn't like picturing the alternative. My cuckolding. With nothing to keep me in the District of Catatonia, I decided to move back to New York. When I told Elisabeth, she begged to come, too.

"Give me another chance. You *have* to. . . ."

What could I say?

We moved into Twenty-fifth Street just after Christmas, full of New Year's hope. I set up house again—arranging all the furniture, putting up pictures, unpacking books. The idea was that I'd keep sending TV pieces to the *Washington Times* while trying to get a freelance career going. Elisabeth had a job interview that seemed promising. We had a future again.

That first week of January, when she was off at her tryout, I went to see *Godfather III* at the Chelsea. I came home to her coiled on the couch, staring at CNN like she wanted to crawl inside the TV.

The U.S. had begun bombing Baghdad.

"Just when we thought we were out—" I said, giving her a little of my Michael Corleone.

"Shhh," she said, without looking up.

I don't like being *shhh*ed. We watched smart bomb videos for hours, hardly speaking.

"Let's go to bed," I said, finally.

"You can," she said, still not looking at me, and drew her bare, white legs up under her T-shirt tepee.

I waved good night. The old trouble was starting again. This was a mistake. Just when I thought I was out, *she pulled me back in.* I willed myself to sleep. The sound of Elisabeth's voice woke me up. The TV was still on. Was she talking to it now?

I shuffled into the living room.

"I've been trying to get through for an *hour*," she was saying. "Riyadh Hilton! *Fine*, I'll try again in five minutes."

"Who were you calling?"

Now she looked at me, eyelids fluttering in a way that I once associated with flirtation but now knew meant defiance.

"Drew," she said. "They sent him to the Gulf."

Just a friend.

"He works for a talking head," I said, determined not to show the effects of this sucker punch. "On a *local* public affairs show."

"He may be in danger."

"At the Riyadh Hilton?"

"Maybe!" she said to my back, as I retreated to the bedroom and sat on the edge of the sleigh bed.

After a minute or so, Elisabeth's silhouette blocked the light from the doorway. I tried to think of something sardonic to say.

"Fool me twice, shame on me," I said.

I let her make her own way to the Metroliner the next morning.

How long had we lasted, exactly? Heartburned, and not just from the paella, I got out of bed and went into my office to check my Week-at-a-Glance.

I flipped to January 16 and squinted at the words I'd written on that date,

GULF WAR BEGINS

On January 17, I had entered the first-ever personal notation in my all-business diary:

E. SAYS, "IT'S OVER." LEAVES FOR D.C. FOR GOOD, UNDER A CLOUD.

I'd bordered the day in black ink, like a death, then on Friday, wrote,

CALL ABC RE URKEL

So it was a big week.

Monday, April 1, 1991. Another red-letter day in my life-at-a-glance. I turned twenty-nine. My parents gone, I hit the Y, downed my comfort gruel and Café *carbolico*—and quit the *Washington Times*. The Moonies had been good to me, but three years seemed like all my self-respect and so-called career could take. My birthdays are littered with crumpled resolutions and broken promises to myself, but this time I couldn't be talked out of freelancing. Professionally and personally, I wanted my lance free.

Plus I'd just landed a big baldness-cure assignment for *GQ*. Viv, the editor, had complained I wasn't follically challenged enough—not even a bald spot. But I talked my way in, persuaded her that my once-magnificent locks were clogging my shower drain. So when the mailman buzzed from downstairs with a package, I expected my first shipment of Rogaine. But it was from Elisabeth. I squeezed the padded envelope, then ripped it open.

American Psycho, in paperback, with an inscription.

> Hope this doesn't happen to you.
>
> Happy Birthday,
> Elisabeth

Was this an April Fool's joke? Did she somehow hear about Chloe? Never underestimate a woman's clairvoyant powers.

Whatever its intended effect, Elisabeth's twisted birthday offering inspired this Canadian Psycho to spin his own dark yarn. Instead of grinding my way down my To Do list, I started a new file on my IBM XT and typed up the whole Chloe episode. I printed out a slim accordion of form-feed paper in faint dot-matrix type, which I put in a green hanging file labeled Bachelor Hell.

This diary, I daydreamed, would be the basis for my *opus bachelorum*—a novel that would catapult me from obscurity to a velvet-roped VIP lounge where the damsel of my dreams awaited with her own all-access laminate flashing in the strobe light. At last, I'd found my subject, the "material" I always felt I'd been lacking.

In an age of dysfunction, I grew up, by definition, *not interesting.*

Only child of doting older parents. Raised in cozy captivity behind a white picket fence in the "world's most livable city." Never molested by the baby-sitter (I wish). Never even *had* a baby-sitter. My mother stayed home to devote herself to the important work of my care and feeding. My father always had time for me. . . .

Doomed from the start!

My issue was that I had no issues. Oh, I got asthma when I was three—that was a bit rough in the days before inhalers. But I was healthy enough to play baseball and road hockey and indulge in light hooliganism. I was a regular kid, though close inspection of my hobbies might have exposed me as a closet shut-in. Reading, stamp collecting, coin collecting, bottle cap collecting—just about anything collecting. Those plastic price thingies on loaves of bread? I had a shoebox full of them.

But I yearned for a wilder, more romantic life beyond my bread-thingy world. Shy and cosseted, I developed a wide-eyed attraction to anything exciting or damaged, idolizing women with those qualities, but ill-equipped to deal with them. I didn't even butter my own toast until I left home for university. No wonder I became a magnet to women who *threw* toast.

The book would be "semiautobiographical." My stand-in narrator would share my weakness for wan brunettes, *Godfather* obsession and compulsive habit of pointing out famous Canadians. His apartment would be spare and neat—almost, but not quite, gay. Decent-looking guy—hair holding up, though preoccupied with losing it. . . .

Orson Welles said men made civilization to impress their girlfriends. I would amend that to, "to *get* girlfriends." Which was what I needed to do now.

Spring was giving way to summer. Layers were peeling off every day. Bare legs led to bare arms to bare midriffs. . . .

My Bachelor Hell diary was heating up. Or I was.

April 19

Canadian model encounter. Astrid. Asks for the time, then for the subway to 23rd Street.

"We're on 23rd Street," I say.

She's en route to a *GQ* shoot requiring her to pose in a bathtub wearing only a pair of men's shoes.

"I'm doing a piece for *GQ*."

"On what?"

"Baldness cures."

"Oh."

That's not going anywhere. I detect a familiar accent.

"Where are you from?"

"Montreal."

"Did you go to McGill?"

"I finished high school!"

Oops.

"Coffee?" I say.

"I'm really late."

"Can I call you?"

"I'm not allowed to give my phone number out. Sorry."

May 10

First laundry-room pickup. Valeria, a WWF makeup artist. Reddish hair. Strong, Slavic nose and face. On the edge of beautiful. Pre-verbal though. Can't even manage mindless bim babble. Walk her to her building on 26th Street. Stop at the door.

She says, "Where do you think you're going?"

May 12

Film Forum, alone, to see *Ace in the Hole.* Navigate into line in front of petite cutie in shorts and a tank top.

"Big Billy Wilder fan?" I say.

"I'm seeing the French film."

Betty—a dental hygienist. Small and blonde, with the soft face of a nun.

Drink after?

No, girlfriend coming down.

Phone #?

"I don't usually give my number out, but you seem like a nice guy. . . ."

At last! A number. My first prospect since Chloe.

I showed up at Betty the Hygienist's West Village apartment around 7:00 on a cool April evening. Here's a heartbreaking thing about dating: picking a girl up for the first time. The door opens and you see her dressed and made up as pretty as she can be and always a little nervous. What happens next is anybody's guess, but that moment at the door is charged with hope and the triumph of optimism over experience on both sides.

So it was with a forgiving eye that I noted her pilly V-neck sweater, jeans tapered and faded where they shouldn't have been, and heels that didn't really go. That she was no fashion plate shouldn't matter, I told myself. I can get past it, not be so superficial. But I didn't really believe that. *Vogue* was as erotic a publication to me as *Playboy*. Women who assume men are oblivious to the nuances of fashion—this season's sandal, last season's hair—do so at their peril. But I concluded, in my state of sexual dehydration, that, if not an ingeniously sexy outfit, she was trying. I took her to Time Café, on Lafayette Street, and we sat against the black-and-white mural of some western cactus scene. She didn't drink. I did. Perhaps too much.

"I'll have a martinus," I told the waiter.

"You mean a martini, sir?"

"If I wanted two, I'd have asked for them," I said.

"Oh-*kee*," the waiter replied, with what sounded distinctly like insolence.

I turned back to my date, who seemed to be on the waiter's side.

"It's an old Wayne and Shuster joke," I said.

"Who?" she asked.

"Canadian comedy team. It's from their famous Big Julie Caesar sketch. . . ."

Mental note: Lay off Canadian comedy. Instead, I extracted the details of her biography and the biographies of her extended family and friends. I'm an interviewer, not a monologist, at heart. I prefer to get information than give it. I seem *interested*. And I am, I genuinely am, at first.

"I feel like I'm being interviewed," Betty said, at the end of dinner, as I delved into the arcana of her mother's first marriage.

I'd gone too far. When I dropped her off in the cab, she ran away without so much as a good night kiss.

Here's another heartbreaking thing about dating: going home alone, kneading Rogaine into your scalp and watching the 976-PEEE girl on Channel 35.

"The extra *e* is for extra *pee*."

Memorial Day—the wedding anniversary I no longer celebrated—came and went. The days got longer and hotter, with no closure in sight. And not for lack of trying. At work and at play, I was always pitching. During the day, *Spy, Premiere, Esquire*. At night. . . .

Trappist Torrence—a kindergarten teacher who spent mute weekends at monastic retreats and said I had "issues with women" because of how I played Ping-Pong. My tricky spin serve, I guess. Or my triumphant flamenco stomp before smashing a high ball. I should have let her win.

The Mayflower Mademoiselle—Newport-bred and slumming in the Brooklyn DA's office. She seemed promising until she came by my place late on a boiling Sunday afternoon with an unusual request. "Do you mind if I wash my feet?" I pointed her to the bathtub. At dinner, she had an unusual question. "Did you know there's a special section at the video store for anal intercourse?" From her I got a good night kiss. An invitation to Brooklyn seemed in the offing. But as we stood outside the Christopher Street subway, I was compelled to wonder, *Did I just hear her fart?* It is possible to sleep with a woman after almost anything, but that? I let her descend into the subway alone.

Tall Alice—whose job was putting bird sounds on golf games. In a letter to my parents, I wrote,

Tell me: how do I attract these women?

But I knew how. Relentless scheming, plotting and premeditation.

When I first came to New York, I used to Walk the Route before each date—from bar to restaurant to after-hours club. I mapped out every move, then pretended I was making the whole thing up as I went along. Churchill used to stand in front of his bathroom mirror saying, "I did not intend to speak today." That was my approach: rehearsed spontaneity. Now that the city's nightlife grid was no longer unfamiliar terrain, I mentally rather than literally went through my paces, still leaving nothing to chance. I made daily phone calls, worked it like a second job. No, like it *was* my job and freelance writing was something I did on the side. With women whose attention was drifting, I did the whole marriage business.

Apparently my impending divorce made me seem redeemable. I'd shown a willingness to commit, even if it hadn't worked out. Whenever I told Daly about a new girl, he'd ask, with his skeptically inverted commas, "Did you 'take off your glasses'?" This had become my patented move, or moves. The Earnest Swipe (always right to left), the Pensive Nibble, the Rakish Helicopter Twirl—a whole repertoire. I turned my suffering into faked sensitivity.

And still I couldn't close.

This is every man's clean little secret: night after night of exhausting conversation, chasing a few fleeting moments of satisfaction, then not even getting that far. Dating is a salesman's game. One in ten is a good month. Most of the time, you feel like Willy Loman.

The only way a guy can deal with these losing streaks, short of lying, is to mythologize them. I started celebrating my quixotic misadventures in overheated correspondence with a similarly nookie-less writer friend in Toronto, David Eddie.

An update from perdition, dated July 19:

The city is like a kiln. As my drought stretches to Ethiopian proportions, I am struck by this cruel Catch-22: the more time I spend with Betty the Hygienist, the greater my chances of closing but the less attracted I am. Her prudishness has all but killed my desire! And momentum. I have begun to see flaws I would normally have held off noticing until after having sex. Like, as we spend Saturday aft. in Central Park, the dark stubble on her stout calves. . . .

In a cavernous black box at 21st and 11th across from an S&M club, four bottle-blonde Brits with Brian Jones haircuts assume the stage, vocals barely audible. I stand us as close as possible for maximum impact. She's immobile, barely able to speak. I lodge myself next to the Appalachian redhead who got me the tickets. Jeffrey-Ann, a Rolling Stone *scribe, is gyrating in a spandex tube top. When it's over, we all stagger out. The Platonic Hygienist is a blur, running along 21st Street toward civilization, bleeding at the ears from the sonic assault, sobbing something about a cab. I bid her farewell and, thus liberated, go for a nightcap. Noting the lift in my spirits, Jeffrey-Ann shares some of her backwoods wisdom:*

"Chick like that, if you'd hung in for the sex, the sex wouldn't been worth hangin' in for."

And so the days baked and boiled. Thank God for Billy's Topless.

WHAT CAN I GETCHA, HON?

WELCOME ALL OUR FRIENDS

FROM NEW JERSEY

The hand-lettered sign on the wall told you Billy's Topless did not aspire to class. Conveniently situated on the southwest corner of Twenty-fourth and Sixth—a block and a half from my apartment—Billy's had none of the trappings of a "gentlemen's topless lounge." The bouncer did not wear a tuxedo. No lurid carnival barker exhorted patrons to "please welcome *Tia* to our *champagne stage*." There was no cover. But there was always entertainment. A mariachi band. Minor celebrity sightings. (Joe Jackson in a trench coat, trying to blend in.) And a buffet every Friday, though I was never starved enough to approach its sweaty chafing dishes. If not exactly clean, it was a well-lighted place. Strings of Christmas bulbs gave Billy's a year-round festive feel, though from the outside it looked like a biker bar, and for a long time I was too chicken to go in.

Tad got me over that.

I met Josiah O. Low IV—Tad's official WASP name—on a trip to the Cayman Islands in the middle of June to "cover" the swimsuit edition of MTV's *House of Style* and its host, Cindy Crawford, for *Mademoiselle*. Tad was a segment producer and occasional on-air talent. We spent a lot of time together, night crawling and plotting our own TV show. Both activities continued in New York.

It was the end of the day when I showed up at Billy's for one of our creative meetings. Tad was already at the bar, scribbling notes on one of the pads he always carried in his back pocket. He was wearing faded Levi's, cowboy boots, a blue-striped button-down and one of those L.L. Bean duck-hunting jackets. The look was sort of a mixture of Old West and Old Greenwich.

"Yes! Very nice, ladies and gentlemen!" he applauded my entrance.

On or off the air, Tad acted like there was always a camera and a live studio audience taking in his every move. Hanging out with him was like being a guest on his own private talk show.

The barmaid—a gum-popping, leather-haltered Pat Benatar type—was on me in seconds.

"What can I getcha, hon?"

Window-shopping was not encouraged at Billy's.

"Beck's, please," I said.

I'd spent the day on the "hair piece" for *GQ,* interviewing lab-coated transplantologists, tricologists, weavers, thatchers, spray painters. I paid a visit to the Hair Club for Men's Sy "I'm Not Only the President, I'm Also a Member" Sperling. From an old-fashioned rug merchant, I learned the difference between a "Captain Kirk" and a "T. J. Hooker."

I was beat.

"What are you writing?" I asked.

"Notes on our show," Tad said.

The show we had come up with was called *Out There*. It would be a "reality-based comedy"—the kind of investigative humor Tad was already doing as a reporter on *MTV News*. Offering pedestrians who were talking too loudly into their cell phones a quarter to use a payphone, getting people to divulge their obsessive-compulsive disorders, quizzing women about loofahs. Tad was obsessed with loofahs.

Write about TV long enough and you want to be in it, though I was happy to stay behind the camera. In our partnership, Tad was the "idea guy" and I was structure, organization and writing—the weaker link. He was the aggressive front man. As an intern on MTV's *The Big Picture,* Tad once suggested replacing the host, Chris Connolly, with . . . Tad Low. The suggestion was ignored, but I saw his confidence in his own genius as my ticket out of journalism, which I was coming to regard as a mug's game.

Tad had set up a pitch meeting with a development exec at MTV. We were busy honing the proposal.

"Whaddya got?" I asked.

He looked down at his pad, reading his notes. " '*Spy* meets *USA Today*' . . . 'a *Laugh-In* for the nineties.' "

"Like it," I said. "Very high-concept. Any segment ideas?"

"How about the Not-So-Special Olympics? Sports stars compete at fussball. Rappers play Scrabble."

"How could they *not* greenlight this?" I asked.

"They're lucky we're offering it to them. But I have bigger problems right now."

"What?"

"I'm being followed."

"Who's following you?"

"Tamra's ex. That's him."

Tad rolled his eyes toward a guy in shorts and a white polo shirt with a tennis racket under his arm.

"That's not him," I said. "I've seen his picture in her bedroom."

"It sure looks like him," Tad said.

"You gotta dump her. *She's still sleeping with her ex.*"

That wasn't enough reason for Tad, a strange blend of egomania and empathy.

I took out my notepad, flipped past pages of baldness notes, then wrote, Tamra's Good Points and underlined it.

"Okay, good points first," I said. "*One.* No . . . artificial . . . limbs."

"Good," Tad said.

"*Two*," I continued. "Good shoes."

"*Very* good shoes," Tad said.

"*Three.* Good nails."

"Excellent nails. And teeth. That's the first thing I check. It's the only time you get to look directly at someone's skeleton, or DNA."

"*Four*?" I asked.

"Sexually inventive," Tad said.

"That should be higher on the list."

"For number five put 'can cook,'" Tad said, sipping his Beck's. "She makes an amazing chicken-fried steak."

"Got it," I said. "Anything else? No? In that case, I'm starting a new heading."

Bad Points, I wrote, underlining both words.

"Oh, boy," Tad said. "This is gonna come back to haunt me."

"*One*: journal thief. *Two:* picture of ex in bedroom. *Three*: still screwing ex—"

"We don't know that!" Tad said.

"*Four*," I said, relishing my bad-cop role. "Fanatical jealousy— especially bad considering number three. *Five*: boring friends. *Six*:

not funny. *Seven*: actress. *Eight* and *nine*: listens to 'lite-FM' radio. And number *ten* in the Top Ten Reasons to Dump Tamra—you know what this one's gotta be. . . ."

"Can't ride the Reference Train," Tad said.

"Can't . . . ride . . . Train," I wrote, underlined three times.

Riding the Reference Train was a term of Tad's invention. It meant that if he started in on a riff, you had to follow, lead or get out of the way.

"That's a big one," Tad said. "Just last night, I was trying to get her going on loofahs. You know, what's it really made out of—coral? sea sponge? vegetable root?—and how often do you replace your loofah? What parts of your body won't you loofah? Are you an up-and-down, side-to-side, or circular loofah-er? Do you pre-moisten your loofah or enjoy a dry loof? All she said was, 'I never really thought about it.' "

We sipped our beers. AC/DC gave way to James Brown. The music was always good at Billy's. We watched the three "dancers" pick up their tip money and the clothes they'd piled by the mirrored wall behind them and move one station over, or off the stage. They were all shapes and sizes. Well, no three-hundred-pounders. But they weren't all five-foot-five silicone blondes from Boca Raton. That was a rule of the owner, Milton something. (The original Billy was long dead.) Milton was a little old Jewish man—a former Garment Center guy—with an office in the Flatiron Building. His rules were: no breast enhancements, lap work or table dancing. It was like a regular bar, with naked chicks. Our Cheers, only nobody knew your name. And it was here that my inner circle of hardcase single friends could gather to lament our single plight, as if we hadn't chosen it.

Pat Benatar was frowning at our empties.

" 'Nutha round, guys?"

"Keep 'em coming," Tad said.

———

Dousing myself in Rogaine, I crawled, ragged and parched, across the sands of my arid sex life towards one tantalizing mirage after another.

August 13. Nary a drop of juice to enter in the Bachelor Hell diary. I sat at my desk, hunched over the *Times*.

> New York: Today, hot, humid, hazy,
> high 97. Tonight: warm and muggy,
> low 81. Tomorrow: sultry, high 95.

Sultry. The weather was getting more action than I was. Wait. Moira Kelly! No up-and-coming starlet had offered me her number before or since. Why had I let that slide? I knew: fear. I didn't have the stomach for rejection by the fame world. It's one thing to be cold-shouldered by a Trappist kindergarten teacher with no eye-hand coordination, but to be turned away at the velvet rope by an actress. . . .

I sent a copy of my (puff) piece, care of her publicist, with a note. A week later, an airmail envelope came, postmarked Long Island, NY. The letter was typewritten. It thanked me for my "exceptionally flattering" words and said she was flying to the Pacific Northwest to shoot *Fire Walk with Me*—David Lynch's *Twin Peaks* movie—and would need a cup of coffee "and a slice of cherry pie" when she returned. The coffee and pie were, of course, references to well-known bits of *Peaks* mythology. I preferred to think of them as the first entries in the phrase book of in-jokes we would soon be compiling.

She signed off with her parents' phone number.

I called.

"You want Moira?" an older female voice said. "She's in Seattle, I'm afraid."

Two weeks later, when Moira was supposed to have returned, I left another message. No call back. If only I'd phoned sooner! She'd gone Hollywood now. She'd be having affairs with co-stars.

I'd blown my shot.

For the first time in my life, I composed—with Daly's assistance—a personal ad.

> Moderately insensitive bachelor,
> 29, seeks vivacious female with
> highly developed sense of irony.
> Should have seen at least three
> Fassbinder films, without liking
> them. No vegans or spiritually-
> inclined respondents, please.
> Appreciation of P. G.
> Wodehouse, Pee-Wee Herman
> and lingerie an asset.

We wrote it on a plane to London, en route to the Edinburgh Festival—two weeks of high and low culture that are also known for a more-than-usual amount (even for Scottish people) of drinking, fighting and public vomiting. Daly was half-Scot and I was a quarter, freeing us to drown our sex sorrows in whiskey and fish-and-chip oil.

I never placed the ad.

I LIKE CRUNCHY
BETTER THAN
SMOOTHY

We stayed a long bus ride from town with one of the many Daly aunts, who fed us good-natured rebukes and haggis, which suited us fine. Our trip to Edinburgh was not to find women—despite the daily temptations of the translucent-skinned, flame-haired local lasses—but to escape them.

The Soviet Union was crumbling. The papers were running pictures of huge statues of Lenin toppled and desecrated. Every way of life, no matter how corrupt, usually has some guru whose philosophy is either followed to the letter or perverted by his demented followers. Ours was a stand-up comedian named Bill Hicks.

Hailed as "the comic outlaw from the U.S.A.," Hicks wore black jeans, black cowboy boots and stalked the stage of his tent show with the furor of a televangelist. He delighted in offending the woolly, lefty Brits with his pro-smoking, pro-meat, pro-porn politics and drawling, demonic anthems. Daly and I weren't offended. When he performed his song "Chicks Dig Jerks," we felt like he was reading our minds:

> *Hitler had Eva Braun*
> *Manson had Squeaky Fromme*
> *Ted Bundy got lots of dates*
> *Don't know what I'm doin' wrong . . .*

> *I don't pretend to understand*
> *Women's little quirks*
> *There's just one thing I know for sure*
> *Chicks dig jerks.*

After the show, we ran backstage to pay homage. Expecting to fight our way through a throng of devotees, converts and idolaters, we found him standing alone on the grass outside his trailer, puffing away, lamenting his life in Los Angeles.

"Look, it's not even September over here and it's already *fall*," Hicks said, opening his arms to the cool night air. "I love the fall. In L.A., it's eighty-five, sunny and hot. People say, 'Isn't it great?' What are you, *reptiles*? I'm a *mammal*. I have the soul of a poet, not a gila monster! I'm sick of those leather-skinned iguana blondes. I want a witch woman, pallid, with wrist scars—"

"You're describing his ex," Daly said, laughing.

"Except the wrist scars," I said.

"I want wrist scars!" Hicks railed. "I want one with *character*."

"Do you have a girlfriend?" I asked him.

"I think I'm at a point maturity-wise and career-wise right now where I could make a good woman's life a living hell," he said.

"I know what you mean," I said.

Hicks kept chain-smoking and complaining about British food and seemed happy for the company. He was only thirty, but seemed ten years older than us. And wiser. We took "Chicks Dig Jerks" as a *validation* of bad behavior, opting for a literal, rather than ironic, reading of his message.

That was when we instituted the "shot clock."

"You've got thirty seconds to start a conversation and get somewhere—a name, a number—or you have to move on," Daly said, in a Princess Street pub after the show.

"I dunno. I'm not exactly Mr. Goodbar."

"How many months has it been?"

"All right," I said, tilting my pint in the direction of the bar. "That one looks unencumbered."

"The blonde gal?" Daly said. "Looks like she's in high school, too. But if you insist. The clock's ticking. Thirty seconds."

I pimp-rolled over and asked, "Are you with the bride or the groom?"

A horrible line, but if delivered with enough confidence it can throw a chick off and buy some more time.

"Neither," she said, with a hostile look.

Dead air. My ego dangled in the air like a piñata.

She took pity on me.

"I was at the Bill Hicks show," she said. "Fuckin' awesome."

"Us, too," I said, detecting a familiar accent. "Are you by any chance Canadian?"

The look softened to appraising.

"Nova Scotia born 'n' bred."

"Toronto," I said. Then, so she wouldn't think she was dealing with just another hick from the old country, I added, "But I live in New York."

The clock was ticking. How long did I have? Ten seconds? Five?

"*Ooh*, I'd love to go to New York. *Spy* is like my favorite magazine."

"Really," I said, seizing the opening. "I write for them."

Guinness sprayed everywhere. She'd done a spit take! Like she was Jerry Lewis or something.

"I love *Spy*!" she said, dabbing foam from her chin.

We traded names as Daly came over tapping his watch.

"Daly, Kim. Kim, Daly. She's a Bill Hicks fan."

"The perfect woman," he said. "What else can you tell our intrepid reporter here?"

"Well, I like crunchy better than smoothy. I'm a fit model . . ."

Now my eyebrows must have looked like McDonald's arches, though I didn't exactly know what a fit model was. I gladly let her explain. Fit models were a subspecies of women blessed with bodies good enough for designers to test-drive their wares on but barred from runway or catalogue work by some petty imperfection. Something about her nose, she said. It looked fine to me. All of twenty-one, Kim was winding up a backpacking tour with a friend who'd gone home a few days ago. She was staying in a Catholic hostel/hovel for girls. No men allowed.

"This is very dangerous," she whispered, sneaking me in a little after 2:00 A.M.

"Danger is my middle name," I said, in my best Sean Connery.

"Mine's Pussy Galore," she said, stifling a giggle.

We tried to keep quiet, insofar as you can keep the sound of a dam bursting quiet. Four months is a long time. After a few hours of apocalyptic carnality, she regaled me with tales of her previous love mate, a pervert lawyer whose nocturnal needs required her to kneel behind him and administer an asphyxiating headlock while he flipped through her Victoria's Secret catalogue.

Who *are* these guys? Why would they need any of that sicko stuff in the presence of these toned calves, these gravity-mocking breasts? With, in short, a twenty-one-year-old?

"I'm very boring," I said.

"Not!" she said.

I was beginning to appreciate the seductive power of the Older Man. I could now get the girls who were dating guys my age when I was their age. Maybe it was just that I was employed and heterosexual. . . . My reverie was rudely truncated when one of the nuns raided our room and started prodding me with the business end of a broom handle. I guess we hadn't been that silent. As I fled the building into Edinburgh's cobbled streets, I yelled to Kim to come visit me in New York sometime.

"I just might, eh?" she called after me.

Daly and I took the train down to London the next morning, looking forward to a couple of wholesome days of detox at my sister's place.

"The Bachelor Beelzebub works in strange and mysterious ways," I said.

"What's that?" Daly said, looking up from *The Scottish Sport*, a tabloid whose front page was adorned with a "sexy stunna," topless, in a garter belt and red stockings.

"Did I mention she claims to have the sex drive of ten men?"

"A few times," Daly said. "Do you?"

WHERE'S THE
BEDROOM?

My losing streak was over. When I got
back to New York, Tad gave me the news. MTV wanted a half-hour
pilot based on our *Out There* proposal. A greenlight! We found a
lawyer: John Dimes. "Johnny Ten Cents," as we called him. He handled the "deal memo," though neither of us knew what one was,
and an almost negligible sum was involved. Nowhere near enough
for me to restructure the Third World debt I was accruing as a freelancer. Once the show was on the air, we figured, the big dollars
would roll in. We were Hollywood now. Or something. Because
soon my answering machine was lighting up like a pinball machine.

Beep. "Hi-hi, it is me Electra. It was very funny to be talking
with you and your friend Tab at the UN party last night. I certainly
do hoping to see you again. Call me. *Ciao!*"

Beep. "You ol' poon hound. This is Jeffrey-Ann. Ten to eleven

on Monday night and I have a favor to ask. Find me somebody to
have an affair with! I'm sick of my boyfriend. I'm goin' outta my
mind!"

Beep. "Hey, cutie!" *Beep.* "Hiya." "Howdy, pardner." " 'Allo,
luv." "Just checkin' in." "Wanted to see what you're up to."
"Gimme a call sometime." "I'll be home all night." "You can call
late." "Call me!" *Beep-beep-beeeeeep.*

Phone numbers were falling out of my pocket like confetti. I
was working in volume, to make up for lost time and heal my
wounded ego, accumulating trophy vixens and, when I couldn't
pick them off, separating the weak ones from the herd. My letters to
Dave Eddie took on a new tenor:

> *Bachelor Hell rages on, but with grinning twists and randomly*
> *uplifting surprises.*
>
> *Tiina. Two "i"s. ("The extra 'i' is for extra . . .") It's Finnish,*
> *though she's from here. A cultured, balletic creature six years*
> *my elder. Small, bowlike mouth. Met her at a party devoted to*
> *variations on the theme of Finlandia vodka. Thanks to that*
> *nourishing beverage, I soon found myself in an X-rated*
> *embrace on a piece of Scandinavian furniture. Bonus turn-ons*
> *included the facts that she a) has a Ph. D in Eng. Lit. and b) is*
> *opening a restaurant uptown. It's called "Kahdeksantoista*
> *Nalkaista Pyoraa." And you know what that means. "18 Hun-*
> *gry Bicycles." (Tiina thinks it sounds "surrealistic.") No, what*
> *I'm talking about is free dining any night of the week! Needless*
> *to say, I haven't let the lady in on my penurious financial sta-*
> *tus, only because I haven't boffed her yet. Once she has a stake*
> *in me, then and only then do I unlock the bank statement.*

In the middle of this frenzy, I barely noticed the call I'd so des-
perately wanted a month ago, at the end of that long, hot summer.

Beep. "It's *Kim-my.* Just got my ticket. Be in NYC in two weeks. Rest up, eh!"

MTV put us in its satellite building at 1775 Broadway—ten blocks up from its Times Square headquarters. The only "staff" they assigned us was Jill, the production manager whose job was to keep the pennies pinched and report our budget to high command. The receptionist we were permitted to cast ourselves, and did so with maximum immaturity.

Tatia—Tad was ready to hire her on name alone—was a sullen, exotically punctured Eastern-Bloc exile who answered the phone, "*Outs Air.* Whom is callink, please?" I could have listened to her say that all day.

We were having one of our brainstorming meetings in Tad's office when he called Tatia in, ostensibly to try out one of our segment ideas on her, but really so we could watch her take notes in one of her motion-constricting vinyl skirts.

"Okay, Tatia, check this out," Tad said, leaping up to the cork wall where we had all the show's segments on colored index cards. "Have you ever seen those girls in the background of hard-rock videos, gyrating on the hood of a sports car, or trying to dance while this jet of pressurized water sprays against their bikini-clad bodies? Well, not that *I've* noticed or anything. But what if you had rock video girls in your everyday life, *even during life's most mundane activities?*"

Tatia jotted in the glitter-covered notepad resting on her knee.

"Like doing your laundry!" Tad said. "Or making your bed. Or reading your morning paper! And you've got these . . . rock video babes dancing around you."

He mimed a guy reading the paper, with strippers cavorting around him.

Tatia turned a page and kept jotting.

I'd heard Tad's spiel before. We'd been planning this segment for a while. Someone had put out a tape called *Rock Video Girls* and three of its stars were available for promotional stunts.

Tatia's short fingernails were painted a cobalt blue that matched her toes, which matched her bobbed blue-dyed hair and peasant blue eyes—not that *I'd* noticed or anything. I took off my glasses and gave them a twirl.

I seemed to have a thing for receptionists.

"Do you get all that, Tatia?" Tad said, breathing heavily from his exertions.

She shook her bobbed head no.

"What part didn't you get?" I asked.

"Everythink after he say, 'Check this out.' "

The plane was due in from Halifax on Friday evening, at 7:21. I was at gate ten at La Guardia an hour early. Kim was a chick you didn't want to leave unattended. At 7:49, she deplaned in a black mini, white baby-T pulled taut by the world's second smallest backpack, sandals whose vertiginous tilt might have toppled lesser vessels—and this was her *traveling* outfit.

"Hey, you!" she said, throwing her arms around my neck in a sort of "fleet's in!" greeting. She stopped just short of wrapping her legs around my waist.

"Hey," I said, wondering if anyone enjoyed being addressed as *you*. "That's all you brought?"

I picked up the smallish black vinyl duffle bag she'd dropped at her feet and almost dislocated my shoulder. What was in there?

"Just a few essentials," Kim said.

"No jacket?"

"Will we be spending a lot of time outside?"

As Kim passed through the limo gauntlet, I think I saw one of the humid-haired drivers drop his sign. So exhaustively did we reacquaint ourselves with each other during the half-hour cab ride,

I was afraid there'd be nothing left when we finally skidded up to 126 West Twenty-fifth Street.

Carlton was on duty. "Crack mama! Crack mama!" he said, eye-balling Kim and shuffling agreeably out of the vestibule.

"Get outta here!" I said, implying sternness but also, *If you do have a knife, I'm not actually all that angry.*

"That's *Noo* York for ya, eh?" Kim said, with more of the hick Canadian in her voice than I remembered from Scotland.

I knew all too well the effect of beer goggles, but was it possible to have beer *earplugs*? Sex was like crack. You were always trying to recapture that original high.

I followed her up my five flights, mesmerized like a hypnotist's stooge by the metronomic sway of her fit-model haunches. *Must submit to basest desires. Must remember to turn off answering machine.*

"This is the place," I said, panting as I unlocked the heavy black door.

"Where's the bedroom?" Kim asked.

"There," I said, dropping the black bag and rotating my arm to see if I still had the use of it.

She slung the bag onto the bed and pulled the zipper. First came the scented candles, then the erotic potions, safe-sex love oils and mysterious Euro unguents. She inspected each bottle, jar and tube like a commando doing a weapons check, and lined them up on the bedside table. For customs purposes, Kim's luggage might as well have been labeled "dirty weekend."

"You sure you're allowed to bring those into the country?" I asked.

"*Mmm*, flavored condoms," Kim said, extracting a bandoleer of foil packets. "Be right back, lover."

She whipped out a kimono and disappeared into the bathroom.

"No rush," I mumbled.

Was I up to this? Tantric foreplay, aromatherapeutic sexcessories—ritualistic theatrics? Play-acting rapture with a near stranger—that was *my* performance anxiety.

As soon as she came back in, I "took" her, in the suddenly-and-forcefully manner of a romance novel. That much I could act convincingly.

"Do you want to go out?" I asked, riveted by the brick wall outside my bedroom window. "Get some dinner? Drinks?"

"No, I really like this closeness," she said. "Remind me to talk about how I'm feeling about you."

Now she was losing me. How does a few hours of randy spelunking qualify as closeness? She was already on our honeymoon.

"Me, too," I said. "Sure you're not hungry?"

It was getting late. Past 11:00. We weren't going anywhere. She was in the greatest city in the world and didn't want to go out. I smelled like a Thai whore, oiled and unguented within an inch of my life.

"Someday," she said, dozily, "I'll show you Newfoundland."

Not! I thought, wondering what had happened to the tart-tongued spit-take girl. Women have two personalities, the one they meet you with, and the one you meet later. The "later" personality was staying with me for three days.

I woke up in the morning fully moisturized and determined to have a better attitude. *Behold this spray of blonde on my pillow-case!* I exulted. The slender bangled arm resting softly on my chest! Skin the color of golden topping against my white sheets! Panning over all these tantalizing excerpts of womanhood, I thought, *I should be on my knees with gratitude.*

I wondered how long I had before she came to.

"Hi, you," she said, stretching one of her knife-edged calves and drawing lazy circles in the air with her lacquered toes.

"Hi," I said, forcing a cozy smile. "Think I'll just take a quick shower."

"Whatever floats your boat," she said.

I slipped on my boxers and detoured to the kitchen to grab the cordless phone and smuggle it into the bathroom. Turning on the tap in the sink, I speed-dialed Tad.

"*Help,*" I said.

"Why are you whispering? What's that, water running?"

"I'm in the bathroom," I said. "I don't want her to hear. What are you doing tonight?"

"Why? Didn't she just get there?"

"A few hours ago," I said.

"Where is she now?"

"In the bedroom," I said. "Look, I can't be alone with her anymore."

I flushed frantically.

"Was that the toilet?" Tad asked. "Are you taking a leak while—"

"No! You don't understand. I've *run out of conversation.*"

"I thought she was the hottest chick you'd ever met," he said.

"Well, yeah. That's not what I'm talking about."

"Can't do it," Tad said. "Tamra's coming over. We're back together. Which reminds me. About that list—"

"Tomorrow morning, then," I pleaded. "Brunch. Meet us at La Bonbonniere."

"*That's* where you're taking her?"

"She likes greasy spoons," I said. "It's one of the topics we've exhausted."

"I'll try," Tad said, weakening. "I'm not promising anything."

As I clicked off, the door opened. How could I not have locked it? Kim had a towel turbaned around her hair and nothing else. "Want company?" she asked.

I dropped the phone in the sink. The batteries clattered out.

For the rest of the weekend, I contrived to have friends shadow our every movement. By Sunday, we'd stopped having sex—the original reason for her visit. But this is another of every guy's clean little secrets: *sex is not enough*. After two days, the sight of Kim trussed up in her mail-order mantraps was leaving me cold. In fact, I couldn't have been less warm, affectionate or anything she might have hoped for. I knew it was wrong and unkind. She was a sweet girl. But I couldn't face a day of basking in the afterglow or any of that.

Her plane was leaving at 4:00, Sunday. That morning, she said, "I'm trying to decide whether I should let myself get really crazy about you."

Kim professed to be crazy about everything about me, but didn't know anything about me because she *never asked*. Never showed the slightest curiosity about "the man of her dreams."

"I think you're expecting more from this than there is," I said, experimenting with a new policy of openness and instantly regretting it. "I mean, I think you're—"

The phone rang. I stared at it. The machine picked up.

"Hey, there. It's Tiina. I read your piece in *TV Guide* and I thought it was pretty good. I think you certainly give these things as much pizzazz as one could hope for. I'm a hundred percent sure you're busy, but if you want to have dinner at the restaurant give me a call."

My first thought was: *"Pretty" good?* I'd like to see her write five hundred words on the Diet Pepsi Uh-huh Girls. My second thought was: *Kim heard that*.

"I thought you were a nice guy," Kim said, waterworks flowing as she flung her pornophernalia back into her bag and zipped it shut.

Which is worse: to be with a guy who acts like a bastard or one who acts nice then turns out to be a bastard? Men have two personalities, too. I could see in Kim's eyes the awful gap between her expectations and mine. Her flight wasn't for five hours, but she wanted to go *now*. I walked her to a cab. Of course, as soon as I'd gotten rid of her, I wanted her back.

In hopes of drawing some life lessons from my Kim weekend, I repaired to Billy's.

"No man enjoys morning-after brunch," Tad said. "There's never anything to talk about."

He took out his notebook.

"Fuck . . . brunch!" he said, a little too loudly, jotting the words down.

From a stool by the door, the bouncer we called Baby Huey gave us his demented, carny glare.

"Hey, I just had an idea for a recurring segment on the show," Tad went on, still writing. "Mating Rituals. The first one'll be on why men hate brunch."

"It's not just that," I said. "Women blame men for acting fake. Interested when they're trying to get them in the sack, then not spending the night, not wanting to cuddle or spend the day together. But women are the ones speeding from zero to intimacy like a Ferrari. Which is more artificial?"

Tad did his talk-show applause and waved to an offscreen sidekick.

"What could be more *un*natural than sharing a bed with someone you met in a *bar*, when you were both *drunk*," I kept on my rant. "How do they get the moral high ground on this? We *acknowledge* the false intimacy of the situation."

"So how do you avoid the brunch torture?" Tad asked.

"Maybe if you actually liked the chick, you wouldn't mind," I said.

YOU CAN'T BREAK UP WITH ME ON THE PHONE!

The offices of Max P. Markowitz, Esq. & Associates were on the thirty-first floor of the Empire State Building. I knew this was a quality operation when I saw, on the wall of the waiting room, a framed copy of the firm's NYNEX Yellow Pages ad.

Max P., a whale of a man with the look of a bail bondsman, had gotten a friend of mine out of his green card marriage and I was hoping he could do the same for me.

"You been married how long?" he asked me, once he had successfully berthed behind a desk piled high with papers, many of which were take-out menus.

"Three years. Four, I guess. Separated nine months, since January."

"Four years," he said, and wrote it down.

After ascertaining the facts of my case, my legal counsel said a divorce would cost me eight hundred dollars.

"Sounds good," I said.

"You are confident that it will be uncontested?" he asked. "That the spouse will be amenable?"

"No problem there," I said, thinking, *problem there.*

Our relations had not been unamicable, if that's a word, since the *American Psycho* incident, which Elisabeth insisted was just a "little joke." She called me, wrote me. I called back, wrote back. But for reasons I could not fathom, my spouse was resisting legal termination of our marriage.

"I'll have my associates draw up the necessary documents and send them to you, pronto."

On the elevator, I hoped the documents wouldn't contain words like *pronto*, and wondered how the hell I was going to get Elisabeth to sign.

At home, I pulled my Letters file—I kept copies of all correspondence, with everyone—and looked at what I'd sent her over these last nine months. From the beginning, I was conducting a perverse kind of "de-seduction," designed not to win the girl, but to *lose* her. It was like defusing a bomb. The first letter was dated February 14. Valentine's Day.

Please don't think there was any kind of edge or hostility in my voice or that I hate you or that my friends are all whispering evil things about you in my ear. None of that is true. I miss talking to you about everyday things, watching TV, sitting around the apartment together. I'm very concerned about you and worried about whether you're doing okay.

Treat yourself well and don't do anything you know is self-destructive. . . .

Typical, I thought. She leaves me and I'm comforting her. I pulled out another, much later, letter from August 11.

> . . . *For the record, I never tried to persuade you that things could have been solved in "a few soul-searching conversations." And do me a favor: don't mention Drew's name in a letter.*
>
> *Sorry if that sounds curt. I have reason to be.*

Guilting her. Playing the injured party. All very calculated and deliberate. And true. And having no effect. Enough dancing on eggshells. I needed to advance the game, close this chapter, *get it done.*

I started typing a new one, dated November 2, 1991.

> *A couple of things I want you to know. If a cold tone comes over my voice when I bring up the D-word, it's as much for my sake as yours. A degree of dispassion is required to go through with it. Not because I can't wait to be rid of you or anything like that. Just because I don't like this limbo state of neither being married nor not married.*
>
> *The sooner it's over the sooner we can move on to whatever the next phase is going to be.*

I finished with some breezy career updates. No lawyer talk. I'd wait till I had the papers. Serve them in person, like a subpoena. Addressing the envelope, I was once again amazed and irritated that she was still using my last name, with *his* address.

I wanted it back.

I didn't tell Elisabeth about my technical infidelities—the glasses scamming, the inane conversations, waiting jadedly for sex, the empty, hard feeling after.

I mailed the letter on the way uptown to see Tiina. Knowing I wouldn't be paying for dinner, I splurged on a cab to Sixty-sixth

Street between Third and Lex. Tonight was the long-awaited open-ing of Pyoraa. Tiina's partners had prevailed upon her to shorten the name. In the couple of dates we'd had since the Finnish con-sulate, my idealized vision of her as the cultured older woman who would cure my bimbo fever had begun to crack around the edges. I'd seen flashes of neediness, humorlessness, pretension. Which brought out in me flashes of disdain, acerbity and superciliousness. But as she greeted me at the door with her bowlike smile, I reminded myself that, for the moment, she was my best hope.

"Come, darling. I'll give you a tour."

The tour started and ended with the ladies' room. Before I had time to check out the sleek Scandinavian fixtures, my back was against the door and she was looking up expectantly from her knees on the white tile floor, asking, "Why do you like me?"

The service she was performing certainly went above and beyond her duties as a restaurateuse.

"Why not?" I said.

"I want to hear the words," she said, in a breathy voice.

I sensed she was trying to fulfill some "transgressive" fantasy with this Kim Basinger–Mickey Rourke moment. But it's a fine line between sexy and debasing. The whole thing felt a little canned, as it were.

"You have great hair," was all I could muster, and my eye wan-dered to the sign that said EMPLOYEES MUST WASH HANDS.

Waiting at our table, when we got back to it, were her friends Seamus and Bridget Byrne. Like Tiina, they were older (late thirties). An ambassador's son—raised in South America—who said he'd considered going to work at "State" but preferred to serve his coun-try as a nightclub consultant. She did nothing, unless you count drinking with abandon. They seemed highly decadent and worldly.

"I only drink on two occasions," I quoted, raising my Finlandia shot glass. "When I'm thirsty and when I'm not."

"Brendan Behan!" Seamus said.

"Darling," Tiina said. "I was at this—"

"Behan indeed!" I said.

"Good one," Bridget said.

The Byrnes were into their Irish heritage and I was eager to impress. A little pretentious maybe, but I had nothing on Tiina, who had been telling me what unreadable books she was "in love with" and peppering her conversation with Britishisms.

"Darling!" Tiina said, again, more empathically. "I was at a *drinks party* in London a couple of months ago—that time I went over for the week-*end*?—when this enormous *row* broke out over the new A. N. Wilson. *Flaubert's Parrot*? Darling, are you paying attention?"

There were four of us but she kept trying to pull me into a private conversation.

"It's by Julian Barnes," I said, cutting into my reindeer in cloudberry sauce. "Not A. N. Wilson. It's not new."

I hadn't read it, but that didn't stop me from being annoyed. The Byrnes were ordering another bottle of Finlandia.

"If you don't talk to *me* more, I will *stop* seeing you," Tiina said, in a stage whisper.

"Don't *expect* me to talk to you," I said, surprised to hear myself laying into her. "Say something interesting that will make me *want* to talk to you."

Her face twisted with anger as she huffed off. Fine. This erratic emotionalism and bossing me around seemed a bit presumptuous. I turned back to the Byrnes.

"Guess she had to check on the kitchen," I said.

"I doubt she knows where it is," Bridget said.

"She's a *silent* partner," Seamus said, winking.

I had a feeling he was trying to convey something decadent and worldly but I had no idea what, and didn't have time to ask because Tiina was back at the table, in her coat.

"Would you take me home please?"

"It's your opening," I said. "You can't leave."

"Yes I can," she said. "I want to go home."

"Have the graciousness not to make *him* go, too," Bridget said.

Reluctantly, I bid farewell to the table.

"Okay," I said, as we walked along Sixty-sixth Street. "I'm walking you home. I'm paying attention."

I thrust my hands in my coat pockets. Winter was coming, if not quite here. She slipped her arm in mine. I stiffened.

"*Brrr,*" she said, putting her head on my shoulder.

"It's not bad, for November."

"I didn't mean the weather."

The Mr. Freeze treatment was having its desired effect.

"Who played Mr. Freeze?" I asked.

"What?"

"Mr. Freeze. On *Batman.* Cesar Romero was the Joker. Frank Gorshin was the Riddler. . . ."

"I don't look at television."

No, you don't "look at" television. You *watch* it. Several hours a day, if possible. Like *normal people.* You weren't *born* in Finland.

"George Sanders!" I said, triumphant.

We turned down Third Avenue. I continued riding my personal reference train as we rounded the corner of Sixty-third Street.

"Did I make you very angry?" she asked.

"You were being a little high school," I said, to my older woman.

We got to her building.

"It's just that I do like you so," she said, pouting her bowlike mouth and leaning her head back against the front door. "Come in?"

I should peck her on the cheek and walk. Sleep with her again and I'll only be giving her more ammo for her next outburst.

"Just for a minute," I said.

She disrobed. I defrosted.

But my eyes were soon rolling in the dark as she nattered into the pillow.

"This is the thing I like to do most in the world," she said. "Lie in bed and talk and make love and talk."

"*Mmm*," I said.

"I finished *Hotel du Lac*," she said, title-dropping again. "Anita Brookner?"

Will You Please Be Quiet, Please? Raymond Carver?

That week, I screened fanatically. At the *Out There* office, I made sure Tatia announced all calls before putting them through. At home, I let my machine face the world for me.

> *There's a man who leads a life of danger,*
> *To everyone he meets he stays a stranger.*

My outgoing message was the theme song from *Secret Agent Man*. That anyone had the patience to wait for the beep is astonishing, especially the work calls. But it wasn't those calls I was worried about. It was all the others.

Beep. "I haven't heard from you." "You were supposed to . . ." "You didn't . . ." "Is this still your number?" "I hope this doesn't mean . . ." "Where did you disappear to last night?" "I thought you were going to call/be at the party/come to my opening." *Beep-beep.* "Are you on vacation?" "Did you leave the country?" "That was kind of jerky." "Don't bother calling back." "You know my number." *Beep-beep-beeeeep.*

Tiina got me over Thanksgiving weekend, from somewhere in Massachusetts.

"This house is filled with marvelous *bibelots*," was one of the things she said before finally blurting out that the house belonged to the parents of "the guy I'm going out with."

Telling me when she didn't have to was obviously intended to make me jealous. A serious miscalculation. I *wanted* to be the Other Man, if anything, not the boyfriend. I was tempted to tell her, but didn't, that while she'd been gone, I slept with someone else— a graphic designer I was already starting to like even less than Tiina.

"But I'll see you when I get back, won't I?" Tiina asked.

"Sure," I said, resolving not to.

I didn't care. I'd been composing a letter to Julia the whole time we were on the phone.

Julia, my college girlfriend and first lost love, had written me complaining about the "crushing boredom" of life in Toronto. Between the lines, I read possible rapprochement when I went home for Christmas. I wasted no time getting back to her:

Such a sweet and funny letter! You stole the opening sentences from my English papers? I forget if I ever knew that, but I'm flattered. . . .

I told her about the divorce and lifted a Somerset Maugham line, from *The Moon and Sixpence:*

"Why do nice women marry dull men?"
"Because intelligent men won't marry nice women."

Julia always liked it when I quoted. While I was at the computer, I wrote Elisabeth another installment in the de-seduction correspondence:

Got your message. Glad you'll be in New York the week after Christmas. Dinner would be fine. I know you're shaken up by this whole thing, more so than me because my feelings about

*finalizing things are less ambiguous than yours. But we can
talk about that.*

*Call me and, if you leave a message, remember to say when
I can call you back. I know you don't like me to call when you-
know-who is home. . . .*

Evie, the graphic designer, was tiny and birdlike and special-
ized in distressed fonts. I met her at a gallery opening. All style, no
substance. Perfect for me, with my superficial emphasis on clothes
and grooming. While I looked at the pictures, she was doubled over
inspecting the "integrity" of the signage. That got old fast. The location of our farewell, preselected by me, was a townhouse on West
Twenty-third, where she was cat-sitting. I'm allergic to cats, so it
was perfect. I started wheezing, sniffling, rubbing my eyes the
minute I walked in. Adrenaline banished my allergies during sex.
(Always get that out of the way first, before the breakup.) But they
came right back again, to the point where I could barely see or
breathe.

"I can't do this anymore," I said, between puffs on my inhaler.

"Why not?" Evie asked

"I need to see other women." *Puff, puff.*

Perhaps mistaking my symptoms for emotion, Evie changed
her expression to what looked like sympathy, or condescension.

"You're afraid of relationships. We can work through this."

"I don't think so," I said, eyes gushing, lungs heaving.

"I guess we both need some space," she said, unexpectedly,
handing me a Kleenex and sending me on my way.

At midnight, the phone rang. My allergy attack had faded and I
felt sporting. I pictured myself in a bamboo POW cage in 'Nam,
tying a red handkerchief around my head as some blood-crazed VC
barked "Mau! Mau!" at me, like in *The Deer Hunter*. I lifted the
receiver to my ear and shut my eyes.

"*Heyyyyy*, it's Tiina."

This was three weeks after Thanksgiving. My usual strategy—the time-honored not calling and not returning calls—wasn't having its intended effect. She said she was off to Finland in the morning. A hurt, choked sound came into her voice when I said I couldn't see her tonight. I told her it was "over."

"You can't do that," she said.

"You're seeing someone," I argued.

"We broke up. He heard me talking to you at his house on Thanksgiving."

"Sorry, but—"

"YOU CAN'T BREAK UP WITH ME OVER THE PHONE. YOU JUST CAN'T. I WON'T LET YOU."

"Yes, I can," I said, slowly.

"YOU HAVE TO SEE ME. YOU HAVE TO!"

Tears may be an effective emotional weapon against men, but screaming only makes us put up the deflector shields.

"I don't have to do anything."

"I JUST CAN'T BELIEVE YOU WOULD. AFTER EVERYTHING WE HAD. AFTER WHAT YOU SAID—"

Never had I been screamed at like that before. I wanted to preserve Tiina's ravings for the Bachelor Hell archive—for my "novel," which had stalled at thirteen pages. If I was going to be attacked like this, I might as well use it. But I knew I'd never be able to reproduce them from memory. For reporting and interviewing purposes, my phone was hooked up to a tape recorder on my desk.

I hit record.

"I WON'T LET YOU. YOU HAVE TO SEE ME. WE HAVE TO TALK. NOW. RIGHT NOW. I'M COMING OVER."

This could be *Fatal Attraction* territory. I might be dealing with a Rabbit Boiler.

"I'm hanging up now," I said. "I'm hanging up now. I'm . . . hanging . . . up . . . now."

I cradled the receiver, gently, and sat at my desk, wondering what she would do next. There'd be a knock on my door and I'd have to let her in. I did the mature, manly thing.

Ran away.

I considered Billy's, but I'm not good at sitting in bars alone, much less topless ones. The Angry Squire, my nontopless local, was just around the corner, and I *was* angry. Or terrified.

I forced myself to stay a full hour, despite the live jazz. When I got back, no death threats were tacked to the door and my machine wasn't blinking.

I erased the Tiina tape—too cruel, even for me. I vowed to stay in and read more. To go out more. To meet a woman who could save me from all the women I'd already met and wanted to unmeet.

A couple of weeks after the rabbit-boiling call, I hit the play button and Tiina's voice popped out.

"Hi, um. I just got back from an exhilarating *jog* across the Brooklyn Bridge and I thought, maybe we can go out for a *beer* and I can, uh, *deconstruct* your misconceptions of me."

Amazing. No matter how total the freeze-out, they always call—in a month, two months, six months. Trying to reconnect with something that was never really there in the first place. Pride alone would prevent me—and most men—from making that call. One last message from Tiina I did keep on tape:

"I guess I should assume from the silence that this is hopeless, but a month has gone by. Pyoraa closed. I was depressed about it for a while, but it's a *beauteous* day and I'm in this self-confident mood, so I decided to ring. Which is a difficult thing to do, especially when one has made one's self look a fool not two fortnights before. So there you are. I'm going now. Ta-ta."

Ta-ta.

Daly came down for a weekend. We were at Billy's and I was filling him in.

"I just had an idea for a punk anthem," he said.

I watched him write in his clear, even handwriting on a Kinko's notepad.

"Pushing You Away"
For R. T. Marin—A Sensitive Guy.

> *I don't call*
> *And I don't write*
> *And I don't care*
> *If what I'm doing is wrong or right.*
>
> *I don't know what I want*
> *I don't know what I "feel"*
> *And I don't know what it is*
> *You expect me to reveal.*
>
> (Chorus):
> *Don't get close to me*
> *I'll push you away*
> *No matter how hard you try*
> *No matter what you say*
> *Don't search for a reason*
> *Don't search for a rhyme*
> *Whatever it is you're looking for*
> *I know you'll never find*
> *I guess I didn't tell you*
> *This happens every time.*
>
> *Another feeble opening,*
> *Another bad cliché*
> *Talking the night away*
> *As if we're in a daze*
>
> *But we're both just wasting time*
> *That's all pretty clear*
> *Pouring all our heart and soul*
> *Into being insincere*

(Chorus)

Each time this gets started
It seems different somehow
But infatuation fades
I guess you realize that by now

But I'll never say "I'm sorry"
I'll never say "I was wrong"
And I won't really feel so bad
Even when you're gone

(Chorus)

It was for his band, Go! Bimbo Go!

The Rock Video Girls shoot for the *Out There* pilot was at my apartment. The crew came first, to set up. Then Tad came with the props: roller skates, Tide, Cheerios, a gallon of milk.

"It's like we're making some kinky, low-budget porno!" he said, jubilantly.

Even more like it when the three girls showed up, bundled against the mid-December morning in puffy down jackets and carrying garment bags. We'd asked them to bring their own outfits, the skimpier the better. Into my apartment they filed:

Shana, an angular blonde, who on the *Rock Video Girls* tape said she got her first job by auditioning underwearless.

Kat, a petite, top-heavy brunette.

And Stacy-Lynn, an ethereal bombshell who wore around her neck the gold key that proved she had been a Penthouse Pet.

They were all from northern Florida.

"You can change in here," I said, motioning our harem into my bedroom.

Tad was introducing me to a whole new class of women. I was getting paid to cavort with professional sex symbols.

I could tell Tad was in awe of Stacy-Lynn. He hung on her pearls of Pet wisdom. "Everything is sexier when you *do . . . it . . . real . . . slow*," she said, her big golden key glinting in the sunlight.

Tad started walking slowly, talking slowly—antithetical as it was to his caffeinated personality.

"So you used a different name in your centerfold," he said, "Diana—I like that. The huntress. . . . Tell me, do you wear the key all the time? Did Bob Guccione give it to you personally in some kind of official ceremony?"

Humor is an overrated aphrodisiac.

Once they'd suited up in their leather bras, cutoffs and spandex, we got down to business. In the basement laundry room, the roller-skated RVGs squirted detergent and frolicked in the suds around Tad, who was earnestly separating his whites. In my bedroom, they pillow-fought in fishnet body stockings, teddies and boxers (mine), as Tad tried to make the bed amid a flurry of feathers. On my dining room table, they performed suggestive acts with Cheerios as Tad attempted to read the *Times* over his breakfast.

Now that's comedy!

No, comedy was me vacuuming the bedroom after the girls had moved on to the cereal scene, or begging them not to spill milk on my wood table.

Tad had to pull me into the bathroom for a talk.

"Who are you, Felix Unger? Are you losing your mind? There are women out there pouring milk on themselves and you're worried about *staining the table*?"

"My pussy's killing me!" Shana shouted from the living room. "That freakin' detergent got down my pants."

"Maybe you should try wearing underwear," I heard Kat say.

Tad shut the door.

"Chicks like this don't go for guys like us," I said. "We're like another species to them. I'm an intellectual because I wear glasses.

You're the court jester. You might as well be jumping around in a harlequin suit and waving a rattle."

"I think Shana digs you, but fine. More for me. I just don't want to suffer by association."

He left me in the bathroom. I knew, objectively, I shouldn't mind the shambles they were making of my apartment, the havoc bimbo fever was wreaking on my life. I should have been working them as hard as Tad was. But the prospect of the time I'd have to put in, with very little guarantee of a payoff—even with Shana, the brainy one—was too enervating, too soul-sucking. That didn't stop me from posing for a full roll of pictures with the Rock Video Girls, after the shoot was over, as they lounged in various attitudes of undress.

That night, I was watching TV when I heard a rustling sound behind me. It seemed to be coming from the big piece of plastic the crew had wrapped up the mess in. Inspecting the thick, clear plastic more closely, I saw something small and brown moving around very slowly in there. I picked up the whole thing and threw it out the window.

A mouse. Gorged himself on Cheerios, then suffocated.

I preferred not to think about the symbolism.

Elisabeth looked pretty and Tweeds catalogish. But I felt no residual longing. I couldn't quite imagine that we had ever been married, let alone for three and a half years. More than four years now, as we were not yet divorced and wouldn't be unless she signed the papers I passed across a platter of supernachos.

It was a freakishly hot Indian summer day, warm enough to eat in the walled garden of Chelsea Commons, on the corner of Tenth and Twenty-fourth. Lunch, not the dinner she had suggested. More businesslike, I decided.

After wiping off a bit of guacamole, she put the papers down on the table without looking at them.

"If I sign, you won't have any reason to talk to me anymore."

I don't have any reason to talk to you now, either, except to get you to agree to a divorce. That's *why* I talk to you, write you, include you in my life after being betrayed and humiliated.

"Yes, I will," I said.

"No, you won't."

Maybe she knew me better than I thought.

"Yes. I will. You know I will. How could I not talk to you?"

A necessary fiction. If she would just sign her name (my name, "Drew's" name) this second, I could move on. Out of bimbo limbo. End this sorry chapter. Find the next ex-Mrs. Richard T. Mar—

"I'll mail them," she said, and stuffed the papers in her bag. "So, are you going home for Christmas?"

I'M EMOTIONALLY VULNERABLE—AND I'M SEEING SOMEONE

Released by the automatic arrivals doors, I searched the sea of faces in terminal three of Pearson International for my father. He was there, reliable as always, in his familiar winter uniform. Brown blazer with wide seventies lapels over a wool plaid shirt. Checked pants. Heavy beige overcoat, the kind with toggles and a hood, slung over his shoulder. A beret—*boina* in Spanish. Always effortlessly dapper, he only shopped during sales or at bargain stores. I spent a fortune on clothes and seldom felt they were exactly right.

"*Hall-o!*" he said.

He put his hand on my shoulder. That I was taller, and had been for many years, always came as a surprise.

"Hi," I said, patting him on the back.

We had developed no greeting adequate to our affection. A

handshake seemed too formal, a hug too intimate. In Spain, hetero-sexual men kiss and nobody thinks anything of it, as long as there's no tongue involved.

A blast of arctic air seized my lungs as we made our way to the parking lot. Instinctively I tucked my chin into my scarf and hunched my shoulders—muscle memory trained by three decades of Canadian winter.

"You look tired," my father said, undaunted by the cold. "Have you eaten lunch?"

He still walked faster than I did.

"No," I said.

He worried about two things.

"Not working too hard?"

That was the other. I considered telling him about the Rock Video Girls. Or my baldness piece, just out in the December *GQ*, with the embarrassing half-page photo of me with white goo in my hair under a transparent "heat helmet."

"No," I said, trying to keep the arctic air out of my lungs. "I'm not."

We found the car, a 1980 Chevette in two-tone blue. I drove, because he hated to.

Screeching out of the parking lot, shifting gears like a Formula One driver, I swung onto 427 South.

"Your mother and I are very pleased at your successes as a free-lance writer," he said. "I feel confident now you'll make it, finan-cially, as your name becomes more widely known."

"Hopefully you won't have to subsidize me forever," I said.

"Don't worry about that. The point is to do what you enjoy. That's really the only way to do your best work."

"I know."

It started to snow. I turned on the wipers.

"I suppose it's the kind of thing you could do from anywhere. Say, Toronto? We keep hoping for a return of the prodigal."

"Not really," I said, irritated but resisting, out of respect, the impulse to be snippy. "If you're not physically there, you're kind of off the radar."

"Too bad," he said. "It would be nice to have you closer to home."

"I know," I said, again.

Never failed. They still wanted me to move back, after six years. I always acted like it never crossed my mind, but that wasn't quite true. It crossed. Toronto was my alternate future—the clean, crime-free simulacrum of Gotham. American film and TV crews have to import their own garbage up here, only to find it swept up the next morning.

I banked east onto the Gardiner Expressway.

"And your . . . marital status?" my father said.

I knew that was coming, too. Relax. It's natural for him to ask.

"Elisabeth has the papers," I said, in a hurry. "I'm waiting for her to sign."

There was no traffic. Would it be so bad to live in the "world's most livable city"?

"No new girlfriends?"

"Some."

I updated him, putting a light spin on my recent escapades (Finnish Tiina's reindeer restaurant), editing out anything too shameful.

"I suppose your successes in that area were fairly predictable," he said, with an amused grin. "You never had any shortage of pretty girls."

We turned away from the waterfront and up into downtown. Church, donut shop, church, donut shop, church. . . . Pulling into our driveway, I admired, as I always did, our house's comfortingly solid three stories of red brick, with its Tudorish top half. When I was doing my M.A., I lived quite happily in the third-floor suite (living room, bedroom, bath) that I'd annexed in high school. Free room, board, car. I couldn't do that again, I suppose. Live at home. I'd have to get an apartment. Or Julia and I would move in together. Get a house in Rosedale, near my parents. Have a couple of cute kids. . . .

My mother was waiting inside, in the hall by the Christmas tree. I kissed her, delayered and settled into the booth in our sunny yellow kitchen. The clock said 12:30 but the hands started turning backwards as soon as I walked in the door. Nothing changed here, certainly not me.

"You're making me the usual, I trust," I said.

"I am, am I?" my mother said.

"How often do you have your only son to cook for?"

"Not often enough," she said, putting on an apron.

This was a little routine we'd come up with before I left home for university, when I'd persuade her to butter my toast for me because soon she "wouldn't have me around to butter toast for anymore." I played, and preyed, on her bemused indulgence. It worked every time.

"Is that a new shirt?" she asked.

"It is," I said.

A subtle gray rayon check from CP Company, a raffish Italian clothier whose New York operation occupied the ground floor of the Flatiron Building.

"You and your shirts," she said. "Incredible."

"I'm the Jay Gatsby of the Sewing Machine Repair Shop District," I said.

My father let out a short laugh.

"Any soup?" I asked.

"Lentil," my father said. "I made it yesterday."

"Excellent," I said, then to my mother: "I'll have that first."

"Oh, will you?" she said, and brought me a bowl of soup.

My mother had already finished her lunch. My father was starting his. I watched him at the stove making his Spanish omelet, his tortilla. Lately, I had begun to mentally record these rituals of his. It wasn't like I thought he was going anywhere anytime soon. He was a physical marvel, though he did take pills for high blood pressure and an irregular heartbeat.

"And Elisabeth?" my mother asked. "What's going on there?"

"Nothing," I said. "Waiting for her to sign."

"So it didn't work out with the kindergarten teacher?" she asked.

Kindergarten teacher? It took me a second to change gears.

"You mean Torrence?" I asked. "That was a while ago."

"It's hard to keep up," my mother said. "I wouldn't have thought someone who spends weekends meditating at a Trappist monastery was exactly your type."

"Not exactly."

"Unless, of course, she was gorgeous and a stylish dresser," she said.

"Right," I said, smiling. "Those are the important things."

My mother and I had a sort of Bond–Moneypenny rapport that dated to adolescence. Like 007 with Q's clever, chiding secretary, I reported in to headquarters every few weeks, slung my bowler on the hat rack (well, baseball cap) and submitted to an arched eyebrow for my wayward, wastrel ways. "How was your night of debauchery?" had been her opening remark the morning after one of my junior-bachelor-pad soirees—one that ended with me and two grade-nine girls squeezed into my twin bed for a few vigorous rounds of chess.

I slurped my soup.

"Well, if you refuse to divulge any interesting information, it's time for *General Hospital*," she said, and took her tea into the living room.

My father finished his lunch. He ate almost exactly the same thing every day, in exactly the same quantity. Tortilla, soup, crackers with *salchichón* (sausage), a piece of fruit, two cookies and tea. Everything in moderation. I have a dim memory of him smoking after dinner, but this minor vice seemed as incredible to me as if he had once been a heroin addict or a second-story man. He had mastered his appetites. I was in thrall to mine. Would I ever be disciplined, restrained—able to stop at half a glass of wine?

Alone with him, I was always aware of a gap between us. It wasn't that he was "unavailable" or "inaccessible" or any of those dysfunctional-dad clichés. Or even the age difference. More that so many years of his life had been lived before I came into the picture (forty-eight, to be exact) and I knew next to nothing about them beyond the basic bits and pieces I used to impress dates. He was disinclined by nature to talk about himself. And I was embarrassed to ask anything "personal," fully aware that someday I'd regret my timidity. Right now, I had the perfect opportunity to tap into his long life experience and maybe glean some wisdom for my own.

"Guess I'll go do some Christmas shopping," I said.

"I suppose it's time for the *BBC News*," he said, getting up to turn on the radio.

I relayered myself and went back out into the cold. A news junkie, he took politics, national and international, seriously. For him and his generation, history had consequences. For me and mine, there were no consequences—another way I fell short in my compulsive scorekeeping.

DM	RM
Knew one of the great figures of twentieth-century literature, Federico García Lorca, and acted in his traveling theater troupe.	Once met self-published poet Crad Kilodny, who peddled his slim, insane volume *Don't Eat Yellow Snow* on Toronto street corners.
Exiled to French concentration camp after Spanish civil war.	Went to music camp. Fled "the world's most livable city."

Married first wife in England during WWII. Fathered two children.	Split up from first wife while watching the Gulf War on TV. No children.
Happily remarried in Canada for next thirty-five years. Has me.	String of meaningless encounters, dead-end relationships.
Long, distinguished academic career. Many books, awards.	Got word rate up to $1.50

I retraced a familiar trail along Bloor Street and down Yonge, Toronto's main drag, making the gift rounds at stores I'd been going to since I was old enough to shop, then detoured for some Christmas cheer.

"Ri*shard*," Dave Eddie greeted me, in the French/British inflection he liked to affect.

My Bachelor Hell correspondent's semi-fixed address was a garret above the Get It On Boutique, an operation specializing in "Rasta Bart Simpson" T-shirts, in the Jamaican section of Chinatown.

"*Daveed*," I said.

He collapsed his six-foot-five frame into an old sectional sofa that the Salvation Army might have rejected.

"Can I interest you in some homemade vino?"

"Please," I said, examining the bottle's stark black-and-white label.

Entre Deux Travaux

Mise en Bouteille

Dans un Appartement Loyé Contrôllé

"Between two jobs," Dave translated. "Bottled in a rent-controlled—"

"I know what it *means*," I said. "We had the same French teachers, remember?"

"Forgive me, Ri*shard*. Two overlapping hangovers are at present competing for my attention, like evil twins."

I raised my glass.

"Not bad," I said, when I finished coughing.

This might not be such a bad life, back here in the Big Donut, spending leisurely afternoons drinking horrible wine with old friends.

"Alas, it's all I can afford. I spent my last shekels on this suit. Snazzy, no?" A thrift-shop dandy, Dave dressed in heavy tweeds, high-buttoned boots, finger gloves. "Someday, perhaps, I'll ascend to your lofty heights of writerly riches and lingerie-clad nubility."

"I'm still cashing checks from my parents," I said. "How are you doing in that area?"

"You mean my soon-to-be-internationally famous novel, *The Sardines of Poverty*?" he asked, with a finger-gloved flourish. "I've spent the last five years writing the first two pages."

"I meant the nubility."

"Alas, I'm in the lowest pit of Bachelor Hell—the ex-begging circle," he said. "And you?"

"I'm having dinner with Julia tonight."

"In-ter-esting. Rekindling the old college flame?"

Three years together—almost as long as my marriage. We were friends first, for a full semester, then that night at the residence Christmas party when we ended up in my room.

"She wrote me a letter," I said. "Complained about the 'crushing boredom' of life here."

What a prize she was then! Many men desired her, but few could handle her emasculating jokes and flaring temper.

"Sad but true," Dave said. "Didn't she used to call you 'the Minute Man'?"

All in fun. We got each other's jokes. Maybe she hurled the

occasional piece of toast. Maybe we had the occasional brawl, me holding her upside down banging her head on the floor. Or was it the other way around? I fancied myself Richard Burton to her Liz Taylor. A *Taming of the Shrew* kind of thing. That was her first play at McGill. Once we moved in together, it was more like *Who's Afraid of Virginia Woolf?*

"She still doing any acting?" I asked.

"Singing in a band now," he said. "I'm told male fans throw their underwear at the stage."

"I never went that far," I said, and coughed down some more wine.

Julia's face was still a geometry lesson of cheekbones, chin and nose. But the angles were less acute. Some of the edges had rounded off.

" 'Bout time," she said, kissing me on the lips at her town house the next night. "They strip-search ya at the border?"

Lip. That boded well.

"You haven't cut your hair, I see."

"My manager wants me to, but I told him he's a big loser, eh."

Still talking like a teenager, in her satirical version of the local "hoser" accent.

She was wearing a leather skirt with a man's white shirt tucked into it, unbuttoned generously, and black boots.

I unzipped my down bomber jacket, supplemented by several sweaters, scarves, and the mandatory Toronto "toque."

"Gotta get my gloves," Julia said. "Go in and talk to Petey."

Julia's kid brother was in the living room.

A mountain of muscle in a rugby shirt pounced on me and said, "I'm in a band!"

He handed me a flyer. I looked at it.

"Kunt?" I said.

"With a '*k*'!"

"So I see. Very clever. What else are you up to these days?"

"I'm going to Asia next month."

"To find yourself?"

"I find myself every morning," Petey said.

Julia appeared, clutching a pair of red gloves.

"I hate to break up this Socratic dialogue," she said.

"After you," I said.

We went to Le Select, a bistro on Queen Street that was still, six years after I left, the place everybody always went.

"I liked your Morley Callahan article," she said, as I congratulated myself for sending it to her. "You know I was his caregiver for a while. I saw his little pink bum."

"Nice image," I said.

She threw a piece of French bread at me. Just like old times!

"What made you write it?" she asked.

"It just pissed me off that here was one of the few great writers this country has managed to produce," I said. "Knocked down Hemingway in a boxing match in Paris in the twenties and his obit doesn't even make front page of the *Globe and Mail* up here."

"He thought Canadians were boneheads," Julia said. "The fact that they didn't get around to appreciating him till he was like ninety really bothered him. I guess he never should have moved back to T.O., eh?"

We polished off almost two bottles of wine. I was feeling so loose, so back to our old selves once I turned off the engine in her driveway, I didn't even see the need for suave seduction.

"Will we be making out now?" I asked.

"N'oh!" Julia said, giving the word two syllables and letting out a short laugh. " 'Fraid not."

I pretended to be undaunted.

"Why not?"

"*Because.* I'm emotionally vulnerable—and I'm seeing some-one."

Funny. She hadn't mentioned that before.

"Who?" I asked.

She named a tall WASPy guy I knew slightly from grad school. "*Him?*"

"Pickins are pretty slim around here, in case you hadn't noticed," Julia said. "It's all so incestuous and gossipy. You know what you said in your letter about how marriage took you away from yourself? How you can lose your basic self-worth and find yourself in situations where you don't even recognize yourself? That's why it's so nice to see you, because it reminds me of a time when I really liked myself, and my life."

This dramatic monologue was reminding me of some of the not-so-good times.

"So I'm just a *mnemonic*?" I said, having more than a little trouble with the word.

"Except when you threw up in Marnie's hat," she said. "I didn't like my life so much then."

Marnie had been Julia's college roommate.

"I didn't know it was hers!" I protested, laughing. "You sure we can't—"

Julia kissed me. Cheek this time. I watched the passenger door shut, then the door of her house. She'll be sorry she settled for some local loser when I'm a *huge television mogul.*

I burned Chevette rubber out of her driveway. There was a Christmas party I could still make across town. As soon as I got there, the host accosted me with two glasses of red wine and a crazed look in his eye.

"I'm desperate to unload this chick I'm living with," he said, jerking his thumb at a woman I once fooled around with in high school. "Interested?"

It was no better here in the hometown, just smaller—without

the constant influx and outflux of women, the eternal chick renewal of the Naked City. Everyone was still re-dating people they'd known since they were sixteen. It was like a biosphere, with no heat. You can't go home, to your old girlfriend, again.

I took the glass of red wine and promised to check her out.

SOMEONE GOOD

On Boxing Day—as my people call December 26—nostalgia for the old country and the old girlfriend was out of my system. I got back to New York ready to face my answering machine like a man.

Beep. "Well, I guess it's a done deal. So you'll have no reason to talk to me anymore. I hope you're out having fun, on a date or something. Maybe I'll talk to you sometime. G'bye."

"She signed!" I said, out loud.

But for some procedural paperwork in the New York courts, I was a free man.

There was only one thing to do. New Year's Eve was in five days. I made it a "Just Divorced" blowout. I put out a couple of relics I'd salvaged from my grandmother's attic after Christmas dinner: a brass hookah and a wooden plaque painted with two monks sipping wine over the inscription, "Commend a Wedded Life but Keep Thyself a Bachelor."

I was standing at my "bar"—a card table with a lot of booze on it—pouring an el presidente, a Cuban cocktail glowing with blue Curacao, when a woman in surgical scrubs came up to me and pulled something out of a black bag.

"If you're going to prescribe those, you better wear this," she said, handing me one of those headband mirrors surgeons wear.

I put it on.

"Doctor," I said, bowing.

She had thick, shortish mousy hair in a sensible ponytail. Expectant, mischievous eyes. A little skinny.

"No, you're the doc," she said, adjusting my mirror. "I'm just a lowly student. My name's Kay."

She shot me her hand. The geeky calculator watch I put down to long hours studying. The other accessory—that black doctor's bag—more than made up for it.

I poured her an el presidente and for my pitch replaced the old Elisabeth marriage material with some budding-TV-genius stuff. Now that I was divorced, I wouldn't need her anymore. But I took off my glasses anyway.

"Your life is so glamorous," Kay said.

"Sorry to be going on about it," I said, after a judicious lapse of time.

Let her move onto her own territory.

Started at Stanford, transferred east to do ob-gyn. *A doctor!* was all I could think as she ran down her résumé. Think of it! In no need of career-coddling. Supercompetent. Engaged in the serious business of saving lives. The anti-Elisabeth. She kept saying she had to go, then staying for another el presidente, blinding me with science.

"You know, there's no hard data showing that pterodactyls really existed," she was saying. "I did a paper in premed at Stanford arguing that they're just a conspiracy dreamed up by some misguided paleontologists."

"Excuse me," I said. "It's time for my medication."

I stood in front of my bathroom mirror trying to think up probing questions, remarkable insights—*anything*. My main concern was not getting Kay to sleep with me, but, I fancied, something bigger. I'd spent so much time "pouring my heart and soul into being insincere," I'd forgotten how to act with a girl I actually liked. Was I giving away too much—or too little?

"It's so much fun talking to you," she said, when I found her still in the spot where I left her. "I can't believe I met someone good."

Neither could I.

PART TWO

"Alas, the love of women! it is known
To be a lovely and a fearful thing."

—BYRON

ARE YOU THE ONE?

"This is insane," I told Tad. "No way is MTV going to let us air leak an internal memo. We *work* for MTV."

Tad did sort of a half roll off the purple bean bag he used as an office chair and flew at the bulletin board, jabbing at one of the colored index cards tacked to the wall.

"Temp . . . Spies," he said.

"Yes, I know that's what the segment is *about*."

Underneath the index card was a photocopy of a memo an intern had leaked us commanding MTV VJs to refer to Michael Jackson as the King of Pop "at least once per week until further notice."

"We're *subversive*," Tad said. "That's why they want our show," he said. "They need us more than we need them. It's part of their identity to make viewers think they're edgy when really they're this giant corporate behemoth."

Jill, the production manager, walked by Tad's door and out of the office.

"Where does she *go* all the time?" I asked.

"Probably spying on us," Tad said.

"I guess you're right about the memo."

He'd worked for MTV a lot longer than I had. Since college, anyway. And he was my partner. I needed a guy like him to take my career to the next level. Fearless in the face of authority. Unwaveringly self-assured. He wasn't sitting around dithering, *I should write a book . . . I should work at a magazine . . . I should. . . .* He knew what he wanted. Kind of like Kay.

"Maybe I can get Kay to leak us some hot ob-gyn document," I said.

"Oh, yeah. Doctors have a big sense of humor about their work."

"No, she's pretty irreverent," I said.

Tad fell back into his bean bag.

"So is she, like, a *licensed* physician?" he asked.

"Just a student," I said. "Second year, I think."

"Think? You've been out three times!"

"Twice. My party doesn't count."

"The night you meet counts," Tad said. "I didn't really get a chance to talk to her, but she seemed very animated."

"I see serious possibilities," I said. "She could be the end of my Year of Living Idiotically. She's really—"

"What I need to know is, can she actually *practice* medicine?"

Tad ran his hand over his closely cropped hair. I sensed an ulterior motive.

"Why?" I asked, looking at him sideways and furrowing my brow.

"I need a prescription. My doctor cut me off. Called my consumption rate 'substance abuse.'"

I thought, for a moment, about what medication Tad could be on. "Prescription for what?"

"Minoxidil."

"*Rogaine?* I'll give you one of the leftover bottles from my baldness piece."

"No good. I don't have time for over the counter. I'm on a super-concentrated dosage. This hairline situation is getting out of control. Yesterday Tatia asked me if I went to Woodstock."

He was cutting it shorter and shorter—the only way to go for the balding guy who wants to avoid the Bozo look. But I shared his pain. You can control the gut, the ass—the other signs of male-pattern aging. But not the hair. Women will say they don't care—but only to guys who are losing it.

"I'll ask," I promised.

At the end of our third actual date, Kay took me to a boring med-student party in Brooklyn. She must have appreciated my sacrifice, because when we got to her building, she invited me up for "hot chocolate."

Cute euphemism, I thought, until she said, "Now you just sit," and disappeared into the kitchen.

Apparently, she actually *meant* hot chocolate.

The apartment, on Sixty-ninth Street over by York, was standard East Side cookie-cutter whose only distinguishing feature was its extreme neatness. Guys have the reputation for being slobs, but I'd seen some scary female living quarters. The promiscuous dust bunnies, impenetrable closets, bathrooms in which every surface inch was occupied by ancient, crusting hygiene and grooming products. What pleasure I got just from Kay's small bookcase. Even though it was filled exclusively with textbooks (not even potboilers or chick lit), the spines were lined up exactly the same distance from the edge of the shelf. As mine were.

The room felt familiar, like I'd been here before. I picked the

Time magazine off the glass coffee table in front of me. It was three months old. The only other reading material offered on the table was *The Diagnostic and Statistical Manual of Mental Disorders*. I hefted it and skimmed the table of contents.

" 'Schizoaffective Disorder,' " I shouted at the kitchen. " 'Shared Psychotic Disorder, Cyclothymic Disorder—' "

"The *DSM*!" Kay shouted back. "Isn't it great? Becky, my psych-major friend, gave it to me. But it's kinda become my favorite new bedtime reading."

I kept reading: " 'Obsessive-Compulsive Disorder, Separation Anxiety Disorder—' "

The kettle screamed. Kay brought out two steaming mugs. I sipped.

"You might want to dip another brown crayon in here," I said.

"What?"

"Old Peanuts joke," I said. "Lucy brings Charlie Brown a hot chocolate and he says—ah, it's not important."

And it wasn't. I saw a bright little girl cramming her brain with empirically useful math and science while I binged on junk culture—cartoons, sitcoms and *The Mike Douglas Show*.

We talked about the party, about her fellow med students. After washing the mugs, she rested her head in my lap. I bent over to kiss her but couldn't reach. She stood up, then started walking backwards towards her bedroom, crooking her finger for me to follow.

"The doctor will see you now," she said.

I knew this place felt familiar. It was a waiting room!

A white cumulus of duvet covered a futon that took up most of the floor. It was like walking into a white-on-white cocoon. I was just getting acquainted with Kay's amazingly firm breasts when she reached into her white dresser.

"That's the second-biggest jar of K-Y I've ever seen," I said, when I saw what she was reaching for.

"Really? What was the first?"

"Forget it. It's an old *Get Smart* joke."

The rest of what she called her "toys" were a first, too. Some sheltered life I'd led.

This was too good to be true—a high-functioning career gal who transformed into a full-on futon freak. Later, in the darkened porn theater of my mind, I ran trailers of our life together. Me in my library of idiosyncratic literary gems. Her thriving practice and prestigious hospital affiliation. Our precocious tots. Hot chocolate every night. *Keep those dirty movies to yourself*, I thought, drifting off. You'll jinx it.

The answering machine woke me up.

"Hey, it's Mike. From the party last night? Just thought I'd [inaudible] and see if you were free this weekend, maybe we could go out and [inaudible] or something."

I sat up in bed and looked at Kay, who was listening, too. I was stunned.

"You gave your number to . . . a guy at the . . . party?"

"Yeah." She stifled a giggle that struck me as weirdly childish. "Don't worry. I'm not going to call him or anything."

"Oh, good," I said, with plenty of sarcasm.

"What could I do?" she said.

"Not give it to him."

"He asked. It was easier. You don't understand. You're not a woman."

She got out of bed and walked out of the room.

I considered making a stand—getting dressed and slamming the door behind me. My half-Latin blood had been roused. But the manly move was to stay, I decided, intensely aware of the symbolism of every move at this formative relationship juncture. I could live with her giving out her number this early in the game. But I needed to eclipse any rivals for her affection.

"You're still here," she said, beaming, when she came out wrapped in a white towel.

I was on the couch by then, reading the *Times* in my boxers.

"I can get to work a little late," I said, pulling her down. "I'm the boss."

"Wha'ho!" Tad said, when I got in, more than a little late. "Weren't you wearing that shirt yesterday? And those pants? And those shoes? Let me guess—"

Tatia appraised me with an expression somewhere in between curiosity and indifference. These inscrutable Slavs. What hidden depths lurked under that blue hair and Goth makeup?

"I'm sure Tatia has work to do," I said.

"No she doesn't," Tad said. "Anyway, this is work. You, evidently, got lucky last night and we, it just so happens, are off-lining the Mating Rituals segment today, remember?"

"Off-lining" was tedious work—watching hours of raw video and writing a log of all usable bits with the relevant time codes for the "on-line" editing session.

"Oh, right," I said, trying to feign enthusiasm. "MTV wants the presentation reel by next week, right?"

"They'll get it when we're ready," Tad said. "Tatia, would you mind coming and recording the time codes?"

She cupped the phone with a heavily ringed hand and whispered, "Lowren is on the phone."

Lauren, the MTV executive in charge of our show, had been calling several times a day in the last couple of weeks. Tad was not entirely diligent about returning the calls. "It'll make them respect us," was his argument. I bowed to his experience in dealing with suits, but pointed out that our suit was a woman and not calling back might set off a train of unpleasant associations. "Or it'll make her want us that much more," I said.

"Say we'll call her back," Tad instructed Tatia, and we got down to work.

The next time I saw Kay, I brought out the big guns: my photo albums.

Relationships are all variations on a school-yard dare: "I'll show you mine, you show me yours." With the unself-conscious egotism of an only child, I gave her the guided tour of my childhood, my nice family, my whole happy life up to but not including the marriage debacle. Those albums stayed on the shelf. I was trying to erase Elisabeth from my permanent record, though her persistent calls and letters made that difficult. The latest said she was marrying "Drew" and could I send some pictures of her family from our wedding? I pulled and mailed the ones she wanted. No letter, no note. Now that she'd signed the divorce papers, I didn't have to worry about hurting her feelings.

Next, the yearbook. I pointed out my high school friends, who I was still in touch with, lost track of.

Kay looked with interest at my graduation photo—and the quotes next to it.

"I like the Jack Kerouac quote," she said, reading. " 'The only people for me are the mad ones.' "

"My *On the Road* period," I said, affecting wry amusement at my jejuneness.

"I don't know if I like the Maurice Chevalier one," Kay said, frowning. " 'Thank heaven for little girls'?"

I eased the yearbook out of her hands.

"Well, I . . . had a bit of a weakness for the younger grades. . . ."

She gave me a worried look.

"I think I read something in the *DSM* about that. The Lolita Syndrome."

"No, it wasn't like that. . . . More like I was seventeen, she was fifteen. . . . We played a lot of chess . . ."

"I'm just teasing," Kay said. "Wanna see how I lost my virginity?"

The yearbook fell on the floor.

———

A few nights later, at Kay's, she offered some reciprocal sharing: a snapshot of herself in starkly clinical profile, naked from the waist up.

"This one was taken in the doc's office, before the implants."

"*Implants?*"

The information rattled me. They seemed so . . . perfect. I felt like an inexperienced idiot for not knowing, but it was my first hands-on encounter with silicone.

"I did the inconspicuous thing," she said, with that slightly off giggle again. "Only went up to a C-cup."

Frankly, I would have preferred a B. Or not to have known at all. But marriage to Elisabeth had made me a sucker for full disclosure. From now on, when it came to women, there was no such thing as too much information.

I handed back the picture. For the bulletin board above my desk, I selected a more . . . innocent shot. Kay at age six, freckled and beaming a manic grin.

I couldn't get enough of her.

We went to movies, made dinner at each other's apartments, were stamped with approval by each other's friends. ("He's great!" "She's hot.") I'd even stopped marking in my calendar the times we "did it"—a habit of my single days I had now outgrown.

Occasionally a spat tested our more-than-willingness to make up.

We were at my place watching *The Appointments of Dennis Jennings*, a short HBO film I was writing about for *TV Guide*. In it, a superneurotic guy is being tormented by his sadistic shrink. Steven Wright and Rowan Atkinson—hilarious.

Not to Kay.

"A real therapist would never do that," she kept saying. "No way."

"It's a character," I said. "It's *co-me-dy*. Do you want to watch something else?"

"No, if you say it's funny," Kay said, "I'm sure it is."

Everything was fine by morning.

Then one chilly Saturday afternoon in late February, we were at the Gap when Kay squeezed into my dressing room, closed the door behind her and said it.

"You're so cute. I love you."

Is it just me or is it always a thousand degrees in these dressing rooms? That was a bit of a leap, I thought. From *cute* to *love*. More than a bit. That was Evel Knievel jumping the Grand Canyon. We'd been dating—what?—six weeks? Things had been cruising along nicely, but this stopped me in my tracks. Did I love her back? I didn't know. I'd vowed not to say those words again except to the next woman I married—possibly not even then. I scrambled to draft a response and threw her a wise, closed-lipped smile.

"You love me," she answered for me. "You're crazy about me."

I ran my hand through her hair and added a knowing wink. That night, in the duvet cocoon, she whispered in my ear.

"Are you the one? The one my mother told me about?"

I offered a nonrejecting but noncommittal reply, smiling with some vigorous eye contact. She was turning me into Marcel Marceau.

Unfortunately, the lights were out.

"Are you the one?" was going into the museum of all-time cringe lines, in the display case next to "Be strong for me." And yet, I wasn't ready to rule her out. I needed advice, sage counsel on how to proceed. Not from Tad. He'd say anything to keep his Minoxidil connection alive. Podhoretz, my old *Washington Times* editor, had just moved back to New York. He had an answer for everything. Not necessarily the right answer. "I give great advice," he often said. "I just can't live my own life out of a paper bag." But an answer.

A large man of infinite appetites (gastronomical, cultural, intellectual), he attended all Broadway plays and musicals in previews, saw every movie, Hoovered *The Times, Time, Newsweek, The New Yorker, New York, National Review, Commentary, The Nation, Vanity Fair, The New York Observer*, etc., etc., the day they hit the newsstand—and still found time to read most important and unimportant new books, maintain a running episodic knowledge of prime-time television, scour the Internet and devote hours on the phone to idle gossip.

I told him about Kay.

We were killing time in the comic book store down the block from the Chelsea Cinemas, waiting for the 2:30 *Wayne's World*. He pulled *Vampire Hunter D* out of the rack and said, "Do you realize guys jerk off to this stuff?"

"You were saying," I said, pulling him back on track. "The Heisenberg Principle?"

"Saying 'I love you' is the Heisenberg of relationships," he declaimed. "The act of observing the thing changes the thing being observed. The woman says, 'I love you' and the man is immediately forced to reexamine his feelings. Suddenly, he's calibrating, considering, reconsidering—"

"Exactly," I said.

"It pushes him one way or the other. But what women don't understand or expect is that they're as likely to push him away as get an 'I love you, too.' "

"They should just hold out longer, stop themselves from saying it too soon," I said.

"In the dance of courtship, the game is to *seem* complete, problem-free. Whoever cracks first loses. The winner gets the power position."

"Who are you, the blind guy from *Kung Fu*?" I said. "I don't want the power position. I want *not* to have to have the power position. I've *been* the problem-free one, remember? With Elisabeth. I want equilibrium, some semblance of normalcy. The female equivalent of me." I flipped through an old *Spiderman*. "We better get going."

"She didn't like *Dennis Jennings*?" he said.

"Hated."

"That's bad."

YOU SHOULD HAVE KNOWN BETTER

Tad and I were in his office watching tape of people from around the world using different euphemisms for sexual congress when Lauren called again. At my insistence, Tatia put her through. Tad's phone was on the floor—he didn't believe in desks—and he pushed the speaker button with his cowboy boot.

"Hey, Lauren," I said.

"We need to talk, Tad."

"Talk?" Tad sounded like a CEO humoring a not terribly bright underling. "Yes, Lauren, we do. We need to talk budget. We're going to need another fifty thou."

"You two need to come down here."

Her voice sounded ominously placid, like HAL in *2001: A Space Odyssey*.

"Pretty tight around here this afternoon," Tad said, holding his date book over the phone and flipping the pages in the air. "How's Friday?"

"No. Now, Tad."

"No can do," Tad said. "Intern interviews all day. It's crazy here."

"We can probably get there," I said, in what I hoped was a calming tone.

"What I have to tell you can't wait." More HAL.

"We'll be there in fifteen minutes," I said, in what I hoped was a groveling tone.

Tad rolled his eyes.

"Yeah, all right," Tad said. "I'll bring the new budget numbers."

"You do that, Tad," she said.

The phone clicked off.

The wind whipped us down to MTV headquarters in Times Square.

Jill, our production manager, was in Lauren's office. She'd been out all morning. It occurred to me Jill had been out a lot of mornings lately.

Lauren sat perfectly still behind her desk and said, "I'm terminating the show."

Tad laughed wildly.

"Look, I'm sorry the on-line is overbudget. It'll be worth it. I think MTV can scrape up fifty fucking thousand more—"

"Tad, you can't use language like that in this company."

"Sorry. Fifty *frickin'* thousand more—"

"You know that's not what I'm talking about, Tad."

As good cop, I finally felt obliged to chime in.

"We actually don't," I said. Reasonable inflection. Play the peacemaker.

"Calling me a . . . 'cunt,' " Lauren said.

Jill crossed her legs. I looked at Tad. He nodded. Instantly, we both knew where she'd been spending her mornings. She was a plant—a mole! She didn't work for us. She worked for *them*.

"No!" I said. "He was talking about my old girlfriend's band. In Toronto. It's spelled with a *k*."

"Please be out within the hour," Lauren said. "Another team needs the space. A car is waiting to escort you. Oh, and anything you've taped so far *is* considered MTV property." She smiled at me. "You should have known better than to pick a partner like Tad."

There was lipstick on her teeth.

The Communicar driver, a mob wheelman type, took us back up to 1775 Broadway, then stood at our office door while we packed up. We took a few pictures to commemorate this dark day. It was the first time I'd seen Tad speechless. Tatia was crying blue mascara. I called Kay.

"You're home," I said.

"Got off early," she said.

I took a breath before breaking the news.

"They killed the show," I said.

"What show?" Kay asked, a little on the impatient side.

"*Our* show."

"Oh," she said, her bedside manner leaving something to be desired.

"MTV pulled the plug."

"I think you'd better come over," she said.

That was more like it.

"I'll be there soon," I said.

The wheelman dropped Tad off at his place on Ninety-first Street and West End, then I gave him Kay's address. Sitting in traffic on the Eighty-fifth Street transverse, I looked through the open window at the wall of stone next to us. I'd been a winner when I met Kay. "Glamorous," she called my budding-TV-genius shtick. I wondered if she'd write me off as a loser now. In the dance of courtship, the game is to appear problem-free. . . .

She opened the door, bathrobed, and forced a smile.

"Can you believe it?" I wailed, collapsing on her couch.

"No." She gave me a weird look.

"Tad thinks we can sell it somewhere else."

More silence. Maybe she *had* written me off as a loser.

Still standing while I sat, she tightened her robe and said, "I have cooties."

I laughed.

"It's not funny. You may have them, too."

"What are you talking about?"

I honestly didn't know.

"Body lice. I probably got them from the cot."

What was she talking about?

"That bed in the supply closet at the hospital? Where you take naps between shifts?"

"Dr. Goldman said I was clean, but I know I've got them."

I tried to make sense of that information.

"But if your doctor said—"

"I just Quelled," she said, pacing a trench in the parquet floor. "You should, too."

"I don't think I need to—"

She ran into the bathroom.

Now I was pacing. I wasn't getting any sympathy. If she wanted to indulge in a hysterical episode, fine. Don't drag me into it. I had my own problems. And "cooties" wasn't one of them.

Kay rushed back in and handed me a dark bottle. I noted the skull and crossbones prominently displayed on the label.

"Rat poison?" I made the mistake of laughing again.

"Read it!"

" 'Overuse can lead to brain damage.' "

I handed it back.

"It's Quell. You need to use it."

"No way. I'm not putting this stuff on."

I was on the other side of the couch now and she was coming after me.

"Yes, you aaaaa-rrrre." The crazed giggle now.

"No, I'm no-oooot."

Five minutes later, I was standing in her shower, shivering and squirming like a five-year-old while she doused me in toxic shampoo. After I toweled off, Kay made me hot chocolate.

She'd already left when I woke up the next morning in her white duvet and a black depression. On the corner of Sixty-ninth Street and York, I passed a crouching beggar holding a cardboard sign.

HOMELESS WITH AIDS

CAN PROVE

How New York, that "can prove." I kept walking, intensely aware of the invisible sign around my own neck.

CAN'T AFFORD CAB

CAN PROVE

Tad and I regrouped at Billy's. "We can sell this show tomorrow!" he thundered. "I'll call Brandon."

Brandon Tartikoff, once the most powerful man in television, was, like Tad, a Yalie. He'd delivered the commencement address to the class of '88. Young Tad had introduced himself, in his inimitable way, and turned down a job in the executive training program at NBC. But Brandon still took his calls.

"Not unless we get all the tapes of our segments back from MTV," I said.

"We'll get them," he said.

"How?"

"We'll go up to MTV and walk in like nothing's happened. The security guy's not going to know we got fired."

"When should we do it?"

"What's wrong with right now?"

Under cover of night, we raided 1775 Broadway, "our" building, until yesterday. Tad flashed his "Mr. Loofah" card at the security guard—a laminated ID with a picture of his hand holding a large, sculptural loofah.

"Names and time in the book please," the guard said, without looking at us. I did the honors, in my least legible scrawl: *Beavis and Butt-head.*

The guard looked up and said, "I don't think so."

"Is there a problem, Officer . . . Lewis?" Tad said, squinting at the badge.

"Officer" Darryl Lewis tapped the photocopy of our MTV IDs taped to the wall of his command center. Our pictures stared guiltily at us like mug shots.

"We just need to go up to the office for a couple minutes," I said, in my most agreeably Canadian tone. "I forgot my inhaler. I'm asthmatic."

"I've been instructed not to let you onto the premises," the guard said.

This guy had been watching too much *N.Y.P.D. Blue.* He gave us a dead-eyed stare.

Tad reached over the desk for the security phone. "Does the name Brandon Tartikoff mean anything to you? Because when he hears about this—"

The guard pried the phone from Tad's hand and rose from his seat, reaching for his gun. Or what would have been his gun if he were allowed to carry one. I think it was a flashlight. I didn't get a good look because Tad and I were running down the corridor to the door.

"Run away! Run away!" Tad was shouting, as he jumped in front of a cab, banging on the hood.

I demanded the driver take us to "William's Demicouture."

"Billy's Topless," Tad said.

"I know it," the driver said into the rearview mirror.

I turned to Tad, as we bombed down Seventh Avenue.

"We need a new plan," Tad said, once we were inside the safety of Billy's again.

We were hatching plan B when Tad cartoon-slapped his forehead.

"I just realized. Magno!"

"What?"

"Magno—the editing house! They have copies of everything we did."

"Why didn't we think of that sooner? Maybe that rat poison did give me brain damage."

"What?"

"Nothing." I wasn't telling anyone about that. "I guess we learned a valuable lesson from this whole Lauren thing."

"And that would be?"

"The worst thing you can do to drive a woman over the edge."

"Call her a cunt?"

"No," I said. "Not call back."

Tad nodded and we watched a pizza guy come in and deliver a large pie to a dancer on stage. She paid him from her tip pile, hardly missing a beat.

Out There Productions was back in business. Our new office was the FedEx on Eighth Avenue. We sent out dozens of demo tapes. To further build industry buzz for our newly freed-up property, Tad planted an item in *Variety*. An item *announcing* the show. They didn't have to know we'd already been fired.

He was pulling every string, his own as well as his dad's—an investment banker with high-level network contacts. We took endless meetings. "I don't want to discourage you, but not in my lifetime," said ABC's president of late night. A VP at Broadway Video, Lorne Michaels's production company, "couldn't wait" to sell it into syndication. We never heard from her again. Another guy sent us to another guy who sent us to two guys named Skip and Bob who called themselves Those Guys International. Two weeks of fruitless meetings. Our *Variety* item was fish wrap. The whole time, I was Quelling nightly. I didn't have "cooties." No signs, no symptoms. I don't think she did either. But it took that long for her to believe they were gone.

To avoid thinking about that, or what it said about her, I cloistered myself in my cell-like home office during the day, thinking about money.

Like most people, I thought about money more than I would admit to anyone, or myself. I performed the mundane calculus of my rent, income, expenses. I made the calls I'd let slide when I thought I was out of journalism for good. Viv, my *GQ* editor, had left a message offering me a new assignment.

"Everyone here liked your baldness piece so much, we thought you'd be great on erectile dysfunction," she said.

"Maybe we should get away from service journalism," I said. "How about an Elements of Style? One of those think pieces on Panama hats or 'the Return of the Walking Stick'?"

"Sure," Viv said. "Got any ideas you can navel-gaze for fifteen hundred words on?"

"Um, Old Spice?"

I whistled the nautical theme from the commercial.

"Retro colognes," Viv said. "Did 'em last month."

"Okay." I racked my brain. "One of your 'great bars' pieces? There's this place in Madrid—Chicote. Hemingway has a story set there."

"I'm up to my ass in great bars," Viv said. "How about a style signature? Do you have one?"

I looked at my shoes, my belt and said, "Suede?"

"*Hmm*," Viv exhaled. " 'In Praise of Suede.' I like it. Can you get some sentimental father-son stuff into it?"

"I have an old suede jacket of his I've been wearing since high school."

"Perfect. I'll send you a contract. But more important, are you available for setups?"

"Well, I'm seeing someone."

"Who?"

"A med student."

"Because I've got someone I know you'd be into," Viv barreled ahead. "I just met her the other night. She's in publishing. Reads everything. And bea-u-tiful. I'd kill for her hair. Let me give you her number."

"I have a girlfriend. I can't take her number."

"What if I give her *your* number?"

"Like she's gonna call," I said.

"You'd be surprised."

I spent the next day shuttling between FedEx and our satellite office, Kinko's. When I got home, my machine beeped a message I never thought I'd hear.

"Hello, my name is Kay. I'm a friend of Viv's and I think you're right, in the nineties, there's no law that says that only you should take my number. So yes, I thought I'd give you a call. It's Tuesday and I'll be home after eleven, I guess. Look forward to speaking with you. Oh, my number is. . . ."

Another Kay—what were the odds? Confident voice, with a flirty lilt. Points for calling, pending subtraction if she turned out to be a dog.

It was after 11:00. I could have called. I was home. But I held off.

We talked in the morning just long enough to settle on a Thursday night drink at Raoul's, in SoHo, before she said she had to go. What the hell, I figured. I had a girlfriend. I took pride in not being a cheater—one of the few values I could lay claim to.

A drink couldn't hurt.

Early, as always, I ordered a vodka-tonic and kept my eye on the door. When a full-lipped brunette stepped inside and marched up to my barstool, I nearly fell off it.

"This is not a date, all right? Viv told me you're seeing someone. Which is fine. As long as we agree this is not a date."

I saw what Viv meant about the hair: a dark shoulder length mane so ruly each hair looked individually blow-dried. She hadn't mentioned the tan, which looked like it hadn't suffered in the winter months.

"Right," I said, taking in the milk chocolate eyes and glints of silver at her earlobes and neck. "Definitely not a date."

Men have nothing on women for sheer venality in the mating world. Viv cooked up this home-wrecking. The luscious creature next to me was a willing accomplice. Then again, I was at the bar, too.

I sensed she did a lot of these. Blind dates, that is. She was wary but friendly, an interesting contradiction of tough cookie and softly stylish packaging. Her thing was "new fiction," so that was our date topic. Unlike Tiina the title-dropper, Kay had a self-deprecating irony about her literary interests.

"Japanese, Indians, Pavlovians—if you can't pronounce 'em, I read 'em."

"Pavlovians?"

"I'm a sucker for hillbilly memoirists, black lesbians and twelve-year-old PFC addicts," she said.

"You mean PCP," I corrected.

"Do I?"

She had exactly one Stoli martini, up, with three olives, then, as abruptly as she'd sat down, got up to go.

"So soon?" I said, throwing cash on the bar and following her onto Prince Street. "I wanted to hear more about Banana Yamamoto."

I was shameless, the Zelig of dating.

"Call me sometime," she said, ducking into a cab.

"I will."

Nice boots.

But I didn't. Like a gambler on a losing streak, I kept throwing more chips at a bad hand.

That weekend, under a sketchy March sky, I found myself on the Triborough Bridge heading to Ward's Island, an East River atoll with two things on it: a park and a state mental hospital.

We weren't going to the park.

Kay, my Kay, was driving, in her Honda Civic, and saying, "Isn't this *fun*?"

"Yeah," I said, with a halfhearted laugh.

When she had proposed this furtive, forbidden visit to a state mental hospital, I thought, sure, maybe it'll be an adventure we can share and laugh over in the years to come. But I didn't believe it.

We parked in front of a cinderblock cuckoo's nest.

"Here it is," Kay said. "The nut house."

"I'm sure it's a respectable institution run by trained professionals," I said, stiffening as we walked past the sleepy guard, who glanced perfunctorily at my guide's black bag and waved us in.

"Don't talk to anyone," Kay said, hushing me. "You shouldn't really be here."

I have an innate aversion to unauthorized situations, being

from a nation of congenital law-abiders and reflexive rule-followers. Consider the motto of Canada's national newspaper: "The subject who is truly loyal to the Chief Magistrate will neither advise nor submit to arbitrary measures.—Junius."

Catchy. I think it means don't cross the street on a red light even if there isn't a car in sight. So I felt more than a little self-conscious entering these forbidden, freakish surroundings.

As far as I knew, Kay had no official business here either. She just thought it would be a fun Sunday field trip.

The central corridor was a gauntlet of filthy gowns and cathetered lunatics. A woman of indeterminate age was sitting in a plastic chair fingering phantom knitting needles like Madame Defarge. Standing next to her was an intelligent looking young man who seemed to be muttering "monkey doodle" to himself, over and over. Another male patient/inmate jumped in front of me and offered to sell the crumpled pack of cigarettes clenched in his gnarled hand. I recoiled like a boxer slipping a punch.

Kay waved at a male nurse. "Have you seen Becky?"

Becky was her psych friend who worked here.

"No, ma'am."

"Oh, thanks," Kay said and stopped in front of a vending machine.

"Want a hot chocolate?" she asked me.

"Maybe later," I said, catching a whiff of something and wondering how long it had been since they hosed this place down.

I used to joke that my number was on the wall of the women's room at Bellevue. I never thought I'd end up with a woman who'd *literally* drive me to an insane asylum. When you're in this deep, you accept all kinds of incremental encroachments on your sanity. You don't notice them until one day you're standing in a shower pouring Drano on your head.

We fast-walked out again. Kay was all charged up. I felt ashamed and vaguely humiliated, just as I had been by the phantom cooties and the industrial-sized tub of K-Y. Well, maybe not the K-Y.

I stopped talking, much, all the way to dinner at an Indian restaurant on Sixth Street.

Kay nervously filled the conversational vacuum.

"I'm masochistic and you're sadistic," she said. "We're acting out a sadomasochistic fantasy."

"I'm not following," I said, thinking it was the other way around.

"That's what the *DSM* says."

This was worse than the Quelling.

"But you don't want to hear about that stuff, right?" she said. "My 'psychobabble'?"

I chewed my *rogan josh*.

"I didn't mean *you* were a psychobabbler when I said that. I was just talking about self-help platitudes in general. Like that chick who said dating me had been a 'personal growth experience.'"

"Chick?" Kay said. "And how am I different?"

There are two kinds of women: the ones who get offended by the word *chick* and the ones who don't.

I stalled with a long sip of Taj Mahal.

"You're . . . *you*."

At her place after dinner, she popped some "tranks" with three Amstel Lights and a box of Cracker Jack. I'd never seen her self-medicate before.

"Our problem is we both want to get married and have babes," she said, stretched out on the couch.

Babes?

"Got any Tums?" I asked, rubbing my stomach and making a face. "Gandhi's Revenge."

"Check the medicine cabinet."

I slugged some Pepto and returned from the bathroom to find

Kay on her futon, wearing only that manic grin from the picture on my bulletin board. The black doctor bag was open. Nearby gleamed the cold steel of a gynecological instrument I knew only by reputation. Her free hand offered me a flashlight.

"Wanna take a look?"

> YOU VANT SPATIAL
> MASSAGE?

"So, so she whips out this, this . . . thing," Podhoretz said as we entered the moist, shvitzy air of the Tenth Street Baths. "Then what happened?"

"I looked," I said.

"No you didn't," Podhoretz said.

"What else was I gonna do?"

I handed the stone-faced Russian behind the counter two day passes.

"My girlfriend gave me these. For a birthday present."

He turned them over in his hand, with unconcealed contempt.

"Lockers there," he said, throwing us a couple of towels and pointing to a sign on the wall:

THIS IS A STRAIGHT PLACE.

Another placard next to it said,

ON CO-ED DAYS, MALE PATRONS MUST WEAR SHORTS OR TOWEL.
BORIS'S WIFE IS WATCHING. THANK YOU.—BORIS.

We squeezed our clothes into the tiny lockers and headed downstairs.

"I'm sure she wouldn't have wanted you to waste the passes," Podhoretz said. "Even if you didn't invite her to your thirtieth. Let's sauna first."

We doused the coals with water and sat.

"So what did it look like?" Podhoretz asked.

"What did what look like?"

"*It.* What you saw when you looked."

"A glazed doughnut."

"Come on."

"Scary. Like something out of *Fantastic Voyage.*"

"So *then* you broke up with her? I marvel at your guilt-free gifts in that area."

"Well, I didn't say it was because of *that.* I waited a few days for an opening. She called me an 'opportunist,' because I went to publicity events for the free booze. 'I'm a journalist!' I protested."

"Not exactly the moral high ground," Pod said.

"No, but I latched on to the insult as an excuse to negotiate a 'vacation from the relationship.'"

"Soft landing?"

"Allegedly. But now I'm getting heavy-breathing phone calls."

"Saying what?"

"That her horniness is 'a medical emergency,'" I said.

"And you told her?"

"Not to worry, that it was just 'separation anxiety.'"

"You are a cruel man."

"Women don't want honesty," I said. "They say they do, but

they don't. You can't tell someone the real reason, or reasons, you don't ever want to see them again. Like they're too crazy or they don't get your jokes. *That* would be cruel. So you latch on to some minor thing and they come away thinking you're the damaged one."

"Very true," he said. "Ready for some real heat?"

We walked out of the sauna and followed another sign:

TO RUSSIAN ROOM

Pod heaved open the vault door. The Russian Room was a furnace, pitch-black and lung-singeing. I staggered to the nearest bench, gasping for air, a burst hydrant of sweat. Podhoretz clambered casually to the top level. How was he *alive* up there? I felt a rough tap on my shoulder. Over me stood a brutish giant in the world's worst turban—a towel he removed to resoak in the bucket of twigs at his flip-flopped feet.

"*Platza*," he said.

Was this Boris?

Before I had time to request a UN translator, I was being beaten about the head and shoulders with the soapy branches.

I closed my eyes and forgot about everything.

On our way back upstairs, Pod asked how I liked my *platza*.

"Fantastic," I said. "I feel . . . cleansed."

The massage rooms were on the second floor. Red lightbulbs told you whether they were available or occupied. Each door was marked with a Polaroid. Pod got a pouting peasant girl. Mine had no Polaroid. When I got inside, I saw why.

A burly, flat-faced woman who could have been thirty or fifty went to work on my neck, shoulders and spine. I inferred from some primitive hand gestures that she wanted me on my back. I rolled over, demurely adjusting my towel.

"You vant spatial massage?"

"Sorry?"

"*Spatial* massage."

Another primitive hand gesture left no doubt as to her meaning.

"No thanks, thanks," I said.

I'd had enough weird sexual encounters. She shrugged and went back to punching my left thigh. Was this Boris's wife?

About forty minutes later, Pod and I were back in front of the stony Russian.

"You teep guy beat you ap?"

I looked at him uncomprehendingly.

"You *teep* guy beat you ap?" Podhoretz, an excellent mimic, repeated.

I grasped the reference to the *platza* man and I forked over ten bucks.

Ambling rubber-limbed along Tenth Street to Second Avenue for lunch at Veselka, I could already taste the hot, meaty borscht and mixed pierogi platter. I inhaled the clean April air, feeling liberated, and more relaxed than I had in a long time. I couldn't wait to call Kay 2.

GOOD-BYE, COLUMBUS AVENUE

"**Y**ou've got a bit of nerve."

Not big on hello, I noticed.

"I do?" I asked, into an awkward pause.

"Two months since our blind date and suddenly you call?"

"Six weeks! I was seeing someone! Anyway, I thought that wasn't a date."

"A date's a date."

"I throw myself on the mercy of the court."

"What if now *I'm* seeing someone?"

"Are you?"

"No."

"So you want to have drinks?"

"No."

"Oh," I said.

"But I could be persuaded."

This was the most complex date negotiation I'd ever had. I couldn't pace myself to Kay 2's conversational rhythm. Just when I thought I'd caught up, she jumped ahead.

"How about that café outside Industria," I said. "The photo studio? Braque?"

"No. I never go to cubist cafés."

"Oh," I said, smelling defeat.

"But I could make an exception," she said.

When we hung up, I noticed I was sweating.

For our first sighted date, a gusty spring breeze blew down Washington Street. I sat at a table the size of a medium pizza watching Kay 2's crisp approach. The details came into focus: white Levi's, snug light green sweater set and flat, slipperlike black loafers.

"You're a little warm," she said, skipping hello again but brushing my cheek with hers.

Her skeptical eyes and inviting mouth were like opposing political parties.

"Sorry," I said.

Never walk to a date.

"Merino," Kay 2 said, fingering my long-sleeved polo sweater. "Doesn't breathe. Feel this." She put my hand on her sleeve. "Ultralight cashmere."

I dabbed my brow and was saved by the waitress, who took Kay 2's order, a Stoli martini.

"I was at Tribeca Films," I said. "De Niro's company?"

"I've heard of him."

"My friend Tad and I were pitching TV ideas down there. I had plenty of time, then had to run up—"

"So you met with Bobby?"

"Well, not exactly. Bobby's henchwoman. At the beginning of the meeting, she offered us smart drugs."

"Is that why you're sniffing?"

"No, that's allergies," I said, and blew my nose. "She whipped out a little bottle with a dropper and squeezed a couple on our tongues, like a priest giving communion."

"I'm Jewish, in case you were wondering." She sipped her martini. "Why are you laughing?"

I was working grade-A material here—De Niro, no less!—but kept thinking I wasn't being interesting enough to hold her attention.

Over a second Stoli (progress!) and my third beer, I gleaned the salient biographical details. Born in suburban Philadelphia, on what she called "the Jewish Main Line." One sister, younger but already married with a baby, still in Philly. Daddy took the family envelope business public, then "cashed out." Summers in a rambling oceanfront manse on the Jersey Shore, winters in St. Barth's. The parents spent most of their time on exotic trips organized by the Smithsonian: private jets to the Galápagos with the world's foremost Darwinian as tour guide. After doing her time as an assistant, she had risen to signing obscure authors of her own.

"Preferably MFAs who've never lived outside a writers' colony," she said.

"With brooding book jacket photos by Marion Ettlinger?"

"Preferably blurry and outdoors," she said, tiny laugh lines creasing her cappuccino-colored tan. "Somewhere very cold."

"I bet you never miss a *Paris Review* party," I said.

We were both smiling now. At the same time. Before long, I felt confident trying to extend the date.

"Dinner?" I asked.

Kay 2 looked at her watch, a wafer-thin silver bracelet.

"Ask me how much reading I have to do," she said.

"How much—"

"This was fun," she said. "How glad am I that you called?"

"I don't know, how—" I started to say, but she was already getting up.

I realized her questions were a rhetorical trope. *How happy am I? How fun is this? How great is such-and-such unknown author?*

"I'm cabbing," she said. "I'll drop you."

This was not the kind of woman who let drinks after work turn into all-night sex-and-booze binges—the kind I was used to.

"Nah, I'll walk," I said, hoping to convey an aura of lonerish mystery.

"Call me," she said, ducking into the backseat.

Commuting *à pied* up Eighth Avenue, I wondered how I was going to distinguish myself from the corporate lawyers, bond traders and assorted Jewish American Princes I pictured showering her with baubles and dinners at Montrachet. She was obviously willing to entertain the goy option. But did that extend to marriage, or was it like being lesbian until graduation?

To compensate for my lack of compensation, I concocted an ingenious blend of bohemia and class for our next encounter. My plan called for military precision and split-second timing.

"I've got a gallery opening at Salon Dada," I said, when I called her at work. "A reading of my friend Doug's difficult new novel, *Malaisia*, then a rainforest benefit with a live performance by Sting. Then we could duck into—"

"You never heard of dinner and a movie?"

If the Upper West Side of Manhattan was suburbia-in-the-city, with its strollers and sweats and PBS tote bags and unearned complacency, then Isabella's was its Le Cirque. Which is to say: if you were young(ish), single, on a first or second or whatever date and at least one of you was Jewish, by birth or ability to quote *Seinfeld*, you went to the southwest corner of Seventy-seventh and Columbus to sit inside Mediterranean-washed walls and be served fennel-encrusted tuna medallions by waiters recommending you "do" a wine with an etching of Tuscany on the label and a "death-by" dessert, then slipped the stiff plastic of your frequent-flirter gold card (ribbed for her pleasure with your "member since" date) into the see-through slot with the check and asked, "Your brownstone or mine?"

Not that I'd thought about it much.

Kay 2 and I were waiting at the bar of Isabella's for our eight o'clock reservation in an atmosphere only a Zagat surveyor would call "lively." The Levi's were red this time, with those same slipperlike loafers, and a black sweater shorn from the belly of some rare Himalayan mammal. I knew from our three meetings that she would always dress well, if conservatively, and found this prospect immensely comforting. We talked desultorily. Kay 2 was annoyed about waiting for our table. I asked the hostess cupcake at the reservation lectern how much longer. She said soon. At 8:25, Kay 2 went over to have a word. At 8:27, another hostess, this one more of a Twinkie, led us to our table.

"At least it's inside," I said, once we were sitting. "There's nothing worse than outdoor dining in New York. Inhaling exhaust. Bums begging for your fries."

"Where are you eating, on the Bowery?"

"No, but—"

"What's your favorite restaurant?" Kay 2 asked.

"*Hmm*," I pondered, thinking I probably shouldn't say Billy's Topless.

A waiter intervened, in a denim button-down disturbingly like the one I was wearing. He had blond hair, combed straight back. He dealt us our menus and the wine list.

"Will we be doing bottled or tap tonight?"

I didn't like that "we."

"Tap is fi—"

"Bottled," Kay 2 said.

"Do we like sparkling or still?"

"Still," Kay 2 said.

"Will we be having cocktails?"

Kay 2 got her usual martini. I had a Heineken.

He signaled his departure with a broad wink. I was exhausted and we hadn't even started dinner.

Kay 2 smiled what I suspected was a naturally perfect—rather than orthodontically corrected—smile. One look at her nails—flawlessly even clear-polished almonds—told you Kay 2 had superior DNA. Tad would approve.

I looked at the menu, saw the word *penne* and latched onto it.

"Would you pick a wine?" Kay 2 asked.

When our waiter returned, I employed the Homer Simpson method of wine selection: order the second least expensive bottle on the list.

"Can we talk specials? In the apps, I have a saffron mâche. . . ."

I didn't like that "I." You're not the chef—or the sous-chef or the mâche-chef. It occurred to me that at some point in the recent evolution of restaurant pretension, waiters stopped being unemployable actors and decided to be faux foodies. Bring back the actors.

I was awed by Kay 2's comfort level with service people, able to stop a waiter with a single glance while I was still waving like a castaway at a passing ship. When I was a kid, my parents only took me to a restaurant if we were in a foreign country. I wouldn't dream of sending back the fish. At the end of the meal, Kay 2 didn't make the customary insincere reach into the purse. She waited, composed and content, for me to pay.

"Wanna walk me home?"

Was that an intentional foot brush under the table?

"I thought you'd never ask."

I hadn't even had to take off my glasses.

Home was only half a block away—an imposingly adult prewar

across from the Natural History Museum. We shuffled and swayed under her awning. Peeking into the marbled lobby, I caught the doorman sizing me up.

"I don't have anything to entertain you in my apartment," Kay 2 said.

"Oh, I don't know about that," I said.

Now I took my glasses off—the Rakish Swipe—and smoldered.

"Why do you look like you just swallowed a rotten egg?" she said.

I put them back on, said, "Well, g'night," and leaned in.

She stepped out of range and pouted.

"You're not coming up?"

She turned the key, stepped briskly inside and vanished into the bathroom while I admired my pristine surroundings. Not a warped angle or scuffed baseboard in sight. The furniture was even more spare and minimal than mine, with a Modernist bent. No Conran's knockoffs. The real thing. The walls glittered with silver-framed pictures of Kay 2 and the extended 2 family. I marveled at her casual narcissism. I wanted to be on that wall.

The toilet flushed. She came back out.

"Nice," I said, and made admiring noises in front of a pair of Barcelona chairs.

"I stole them from Dad's old office," she said.

Before he "cashed out," I thought, and walked over to the red-lacquered bookshelf. Amid the writers' colony fiction and Vintage yuppiebacks, I saw some familiar editions of Hemingway, Fitzgerald, Salinger. I pulled out *For Whom the Bell Tolls*. My copy had the same original cover, only ripped and worn. Hers was like new. I flipped it open to check the date.

"Published in 1992?"

"First-edition club," Kay 2 said. "They're reproductions of the originals. I get one every month."

No sign of the *Diagnostic and Statistical Manual*.

"I like your shoes," I said.

"My Belgians?" she said, slipping them off. "Aren't they the best?"

"The best," I said, whatever the hell Belgians were.

She noticed me noticing her wiggle her toes.

"My pedicurist makes house calls," she said, walking over to the doorway to a darkened room. "Wanna watch TV?"

"Okay," I said.

Not really.

"It's in here," she said.

In that case.

I was relieved to discover that the most exotic piece of sexual equipment in her bedroom was the bed itself. A "European king," she called it. A team of Italians had to assemble it on-site. "It's a princess-and-the-pea thing," she said. When it came time to sleep, she put on a black silk mask with fur trim, like a movie star.

In the morning, the No. 1 train hurtled me back to the Sewing Machine Repair Shop District. Cashed *out*? I was barely cashed in. I'd paid off my debts, my parents. I was making money. But I wasn't making *money*. I couldn't afford Isabella's every night, or even every other night. After kissing Kay 2 good-bye on Seventy-seventh Street, with the doorman watching, I had said, "Next time, we're going downtown."

"Don't you love it here?" Kay 2 said. "This is one of my favorite places."

We were at Cafe Luxembourg on Seventieth Street between Amsterdam and West End. (*Zagat Survey* sez: "civilized," "after all these years," "some celebs.") I was staring into a bowl of penne *arrabbiata*. The couple next to us could have been my parents' age. On the other side a bald gay man was watching his much younger date gobble his flounder.

"It's great," I said.

We were in week three already, and had yet to dine below Sixty-sixth Street. I did get her to play "minigolf art" on a course in TriBeCa designed by downtown artists. That was the night I knew I'd become an integral part of Kay 2's closely guarded existence— when she putted into Cindy Sherman's vagina for par and said, "Being with you is like being alone." From her, this was a hole-in-one. Because there was something almost masculine about her, in her spare modern furniture and wariness of intimacy. "Please don't like me no matter what," she had said. "Then there's no challenge." I played along: "Yeah, I hate it when you start seeing each other every night, knowing every boring detail of the other person's life." To which she replied, "That comes later."

Her aloofness was a pose. She was the one pushing us into the dress-rehearsal marriage of "exclusivity." Nuzzling smugly through *Singles*, taking Metro North to visit her newly parenting friends in Hastings-on-Hudson. . . . I didn't mind. I was enjoying this holiday in Normalville.

So here we were on a Sunday night, at Cafe Luxembourg, after an afternoon at the "Googlyheim," as she called it, and the Met, in the same day. I stuck to playing the culture card, even though my *Malaisia*/Sting plan hadn't gone over. "Suggested contribution" was a ticket I could afford. And I got the feeling she liked that I took her on highbrow field trips, though she'd showed signs of fatigue in front of a Mantegna engraving. "The horn of . . . polenta," she'd said, squinting at the title. Her malapropisms were either part of her private comedy act, or for my benefit or both. I liked never being sure whether she was putting me on. "I think that's 'horn of *plenty*,'" I'd said—her willing straight man. Our fights, when we had them, never lasted beyond her next therapy session, her weekly mental manicure. "My therapist thinks you're very good for me," she said. In my experience, a woman is never as nice to a guy as after she's seen her shrink. I called it the Couch Dividend. But I'd stopped making entries in my Bachelor Hell diary. Kay 2 was just too sane.

Between bites of spruce-cured salmon, she was talking about the apartment she'd looked at today—in the Dakota. The dilemma on the table was this: Mr. 2 was willing to shell out, but she wasn't sure if it was "appropriate" for someone her age to be living in one of the fanciest buildings in New York. I respected that she was conscious of those things, like wearing silver rather than gold. She also hinted that maybe she shouldn't be looking at one-bedrooms. Maybe she'd need something bigger if . . .

The Dakota. Titillated by the prospect of borrowing a cup of sugar from Yoko Ono, I flashed to a conversation I'd had with Podhoretz. "You know what you are?" he'd said. " 'Yontrop.' Portnoy in reverse. *Portnoy's Complaint* is a Jewish guy obsessed with a blonde shiksa, right? But to you, Kay 2 is 'the Other.' " That she was. A hothouse flower. An exotic creature from a plush, pampered land where everything is a choice, not a need. I was the young man from the provinces and she represented an immaculately groomed, sublimely American vision of success. Then Pod said, "Of course, you'll have to convert."

"I'm booking you for Mindy and Seth's wedding, right?"

I snapped back into the conversation. Mindy, I'd been apprised, was Kay 2's best camp friend.

"When is that again?"

"July twenty-fifth," she said. "Down the shore. Near my parents'."

"Oh, right—love to," I said, thinking she might as well have asked me what I was doing in the year 2020.

I wasn't a planner. Her Filofax had every dinner with friends, weekend activity and trip entered months in advance. When we walked out of the Met, right away she had to know if we were going to the Eighty-sixth Street or Seventy-seventh Street subway. "Do I have to decide *now*?" I'd ask peevishly. And I'm hardly Mr. Spontaneous. I grew up eating dinner at 6:30 every night. But I had a pleasant vision of me on the beach with my Powerbook, reading and writing; Kay 2 running, sunning, throwing sultry glances and dry asides from behind her designer sunglasses.

At the end of yet another pornographically priced repast, Kay 2 looked up at me with those milky, chocolatey eyes, pouted her irresistible lips and asked the inevitable.

"Are you treating?"

I was writing like a dervish just to be able to afford her. I tallied my output and income for the month of June: eight TV reviews for *Variety*, four features for *TV Guide, Premiere, New York*, book reviews on the side. I placed wake-up calls to Pepa (of Salt N'), decoded infomercials for the *Times*'s new Styles of the Times section, interviewed Sir Mixalot and Billy Idol for *Rolling Stone*'s "100 Best Videos of All Time." I sat twelve hours a day with my headset glued on like a Time-Life operator. . . .

I reached for my wallet.

"May I take those for you, miss?"

"Thank you," Kay 2 said, handing over two large white shopping bags to a very sincere coat check girl.

Picholine, on West Sixty-fourth Street ("wonderful," "inventive," "impeccable"). A significant dinner—my first with Mr. and Mrs. 2. And that afternoon, four months in, their daughter had taken our relationship to the next level. A sample sale.

"Who is this Laura Piano?" I'd asked, as we'd entered the *sanctum sanctorum* of quality cashmere an hour earlier. "I'm a kid in the world of deluxe goat underbellies."

"*Loro* Piana," Kay 2 said. "It's Italian. It means 'then softly.' "

Laura's wares were prized throughout the land, notably the land from Central Park West to West End Avenue. In a twenty-ninth-floor showroom in Midtown, a Casbah of women threw elbows around tables piled high with sweater sets, gloves, socks, scarves. Boiling in my leather car coat from the Gap (American for "now cheaply"), I was feeling the pressure to volume-shop against the clock. *Was it so terrible I wore cotton sweaters in winter?* Kay 2 had found me timidly fingering a burgundy vest just as it was snatched away by a woman stripped down to her bra on the other side of the table. "You don't have *anything* yet?" She'd plucked out another vest in my size and pointed me to the cash register. If this was a test, I had failed. The Canadian curse of deference!

"That vest is very becoming on you," said Mrs. 2—a warm, pleasant woman who was aging fantastically—once we'd settled into our table.

"Thanks," I said. "It's double-ply."

Mr. 2 frowned at a leather-bound wine list. I eyed his blue blazer, the red-checked, spread-collar shirt that fit too well not to be custom and boldly striped tie. The guy had style, I gave him that. He looked like an English country squire, in from a quail hunt.

"Your skin is looking great, Kay," said Mrs. 2.

"Clio's. We went together, didn't we, hon?"

Bad enough she'd talked me into getting a facial. Now she was telling people about it? If my life were a cartoon, not to say that it wasn't, I would have flushed a violent crimson and discharged clouds of steam from my ears.

During my skate in cilantro butter, Mr. 2 started going on about some philanthropic initiative of his. In the middle of his disquisition, Mrs. 2 turned to me.

"Have you had anything in the *Times* lately?" she asked.

I froze. The speech was still in progress. Not to respond would have been rude. I thought maybe I could get away with a quick side reply.

"I just did a piece on Lenny Kravitz."

The Package Potentate stopped and glared.

"I didn't mean to interrupt," I said.

"No," he said. "Let's all listen to what Kay's young man has to say. I'm sure it's fascinating."

My cartoon self cracked and crumbled into a pile of ice cubes.

"Not really," I said.

"Tell me, how do you make money as a . . . *freelancer*? Is that what you call it?"

You write articles and they pay you for them.

"It's not easy," I said.

When the bill came, I was tempted to pay, to show that I wasn't a penniless gold digger, but decided the gesture would have seemed ridiculous. Plus, I couldn't afford it.

Contrite over dinner, Kay 2 made the extreme sacrifice of sleeping at my place.

"Dad can be such a. . . ."

"I had another word in mind."

"You're not from his world. He doesn't understand."

In her own way, she was a rebel, a sleep-mask girl who hadn't stayed in Philly to live the sleep-mask life with some scissor scion or postage prince, but had moved to New York to champion obscure literary finds. I tugged off the mask and we made up. Afterwards, I lay rigid as a dead man by her side, terrified to breathe, until she dropped off.

If only hothouse flowers didn't demand constant climate control.

"Stop fidgeting!"

Some infinitesimal movement on my side of the bed had awakened her.

"Sorry," I whispered.

Too late. The garbage trucks were already picking up their Sewing Machine Repair Shop loads. After fifteen minutes of industrial compacting and idling diesel engines, Kay 2 was out of bed and getting dressed.

"This is why I can't sleep here," she said, suddenly sounding not unlike the Envelope King.

I threw off the comforter as dramatically as a man can throw a fluffy down thing. I was starting to question the price of my cashmere codependency. Sample sales. Facials. Night after night fending off pepper mills the size of baseball bats.

"Hold on," I said, pulling on my jeans and making calming gestures. "I'll walk you to Sixth."

East Hampton is a hundred miles from West Seventy-seventh Street, but not so far, really.

Saturday night, the third weekend in March, and Kay 2 and I were sitting across from the joyously newlywed Mindy and Seth at The Laundry ("unique," "Hamptons scene," "cozy fireplace"). Seth built shopping malls and wore jeans with a white crease down the front and a braided belt. What exactly is the message the braided-belt guy is trying to send? *I wear a suit to the office, but after hours I like to cut loose with some ironed jeans and my braided belt!* We didn't have a lot to talk about. I wondered what they were serving at the buffet at Billy's. I hadn't been there in months.

"I told him," Kay 2 was saying, meaning me. "You've *got* to get out of the city."

"Absolutely," Mindy echoed, tapping the sleeve of my new Loro Piana crew. "You have to."

"I love getting out," said Seth, who as far as I knew, didn't live in the city.

Kay 2 couldn't believe I didn't summer anywhere, like I was a Fresh Air Fund kid or something. I *had* to go in on a share in the Hamptons. She dismissed my protestations that I wasn't going to fry like an egg on the pavements of Manhattan. We took the train,

stayed at an inn with cuckoo clocks. In the morning, Kay 2 had gotten up chipper and bright for a day of house-hunting. That's when
the trouble had started. "When you've seen one four-bedroom con-
temporary in the Springs, you've seen them all," I'd said, refusing
even to go past the foyer on the last three. Getting ready for dinner,
I'd made balky noises about "ponying up *now*" for a rental that was
still two months away. "Are you in or out?" Kay 2 had demanded.
My dithering response—"How long do I have to decide?"—had sent
her sniffling onto the canopied bed. "Is it my money? Is that why
you won't say you love me?" *Inns*—can any relationship possibly
live up to them? I hadn't stayed at one of these doilied torture
chambers since my honeymoon. *Why wouldn't I say I loved her?*
What a question! I should have seen it coming. Ever since Valentine's Day—a fiendish and brutal crucible under the best of circumstances. At One If by Land, Two If by Sea ("intimate," "dreamy,"
"expensive"), Kay had offered her first "I love you" over dessert. I'd
done a sort of village-idiot grin and said nothing. She'd assured me
I didn't have to say it back. She hadn't cried or even seemed upset.
Later, we'd rented *Modern Romance*, the Albert Brooks movie, and
pretended nothing had happened. She was beautiful, funny, moisturized, and was offering herself up to me against her father and the
fact that I wore cotton sweaters in December. How could I tell her
that I wasn't ready to be domesticated, housebroken? That this was
our youth and we were acting like our parents. That she was, with
her carefully ordered life plan, *too normal*? Too much, it turned
out, like me. Not "Other" enough. "*Yes*," I'd said, throwing a doily
off the back of a chintz armchair. "The money's an issue."

"Have you seen *The Lion King*?" Mindy was saying into her
mountain of arugula.

"I got her the sound track," Seth said. "She loves it."

My chest was heaving. I couldn't breathe.

Kay 2 gave me a worried look.

"Must be the smoke. Be right back."

I pushed away from the table, walked past the "cozy fireplace" and sneaked a few inhaler hits on the way out for some air.

About a week after the Hamptons debacle, my grandmother died, at 101. Kay 2 was at a publishing party we'd argued about. I had sensed she didn't want me to come, and called her on it. I could hardly blame her, but I did. I needed someone and she was at a party keeping her options open.

I had that empty-gut feeling. The daunting prospect of starting all over again, telling the life story again, *taking off the glasses again,* meeting her parents again, falling in love again, falling out of love again. The next day, I scheduled a summit, a signing of the emotional papers, returning of borrowed sweaters, contraceptive hardware. I was resolved to make this my first mature breakup. No petty recriminations, vicious parting jabs or hiding behind trees. After dinner at Josie's ("wonderful vegetarian, organic and dairy-free options"), I walked her home and, of course, asked to come up.

"Sorry," she rebuffed me. "This is good-bye, Columbus Avenue."

I admired her maddening self-respect. At home, my machine was flashing. Perhaps she'd changed her mind.

Beep. "Hey, it's Viv. So the new editor in chief *loved* your girl's guide to porn and wants to talk about a column. Call me!"

Viv had left *GQ* for *Mademoiselle.*

I looked forward to a night of unbridled fidgeting.

BANDERSNATCH!

When I told Podhoretz I was writing a how-to on renting triple-X videos, his reaction was: "Let me get this straight. You're giving advice to teenage girls on pornography? You have hit a new low."

I certainly hoped so.

After playing house for just short of a year with Kay 2, I was ready to summon the Bachelor Beelzebub and bargain my soul for some Faustian kicks. As if in answer to my prayers, here I was on a windy fall afternoon at Condé Nast headquarters awaiting an audience with *Mademoiselle*'s newly installed editrix. All I knew about her was that she was planning to abbreviate the name of the magazine to *Mlle.*, and that if she was willing to give me a monthly forum in which to justify the vagaries of male behavior, I was her man.

"So how do you pronounce that—*mllll*?" I asked Viv, as we sat in her office awaiting my anointment.

"Millie," Viv said.

"And how do I say hers? Bebé? What kind of name is that? Beh-*bay*? Bee-bee? Beeb?"

"*Bebby*, actually." Viv lit a cigarette and blew the smoke into the shelf of books above her desk. "She's Tasmanian."

"Bit of a devil?" I asked.

"No, actually *from* Tasmania. Talks a little funny, but I like her."

"Heavy Australian accent?"

"Something like that," Viv said, grinning.

"I'm surprised they let you smoke around here."

"They make me use this thing." She tapped ash disdainfully into a smokeless ashtray. "But I edit three-quarters of the magazine, so they can't fire me."

Every man needs a platonic female friend—a confessor, a conduit to the other side—and Viv had become mine. She bore no resemblance to my febrile fantasies of a women's magazine editor. Her hair was a defiantly unlightened melee. The polish on her nails was always chipped. Her eyewear—round and wire-rimmed—prioritized vision, not fashion. She wore faded jeans and Grateful Dead T-shirts. Busty and lusty, she was more *High Times* than high style. But because she had an idea a minute, they put up with her liberal interpretation of the Condé Nast dress code.

"Want to prep me on the column?" I asked, crossing my legs.

"It's a Q and A. You know, questions like, 'I told my boyfriend I loved him, why hasn't he said it back?' 'Is it true men masturbate all the time?'"

I uncrossed my legs.

"Four of those a month," Viv continued.

"So I'll be giving the flower of middle America a window onto my jaded, sex-mad soul and therefore the jaded, sex-mad souls of all men?"

"That's the idea."

After another upward exhale, Viv grabbed the back of her neck with both hands and winced theatrically—her signal.

"Massage?" I offered, getting up and stepping behind her chair.

"Oh, yeah," she said, as I kneaded her shoulders. "You've got the magic fingers."

"Do all your writers do this?" I said, working my way down her spine.

"Just the men," she said. *"Mmmhhh."*

Being happily married did not stop Viv from flirting. I looked down at the wedding photo on her desk. Her husband, David the Dermatologist, wore a monkey suit. Viv had a garland on her head that she said made her look like Mother Nature in those old "Nobody Messes with Mother Nature" margarine ads.

The phone purred. Viv hit one of the long row of buttons. I wished I had a phone like that, in an office like this.

"Bebé can see you now," said a timid voice on speaker.

"Thank you, Winter," Viv said, clicking off.

"Winter? *Summer* I've heard of. . . ."

"She's Bebé's assistant. Brain the size of a Tic Tac. She's a Rockefeller or something. They all are around here."

"Be sure and introduce me," I said.

We perp-walked down a long hallway to a corner office. One of the thinnest women I have ever seen showed us in.

"Hi, Bebé," Viv said. "Here he is."

Behind an immaculate glass desk was a pixie in slitlike glasses an Eskimo could have used to ward off snow blindness. Her reddish-brownish hair was tied in small knots and protruded at different lengths and angles. She wore a skirt that looked like burlap cut on a violent angle, a white tank top with tiny mirrors sewn into it and heavy, rubber-soled black boots. Viv and I lowered ourselves into a pair of red, plywood Eames chairs. I assumed my customary pose of simulated relaxation.

"Your last piece was absolutely *frabjous*," Bebé said. "You said something so *brillig* about those amateur pornos! What was it again?"

"'Ugly people having sweaty, badly lit sex in messy apartments'?" I quoted, wondering what got people these No. 1 jobs. Were they visionaries? Ballbusters? Operators? I would have given it to Bebé based on that crazy lingo alone.

"*Bandersnatch!*" she said, clapping her tiny hands. "I'm *gimbling in the wabe*!"

Standing by the elevator bank fifteen minutes later, Viv was still chuckling to herself.

"Bandersnatch," I said. "Do you mind warning me when I'm about to meet a space oddity. What's with that lingo?"

"She spent her entire childhood reading *Vogue* and *Jabberwocky*. Her father was some kind of Lewis Carroll nut. There's definitely something through-the-looking-glass about her."

The elevator pinged and opened on four legsome Rockefellerettes in identical black dresses and cruelly vectored heels. Their eyes burned as Viv held the doors open.

"We'll need a contributor's page photo," she said. "Something sexy yet sensitive."

Viv let the elevator close and start its rapid drop down.

After two hours of wishing I had more hair, I settled on a picture Kay 2 had taken on Columbus Avenue. I had on a narrow-lapeled olive blazer I was particularly proud of and an expression I thought suggested knowing honesty. My lips were slightly parted as if I was about to say something refreshingly, seductively direct. I stuck the snapshot in an envelope to messenger to Viv with a note signed, "Jim Dixon"—the hero of my hero Kingsley Amis's great comic novel *Lucky Jim*. Something told me I might need a pseudonym.

WHEN PISCES WOMAN
MEETS ARIES MAN

My last trip coastward had been on my own dime. I'd cobbled together enough freelance assignments to cover my costs and cleaned out my frequent-flier account for seats in row ninety-seven with the goats and chickens. My "hotel accommodations," as the game shows say, were a freshly fumigated room at the Saharan Motor Inn. I recommend it, to anyone who likes falling asleep to the sound of gunfire.

But now *TV Guide* was paying. They had entrusted me with their annual "Summer Stars" feature—five-hundred-word verbal snapshots of actors and actresses who weren't quite big enough to rate the Fall Preview. I flew warm-nuts class, rented a red Mustang convertible and checked into a suite at the Sunset Marquis.

A bellhop wheeled my solitary bag to my suite.

"Will you be in L.A. long, sir?" he asked, as I took in the Santa

Fe décor—all washed pinks and burnt sienna, with sunken modular furniture.

"A few days," I said.

"On business?"

"Yeah."

He gave me a guided tour of the minibar.

"Will that be everything, sir?"

All I had was a twenty. What the hell—I could expense it.

"Thanks," I said, slipping him the folded bill.

"Thank *you*, sir. If there's *anything* you need, my name is Bryce."

Within what seemed like seconds, a manila envelope shot under my door. Inside was a script. Typed on the cover page was:

Who's the Boss?
"Look Whose [*sic*] Bossin' Now!"
Spec script by Bryce Dingle

An hour in Tinseltown and already my first cliché. A blond Sammy Glick had mistaken me for a somebody. Did he assume anyone who checked into the Marquis and slipped him a double sawbuck had industry juice? I went down to the pool to pretend to make some calls. Before the cappuccino hit my lips, Bryce was kneeling beside my table like a sprinter.

"Anything you can do to get my script to Mr. Danza—"

"The show's been canceled," I told him. "It's not coming back this season."

"Are you sure?"

"I write for *TV Guide*," I said.

I continued staring at the harem lounging around the pool with half a dozen long-haired, middle-aged guys in Speedos.

"Foreigner," Bryce said, reading my gaze. "Reunion tour. I already gave Mick Jones's assistant my demo tape. Great talking to you, sir!" He leapt off his mark and sprinted to the lobby, where more guests were checking in.

Foreigner! "Cold as Ice" was practically my make-out *theme* in high school. I gave myself over to a brief, ecstatic memory involving a tawny tenth grader and a shuddering dryer in Andrew Munn's laundry room. A member of the band roused himself from his lounge chair, gut jiggling over his banana hammock, and strutted lazily to the edge of the water. Was that Mick? He jumped in, sunglasses still on. Two groupies as tawny as my laundry-room Lolita followed him in.

To Bill Hicks, this town may have been "*Hell*-A"—eighty-five degrees in mid-October. To a kid from the frigid tundra of the north and the concrete canyons of NYC, it was palmy heaven. I stirred my foam, relaxing in the knowledge that I didn't have to be anywhere until tomorrow.

In a few minutes, Bryce returned holding a small blue piece of paper and reading ceremoniously from it.

"Sir? A Mr. Bing Swinger called. The message is to please call him as soon as possible. Would you like me to bring you a phone?"

"Thanks," I said, slipping him another couple of bucks and turned back to Mick and the girls splashing and laughing in the shallow end.

"And then my proctologist says, 'If you like this, you should work in television!' "

Dan Binswanger slapped me on the back and downed another Maker's Mark.

We were at Jumbo's Clown Room, the last stop on a night crawl that had started respectably enough at Dan Tana's, then devolved to The Frolic Room, Bob's Classy Lady and Jumbo's. These bleak burlesque houses were supposed to be the L.A. equivalents of Billy's. But Billy's didn't have the stench of failure and despair they exuded. A former wire-service reporter, Binswanger had given up hard news to scrounge for network gossip at *Variety*. I admired his mastery of the expense-account lifestyle. He wasn't what I would have called a friend, but whenever I flew in, he was always eager for an evening on the company tab.

Onstage, a zoned-out biker mama in braided pigtails peeled down to her helmet and a leather G-string.

"You've got a million of 'em," I said, chuckling not at the bad joke but the unself-consciousness of the delivery.

"You know I do, you ol' son of a gun!"

The guy was a throwback. At thirty-five, his thick head of hair had already gone almost completely gray. He had one of those perfectly symmetrical, ageless faces permanently flexed in a brilliant smile, except when he got plastered and his eyes turned into two hooded street thugs. Tall and wiry, he was full-on retro, from his Galaxie 500 convertible to his Botany 500 suits—both circa 1965.

"Bastards are just trying to lure you out full-time," Binswanger said, into his drink. "Don't take the job."

The hoodies were creeping over his eyes.

TV Guide's West Coast bureau was trying to recruit me. The suite at the Sunset Marquis and light workload were all part of their seductive soft sell.

"Why not?"

"It ruins you."

"You're doing all right," I said.

"You get sucked into this shit. In a year, you'll be living with a porn star in the Valley."

I weighed cohabitation with a porn star with writing "Summer Stars" for *TV Guide*.

"Nobody respects journalists in this town," he went on. "We're all trying to sell screenplays and they know it. Why *should* they respect us? Try talking to a child actor about his *craft*."

I didn't tell him about my appointment the next day with the star of *Boy Meets World*.

In the morning, I breakfasted poolside with an old Washington friend who was now at the *L.A. Times* and desperate to get the fat sucked out of his chin, and lunched at the Warner Bros. commissary with a publicist I liked because he kept a sign on his desk that said "Failed Writer." In the afternoon, more interviews, with Lois *and* Clark. I talked to the ten-year-old, at length, about his craft. All fairly soul-deadening. But aiding and abetting other people's "creative" endeavors seemed to be the price of a ticket West.

Could I live here? Get a bungalow in the Hollywood Hills with a recovering porn star? Or an ambitious script girl loaded with pep, like the one William Holden falls for in *Sunset Boulevard*.

I called Binswanger.

"On the ol' expense account?" he asked, then, without waiting for an answer, went on: "I figure we'll hit Trader Vic's. I'll get a coupla broads. We'll go out for a coupla laughs."

I realized who he reminded me of: Larry Tate—Darren's boss on *Bewitched*. The consummate three-martini ad man. A winker and rib-poker whose favorite phrase was, "You ol' son of a gun!"

"Pass the poi," I said, sliding into his argot.

"You're at the Marquis? I'll bring the lovelies around six."

I liked how early the night started in L.A. They showed up on the dot and Binswanger made straight for the minibar. Within seconds, he was mixing drinks and telling bad jokes, snaking his arms around the girls' waists. In the divvying of dates, "his" was clearly Dusty—a beachy blonde in a pink sundress who worked the cosmetics counter at I. Magnin. Mine, I determined the moment she walked in, was Vanessa—a bombshell in the guise of a West Coast hipstress. When she took off her coat, wavy russet hair fell negligently over powdery white shoulders. Her tanlessness seemed deliberate. Her generous hips announced that she'd never seen a StairMaster and didn't want to. She did something in "gift muffins."

Binswanger pulled his lady onto the balcony, assuring her the second-story view of the pool was not to be missed, leaving Vanessa and me to get acquainted. We sat on the Santa Fe sectional with our drinks.

"I like your glasses," Vanessa said, brushing her hair off one shoulder.

"Thanks," I said. "I like your stockings."

"The seam is a nightmare."

She frowned at the back of her calf, then brightened.

"Hey, what's your sign?"

They don't waste any time getting to the astrology out here. I was on my second, or third or fourth, L.A. cliché now, but it was refreshing being in a cynicism-free zone.

"Aries."

"The *ram*," she said. "Guess me."

"No idea."

"Go on, guess."

"Virgo."

"Pisces! The two fishes."

She said this as if it were self-evident.

Binswanger and Dusty stumbled out of the bedroom. He was straightening his tie. She was adjusting the straps of her sundress.

"Light the Tiki torches!" Binswanger said. "The Big Kahuna beckons!"

Many active volcano drinks secured me a dinner date with Vanessa for the following night. "Just the two of us, I hope," she whispered, slipping me a business card freshly pressed with violet lipstick. As Binswanger dropped her off in the Galaxie, I watched her hips wave good-bye.

Her apartment, in one of those faux-Norman castles off La Cienega, was like walking into a vintage store. Clothes hanging everywhere. Not messy—on display. The dress she'd poured herself into looked forties, as did her shoes, with their wedge heel and open toe. No stockings. There was something deadly serious about the way she approached this Jessica Rabbit impersonation that was both sexy and a little silly.

"I want to show you a book," she said, tugging me into her bedroom.

Diaphanous fabrics shrouded ornately footed lamps. A collection of old perfume bottles covered an antique vanity. Vanessa was only in her late twenties, but her boudoir simulated a lifetime of doomed romance.

" 'Celestial Bodies,' " I read, examining the cover. " 'The Lovers' Guide to Astrological Compatibility.' "

"Here," she said, standing close and flipping to a chapter titled, When Pisces Woman Meets Aries Man. "I'll bring it."

She suggested a French place with more Edith Piaf décor. In a zodiacal role reversal, I had fish, she had lamb. A meat eater. Good sign.

"Okay," she said, pulling *Celestial Bodies* out of her bag. "I wanna read you this."

She put on a pair of cats'-eye glasses and made a serious face.

" 'The Aries man literally will try to sweep Pisces off her feet,' " she read, with feeling.

"Literally?" I said, taking mine off and giving her the old myopic gaze.

"*Hush.* 'If he is in love with a woman, she will soon know about it. He has a positive attitude to life. Even when the odds are stacked against him, he knows how to pick himself up, dust himself off and start all over again. An Aries man will not take no for an answer.' "

I smiled, positively.

" 'Aries is *all man*. Pisces likes a masterful guy. His honest and basic style of lovemaking will thrill her.' "

Vanessa looked through her cats'-eyes at me. I begged the waiter for more vino. No wonder those Larry Tate sons of guns drank so much in those days, with these bombshells going off all around them.

" 'He is ambitious, too. Success means a great deal to him. He is conventional, though, and loves his home life, too. Pisces will have to let him have his night out with the boys. But he would not be unfaithful sexually on his jaunts, and looks forward to returning home. *There is no reason why this couple should not have a happy, successful life together.*' "

"It doesn't say that!" I said, grabbing the book out of her hands.

But it was all in there. And, as far as my end was concerned, all true.

A third bottle got us up to my suite. She unzipped her dress and stood in front of the sliding doors to the balcony.

"You know who my idol is?" she said.

"Who?" I asked, moving towards her.

"Ann-Margret."

A guy could put up with a lot of astrology for a gal like that. When I got back to New York, Vanessa sent me a picture of herself straddling her Harley in the desert.

But I had other fishes to fry.

Not long after L.A., I was at a party in some part of Harlem that was pretending it wasn't. That was where I met Lynette.

I wouldn't normally have given her a second glance. Not that she was bad-looking, just hard. Hard body. Hard eyes. No makeup. Even her dark hair looked hard—slicked straight back, with one or two strands of gray. I'd gone to the fridge for a beer and she was leaning against the kitchen counter, smoking. She looked like a bartender at some place with license plates on the wall. Because I wasn't worried about making clever conversation, I went the other way, seeing what would happen, once we'd traded names, if I asked the most banal questions I could think of.

"So how do you know the host?" I asked.

"She's a friend of a friend," Lynette said.

"Where do you live?"

"On the Upper West Side."

"What do you do?"

"I'm a secretary," she said.

That explained the nails.

"Where?"

"Columbia."

"My alma mater," I said. "What department?"

"Physics," she said. "I also dance."

Never dated a dancer.

"I saw Lucinda Childs at the Joyce," I said.

An old high school girlfriend had come into town. The dancers all wore pink triangles on their leotards. Susan Sontag was sitting two seats down from me. A horrible experience all around.

"Oh yeah," Lynette said, not quite as impressed by my familiarity with The Dance as I expected.

"What company are you with?" I said.

"Billy's Topless," she said. "Do you know it?"

I tried to steady myself.

"It's right around the corner from me," I said, swallowing a little too fast and feeling beer fizz in my esophagus.

How was it possible that I'd never seen her? Must have been that long period of abstinence with Kay 2.

"I'm not doing it anymore," she said.

"You're not?"

"My boss at Columbia is a geologist and he used to work at night, so I did the day shift at Billy's. But now he's working days. And they didn't have anything for me at night. Those girls make too much money to give up their shifts."

The *day* shift. That explained it! I wasn't spending enough time there during working hours.

"My job's pretty basic," she said. "When I dance, I feel free."

"That must be very . . . empowering," I said, taking off my glasses.

It got me Lynette's number. A stripper's—ex-stripper's—number. This was historic. I had crossed the Rubicon separating real women from the pay-per-view variety—a notch I couldn't wait, in my schoolboy depravity, to etch on the bedpost.

We had drinks, at the Ginger Man, on Sixty-fifth Street. (Even with a stripper I couldn't escape the Upper West Side.) She sat on the bar stool in a short dress that showed off plenty of hard thigh. I listened, rapt, as she described her ambition to become a "professional jewelry photographer." I prided myself on my ability to talk superficially about anything, but this was a stumper.

"So you shoot . . . bracelets and . . . necklaces and things?"

"Yeah, it's why I like geology. But I'm really an artist."

I didn't doubt that. Whether her artistry had anything to do with taking pictures of precious metal was another matter.

"Once, in Niagara Falls, I saw an exhibit of Elvis's jewelry," I said. "That he'd designed himself. They also had his favorite casual suit. It was a brown double-knit leisure—"

"I'm more into rings," Lynette said.

"So was Elvis!" I said, grasping.

"Oh."

I was in another irony-free zone here.

"I'd love to see some of your . . . work," I said, forcing myself not to give the word a sarcastic spin.

"Maybe," she said.

"A friend of mine has a photography gallery in SoHo. Danziger? We should go this weekend."

"Should I bring my portfolio?"

"Well, maybe not this time," I said.

When it was time for her to get uptown to Columbia, I walked her to Broadway.

"Well, thanks for that drink," she said, with flat unreadability.

I saw my shot at a stripper ending right here. My strategy suddenly seemed horribly misguided, pretending to be into her "work." This was a woman who took her clothes off for money. I wasn't going to land her with the glasses-guy bit. I needed a bold player line.

"Listen, I have to go to Miami to interview Vanilla Ice next week for *Spin*. Wanna come? All expenses paid. I'm staying in South Beach. Big record release party."

"Vanilla Ice?"

"I know," I said. "It's a comeback album. He's 'gangsta' now. I specialize in fringe celebrities."

For a split second, she seemed to consider it.

"I don't think so."

"Come on."

"I can't."

"Why not?"

"I just . . . can't. Maybe I'll tell you sometime. But I'm late. There's a cab."

That didn't work. What was it? Boyfriend? She'd claimed no. Was she mixed up with the nocturnal physicist? Did she have a fear of overmoussed white rappers?

I flew to Miami alone. A PR guy met me at the airport and we drove to Star Island, where "Ice," as he now called himself, lived in a white mansion decorated in Early Drug Dealer. I was looking at the tropical fish swimming in the Lucite staircase, waiting for the Iceman to cometh, when I heard, "Wazzup, bro! Wuz goin' *owwwwnnn!*"

Rap's Great White Hopeless burst through the patio doors in

baggy shorts and an oversized T-shirt from Kicker Cab Audio Systems that said, "Listen to the Legend." Bottle-yellow hair, shaved around the sides, sprouted asparagus-length dreads on top. Tattoos snaking up his leg and around his wrist completed the image rethink.

"Yo!" Ice said, punching my shoulder. "I was just on the phone with Bernstein, my accountant. You know what I gotta pay in property taxes? Sixty-eight thousand dollars a year, yo! You wanna do the interview now?"

"Tomorrow," I said. "There's plenty of time."

"Cool," Ice said. "Whatever, bro. Let's *ride!*"

Ice raced jet skis competitively. Then again, he used to claim he was a motocross champion, too, and none of that turned out to be true.

I rode. My buddy 'Nilla's favorite move was to ski straight at me, then turn at the last minute, spraying me with sea water.

Bernstein came to the party that night, along with a few local parasites. Around 11:00, Ice decided to lead a search for "titty ho's" at a local topless establishment. Two hours later, we returned to Star Island *sans* titty-ho's and Ice brought out a bong the size of a grenade launcher while a flunky uncaged his pet mongoose. All grist for the mockery mill, I thought, but as I took my notes, I began to question the point of this article. To make fun of a disgraced has-been for the amusement of *Spin* readers? As a licensed "Men" columnist, I should have been able to rationalize any errant behavior, any lapse into primitive maleness. But the whole scene was too sordid and sad. Getting wasted and chasing strippers.

I couldn't wait to get back to New York, fire up a vodka-tonic (or five) and tell Lynette what she missed.

I reverted to my old strategy with her. I took her to foreign films, awful one-woman shows in the East Village, conjured conversation for hours on end. She was always eager to go out, but invariably held back at the end of the night. Never more than light farewell kissing. I figured she was suspicious of men. I could wait it out.

I finally got her on the couch, with access to hitherto cordoned-off areas. All the long, effortful evenings were going to be worth it, I thought. Then she pulled away.

"I have to ask you something," she said.

"What?"

"What would you say if I told you I have herpes?" she said.

Now there was a question for Lucky Jim.

YOU CAN'T HAVE
EVERYTHING

"It isn't that bad if they're not having an outbreak," Tad said.

"The word *outbreak* isn't something I want associated with the sexual act," I said.

"Okay, but you're ruling out a lot of hot chicks."

An Asian woman in a red peignoir was lifting the world's thinnest waffle from a chafing dish and dropping it on a paper plate.

Billy's now opened at 1:00 P.M. on Sunday.

For brunch.

Our creative meetings had become less frequent. A spin-off of *Out There* called *Out with Elle*, featuring Elle Macpherson, died when our supermodel host ran off in pursuit of a movie career. Tad was spending more time in L.A. pitching shows through sock puppets and other nontraditional means.

I went back to reading my Sunday *Times.*

"Can you stop reading for one minute?" Tad said. "I'm trying to have an intelligent conversation here."

He snatched the newspaper out of my hands.

"Hey!" I said.

"Weddings and *Engagements*!" he said. "You're reading the women's sports pages?"

"I . . . glance at them sometimes," I said, thinking fast how to explain why I'd started scrutinizing these nuptial listings like a perennial bridesmaid. "As . . . pop anthropology. You know. How Rich Bastard X scored Hot Chick Y."

"Have you considered the patch? Because if you're having a testosterone problem. . . ."

Might as well come clean.

"Everyone I know is getting married, having kids, moving on—"

"Not everyone," Tad said, downing the rest of his beer and waving to Pat Benatar Sr. for another round.

"I'll be thirty-two this year," I said. "I need a Woman of Quality."

"Model-quality?"

The Asian Spitfire had ascended to the stage and was writhing to the sounds of Bob Seger and the Silver Bullet Band. The music at Billy's wasn't *always* good.

"First, I gotta get a new apartment," I said. "No Woman of Quality is going to want to step over Carlton the Crackhead and listen to grinding garbage trucks at three A.M."

"You live in New York! You should be glad to have a little edge in your environment. You want to move to Old Greenwich—my hometown? Get a wife named Fluffy with a closet full of tennis whites?"

"With the frilly underpants?"

"You'd be begging for crackheads and garbage trucks." Tad slammed down his liquid brunch.

"All I know is, I need a total life upgrade," I said. "Pad, girl, job."

I had heated fantasies about goings-on in offices. Lasting literary bonds forming between writers and editors—Hemingway–Max Perkins type things. Affairs consummated on desk tops, then consecrated in the *Times*. I was sick of freelancing, always pitching, feeling the four walls of my home cubicle closing in. I was ready for professional monogamy. Unfortunately, this was 1993. I had moved back to New York just in time for the recession. No one was hiring.

"I'm going for some of those waffles," Tad said.

I picked up the paper and turned to the Real Estate section.

I started looking at apartments. A petite blonde from one of the big agencies spent a lot of time selling me from inside walk-in closets. I liked her languid, lackadaisical manner. She wore sheer skirts and sandals that hardly seemed to be shoes at all, just fancifully colored ankle-tilters. Why didn't I ask her out? The closet business seemed like some kind of come-on. But she never had anything good. Those were not the shoes of a realtor.

I found myself spending more time with a matronly veteran who kept telling me, "You can't have everything!"

We looked at a studio on Fifteenth Street. Completely black: black walls, black ceiling, black stage-set platforms. . . . A gay decorator and his boyfriend were splitting up and needed to sell.

"It's a little S and M-y," I said.

"So you'll paint. *You can't have everything.*"

"I could just keep renting."

"You could go out with a different chippie every night, too," my matronly broker said. "It's not the same as *owning.*"

I had the same arguments with Viv.

Ever since the Kay 2 breakup, various yentas had been offering their services. My "future wife" was encoded in every set of seven digits they offered. I took the numbers and found excuses not to dial. I tended to rule out blind dates as a desperation move, like a personal ad, or wearing a sign around your neck saying, "I'm lonely." But the love brokers wore me down with their mating-game syllogisms: *You only meet high-level, like-minded people through introductions. Ergo, if you want to meet a high-level, like-minded woman, you have to go on blind dates. QED.*

"Why the hell haven't you called Cynthia yet?" Viv shouted into the phone from *Mlle.* one morning after I'd faxed in my column.

"I'm . . . busy."

"Oh, I'm sorry she doesn't lap-dance for a living," Viv said. "Does a woman who's getting her Ph.D. in English lit and writes grant applications threaten you?"

"No. I have a master's in English, you know."

"So you've mentioned. Worried about a little intellectual competition, are we? Because—I'm wild-guessing here—*Beowulf* probably won't come up while you're fondling her *huge*—"

"I'm actually more of a leg man," I said.

I was playing hard to get, but how could my interest not have been piqued by an academic who gave new meaning to the word *endowment*. I envisioned our scholarly evenings together, a smile playing about my lips as I gazed with satisfaction at what I would waggishly call her "ivory towers."

"Oh, please," Viv said, with a weary exhale. "Take the number."

I wrote it in my Week-at-a-Glance.

"So how long have you been into . . . Hobbitology?"

Cynthia and I were pumping pints of Sam Adams at the Village Corner.

I wondered if that was the right word for a doctorate in Tolkien studies, then drank off, in many consecutive swallows, the top half of my beer. Anything to avert my eyes from her chest. It was all I could do not to stare. Sadly, not at her breasts, but at the loose T-shirt hanging off them like an awning. It was emblazoned with the head of William Shakespeare and, in Olde English lettering, the words *Will Power*.

She might as well have been wearing a Mensa baseball cap. I mean, we *know* Shakespeare is the greatest writer in the English language, don't we? That's generally been agreed upon, hasn't it? For a few *hundred* years. We don't need to go around wearing T-shirts announcing the fact.

Cynthia had been fine on the phone. Sonorous voice, swift on the uptake. I didn't have to remind her who I was. Now I saw she was a geek blessed (or cursed) with the body of a centerfold, and seemed to have no idea how to handle the combination. Neither did I. I can latch onto almost any common ground or opinion or quirk to justify my lust for a desirable woman. At the same time, the slightest misstep will send me into hypercritical frenzy. What were we going to do on the next date, play Dungeons and Dragons?

But I should follow through just to unveil that magnificent *poitrine*, I thought, as we hugged the jostly bar. The Village Corner was a reliably rowdy joint. The last thing you want on a blind date is quiet. Awkward conversation has a tendency to echo.

"Big Shakespeare fan?" I said.

"Shakes? I only live for him. And *Next Gen*."

I caught the reference to *Star Trek: The Next Generation*. TV was still my main beat. But did she really say *Shakes*?

"I'm more into . . . classic *Trek*," I said. "William Shatner bagging all those alien babes in tinfoil bikinis. He's Canadian, you know—"

"No way. Picard is so much cooler. He's so much more . . . intelligent."

Spicy date conversation!

"Remind me," I said. "Which one is Gandalf, the good guy or the bad guy?"

For a couple of hours she told me, with both of us pumping pints like free weights. Where did she put it? Better not answer that.

Mystery Science Theater 3000 came up. *MST3K*, as the cultists called this cable comedy in which a crew of satirical space cadets make fun of bad B-movies.

At last: common ground, where humor meets geekdom. Cynthia pointed out that it was on tomorrow night. We could watch together.

I took one last look. I might never see their likes again.

"I'll be out of town," I lied.

At the risk of sounding like a traitor to my gender, breasts are not enough.

"You're an idiot, but I've got someone better," Viv said. "Hey, easy on the judo chops."

I always dropped off my *Mlle.* column in person now. Any excuse to escape the four walls. And Viv had become my female confessor.

"It's my new Swedish technique," I said. "Who you got for me?"

"My friend Daphne. She's a freelancer, too. *Ooooh*, yes. That spot there."

"Byline sounds vaguely familiar," I said, as if I hadn't memorized her contributor's page photo in *Vogue, Spin* and this month's *Mlle.*

"Why are you stopping?"

"Sorry," I said and went back to judo chopping.

"You're perfect for each other. She's a freelance writer. Into pop culture. All the same things you are. Knows everyone. She's got an edge."

Dense darkish blonde hair, lips curled between a smirk and a sneer. Interesting. . . .

"Isn't she a bit of a . . . climber?" I said.

Not that that was a bad thing. Inept at social climbing myself, I warmed to the thought of letting some more ruthless summiteer sherpa me to the top.

"You heard that joke, too?"

"What joke?"

"Forget it," Viv said. "It's too mean."

I withdrew my magic fingers.

"All right, all right. What does Daphne say when she's having an orgasm? '*Oh, God*—do you know him? *Oh, Jesus*—do you know him?' "

I laughed.

"Call her now," Viv said. "You can use my phone. I'll go get cigarettes."

"Can't," I said, shaking my hands out and moving back into the chair in front of her desk. "Gotta interview Milla for the *Times* at two-thirty."

"Milla Jovovich?"

"She's just going by the first name now," I said.

"Of course she is. And what, pray tell, has Milla done to deserve the attentions of *The New York Times*?"

"An album," I said. "It's called *The Divine Comedy*."

"Of course it is."

"It's actually pretty good," I said. "I've been listening to it."

"Good Lord. *How* did you get your reputation as a tough interviewer? It's pathetic the way you fall for these chicks you write about."

"I always get in a few zingers," I said, unconvincingly.

"You're calling Daphne tonight. She plays tennis, too. Make it a tennis date."

"All right," I said.

I was daydreaming about whites and frilly undies again.

My rendezvous with Milla was at the Book Friends Café. Milla's choice, I preferred to think, rather than her publicist's. Per-

haps she harbored literary aspirations, too. Her album alluded to
Dante, after all. My Slavic Beatrice was just seventeen and I was
eager to learn what other prodigious talents lay behind that cover-
girl smile.

It was a sleety January afternoon. I arrived early and took up a
post near the back, as far away from the sodden, shivering Book
Friends as possible, so Milla and I could commune in relative pri-
vacy. I dried my glasses with a napkin and pulled out my carefully
chosen literary prop: *Bel-Ami.* Penguin Classics edition. You can't
go wrong with a French novel. This one had an added advantage:
I'd actually read it. I kept my eyes on the door, and my watch. Three
o'clock came and went, then 3:30. They're always late. Was that
her? For our brief encounter, the minx had disguised herself as a
thrift-shop waif. Black Converse sneakers peeked out from under
her long black skirt. She peeled off a green army jacket and looked
around. I buried myself in my Maupassant, then looked up with an
expression of distracted surprise, signaling her with my hand.

"Hi!" she said, loping up to my table and leveling me with the
Medusan gaze of a professional beauty. "I'm Milla."

A misshapen sweater was pulled tight over a white T-shirt. A
butterfly-shaped barrette pinned down her wet brown hair. All in
all, a horrible ensemble, but on her. . . .

"No problem," I assured her, though there had been no apology.
"I needed to get some reading done."

I put down my book. She glanced at it.

"I *love* Flaubert," she said, fanning the pages. "There aren't *any*
good bookstores in L.A. What's this about?"

"Young man from the provinces comes to Paris, falls into a
newspaper job and sleeps his way to the top. Maupassant was
dying of syphilis when he wrote it."

Shock her with mature, adult banter.

She dropped into the chair opposite me and lit a cigarette, not
seeming too shocked.

"So you work for *The New York Times*. That i

I saw a way in. The sexpot yearns to be taken

couples with the "serious" writer. Like Marilyn ar

But he was already famous. Maybe we should st

trading intimate opinions on French literature. I consulted the list

of questions in my Reporter's Notebook.

"How would you describe your album?"

Milla waved her hands nervously and spoke in an adolescent, Californian rush that belied her exotic provenance. Born in Kiev, the only child of a Russian actress and a Serbian doctor. . . .

"Omigod. Ethereal but twisted. *Um*. Pure but not pure."

"I know what you mean."

I had absolutely no idea what she meant.

Over a steaming pot of herbal dishwater, we discussed her art. I recalled what a Harvard MBA friend of mine called his "null set" theory. For a long time, he believed that there was an artist or a poetess out there who would be attracted to a management consultant like him. Then he realized there were no such women. None. Zero women. In math terms, the number of poetesses who find McKinsey associates sexy is "null set." But I was no management consultant. I was an emissary of the Gray Lady.

"So," I asked. "How long have you been playing the hurdy-gurdy?"

The Sunday my piece came out, Milla and I were not savoring it together in bed over herbal tea. So I kept my tennis date with Daphne. We were playing at the U.S. Open indoor courts in Queens. She drove.

"What the hell's a hurdy-gurdy?" Daphne asked, cutting off an angry Land Rover as we headed over the Fifty-ninth Street bridge. "And who's your editor at the *Times*?"

"John Capouya."

I liked that she had a car, even a beat-up Civic, and enjoyed tching her matter-of-factly change gears, not making a big deal out of driving standard like men do.

She sped through my Rolodex and bank statement.

"Hey, how much does *Rolling Stone* pay you? Two bucks a word?"

I looked at her slobby Condé Nast T-shirt, beat-up sneakers and purple gym shorts. Kay 2 wouldn't have been caught dead in gear like this. Why did I break up with her again?

"Viv told me you and Jerry split up," I said, trying to veer us onto more personal terrain.

"He was a loser. Sat around all day polishing his National Magazine Award. I told him he was acting like a has-been at forty-five."

Daphne braked and geared down in rapid succession, from third down to second to first. Every time she pumped the clutch, I looked down at her legs. The calves were fine. But there was no getting around the long black hairs on her thighs. Was this some kind of political thing—no hair removal above the knee? More likely just a practical time-saver. The only people who were going to see her thighs weren't people she was going to do business with.

She beat me 6-3, 6-0. I'd lost interest before we started playing.

"A little hair!" Viv said, as I stood behind her chair and pressed my thumbs into her traps.

"I couldn't get past it."

"The depth of your superficiality never ceases to amaze me," Viv said, tensing her shoulders. "Some model/actress/hurdy-gurdist shows up an hour late for an interview and you're all over her. But a *real* woman has one little flaw and you write her off. This is what makes us scream ourselves to sleep at night."

I worked my way up to her rigid neck muscles.

"I wasn't so crazy about her personality either," I said. "It'd be like dating the little voice in my head that kept telling me I needed to network more."

"It's not bad enough that a woman has to compete with all the other women out there. She has to compete with . . . *Milla*? Thank God I married David."

She lit another cigarette.

"So who's next?" I asked.

"In your dreams," she said, shaking the match and throwing it into her smokeless ashtray. "You're too picky, especially for a guy who has no idea what he wants. You're not ready for a relationship. No more setups. I want to write a book on men titled *You Call This a Gender?*"

She spun her chair around and went back to work.

No matter. I had other double-agents in the field. Half the female magazine editors in New York were gathering intelligence and recruiting on my behalf. I went on a nightly montage of one-drink stands. There was the wafer thin beauty editor who brought a miniature blender to my apartment because it was time for her protein shake. The ad-agency account exec who told me, "Last time I was in this bar was when I kidney punched my boyfriend." The former *Saturday Night Live* comedy writer starring in a one-woman show called *It's Not Me, It's You*. All brokered by their *agents d'amour* as smart, successful catches who just really needed to meet a "nice guy." Translation: "Self-destructive basketcases who always date assholes." But I made the calls, went on the dates, dutifully worked my material, then went home and thought about Marisa Tomei.

Allure wanted me to profile her. This was a biggie: photos by Herb Ritts, possible cover. My first. I began the ritual preparations, poring over a thick sheaf of Lexis-Nexis'd clips sent by the magazine's research department. Every night for a week, I rented her movies. A screening of her new one, *Only You*, was held especially for me. I watched jealously as Marisa lapped at Robert Downey Jr.'s chest so furiously I expected her to cough up a hairball.

Our arranged romance began, aptly enough, at a Valentine's Eve theater benefit. I watched her play a bit part with a sexy French accent, but, despite lingering in the lobby like a stage-door Johnny, scored no face time. Date two was a bizarre off-Broadway meditation on homophobia, cannibalism and the films of Katharine Hepburn. Again I'd hoped to nip backstage, but Ms. Tomei fled the theater before I could offer my congratulations for her double role as a porn star and a child psychotic. I wasn't worried. These stalkings, sanctioned by her publicist and my editor, were just to gather background material for the interview itself.

The consummation of our hitherto one-way relationship was set for Cafe Mogador, a hummus-and-couscous dispensary in the East Village. She arrived a little after 4:00, only half an hour late, and kissed my cheek hello. I forgave her instantly. Her navy pea coat, white jeans and black combat boots was hardly the Halloween costume you'd expect from someone who made *People*'s Worst Dressed List.

I put my microcassette recorder between us and jumped right in with the tough questions.

"So, tell me about *Only You*."

Marisa took a deep breath, like someone about to burst into a complicated yoga pose.

"It's about—the theme of it is, like, can you find your true love and should you hold out for that?"

She bubbled out a squeaky giggle and blinked at me as if I had the answer to this question. Viv might have pointed out the inherent contradiction in rejecting crazy and/or annoying women while lusting after Marisa Tomei. But how easily is the seducer seduced! I knew, objectively, that she was playing me. I also believed she was truly interested. Whoever defined intelligence as the ability to hold two contradictory ideas in your head at the same time was wrong.

A nose-studded waitress moped over.

"I'll have the Moroccan hot cereal," Marisa said.

"That's on the brunch menu, and we stopped serving brunch at four."

"We were *here* at four," Marisa said.

A glimpse of the diva.

"I'll see what I can do."

We were alone with our pita bread again.

"She didn't seem to recognize you," I said, slipping accidentally into journalistic mode.

"I did one fuckin' movie!" Marisa said, slipping accidentally into *My Cousin Vinny* mode. "Why should she recognize me?"

But she soon regained her composure and was bubbling and squeaking again.

"I've met, like—I've gotten to be introduced to the cream of the crop of really talented people. And that makes me, like, totally—it sets me on fire. . . . You see how much people attack each other and forget that this is about everybody's growth."

"Did you do a lot of . . . research for the role?"

I recorded her acting theories, her arc and charts and her graphs, as I looked at her insouciantly cropped hair and giant dark eyes. She asked me questions, too. The smart ones always do. What other magazines I wrote for. How long I'd lived in New York. Whether I had a girlfriend. We got along . . . famously.

Famously enough for me to walk her home. And for her to linger in front of her West Village brownstone, telling me about the playwright she'd dumped while shooting *Only You* in Italy. I pressed as hard as I dared but she refused to divulge his name. So I shifted the conversation back to me.

"Yeah, I don't really like to talk about it," I started to say, reaching for my horn-rims.

I noticed she was staring at my jacket pocket. All of a sudden, she took a step back.

"You're *tapin'* this?" she said.

My Cousin Vinny again.

I looked down at the telltale red REC light. *Damn.* A truism of the celebrity interview game is that you get your best stuff before and after the official interview. I always kept the tape rolling. The thing must have shifted in my pocket.

"I can't fuckin' believe that," Marisa said.

"I know. I mean, I guess it was just on."

"*Yahright.*"

Her black combat boots stomped up the steps of her brownstone.

"Don't worry, I won't use it!" I shouted after her.

Even at work, I was in Bachelor Hell.

Back in the home cubicle, the walls closed in a little more. I sat at my computer thinking about all the dumb stories I had written, all the dumb stories I had agreed to write, this month alone. I turned off my computer and went through my mail. In the new *GQ* was my profile of the infotainment visionary who founded the E! Channel. They'd titled it "La Triviata." In a manila envelope was an editing test from the *New York Observer.* This pink-papered weekly tip sheet of the rich and media-savvy had a job open. I'd gone for an interview at their offices—a cramped East Side brownstone that seemed like working out of someone's apartment. I was already doing that. I looked at the test—a two-thousand-word article on zoning laws—and glazed over. I called and said the job wasn't for me. The editor there seemed slightly offended, but I was glad I'd held out. Why *can't* you have everything?

Because Citibank wouldn't give me a loan. I'd gone to my branch to see how much I could get, so I'd know what I could afford.

What I could afford, apparently, was nothing. I ripped open a letter confirming the rejection of my mortgage application.

Another letter, this one from my accountant, also said I had money problems. Not too little—too much. I needed to shelter it.

"I average ten thousand dollars a month," I'd told the Citibank technocrat. "That's a hundred twenty thousand a year."

A slight exaggeration. I had made, through a lucky confluence of late payments, ten grand *this* month.

"I understand that, sir. But with no regular employer, the bank has no secure guarantee of future earnings."

"But I can't be fired! Aren't my future earnings more secure than people who are at the mercy of their employer?"

"Sir, I will gladly bring this matter to my supervisor, but it is the policy of the mortgage department. . . ."

No job. No apartment. The Life Upgrade was not exactly going according to plan.

*B*eep. "Mr. Dixon, sir. This is Tabitha—Viv's
intern? My leader says we have to sub the last question in your column. Seems the young women of America no longer want to know
why their dudes are nice to them when they're alone, then treat
them like crap in public. Instead, they must be told why, once their
dude has *his* orgasm, he has, quote—zero interest—unquote, in
hers. Please advise."

I played it again. Its youthful cadences and chirpy irony
calmed my jangling nerves. I spent my usual fifteen minutes writing
a new answer, then called to make sure they got the fax.

"Oh, hey," I said, when Viv picked up. "What are you doing
answering your own phone?"

"Disappointed?"

"What do you mean?"

"It's fairly obvious," Viv said.

"It is?"

"May I point out that Tabitha is twelve."

"Twenty-two!"

"It's sad that you know that," Viv said. "Listen, you need someone who *has* an assistant, not someone who *is* an assistant."

"You were twenty-two once," I said.

"There's no need for that kind of talk."

"I just mean you were the same person then that you are now. Would you have wanted David to rule you out as wife material because you were a little younger? My mother is ten years younger than my father. They've been married for thirty years. Aren't women supposed to be that much ahead of us emotionally anyway?"

"I think she majored in Frisbee at Bennington," Viv said.

"Hey, just because she hasn't been beaten down by single life in Manhattan," I said. "It's like the baggage carousel at JFK out there."

"It's not *that* bad," Viv said.

"Not that bad? Your friend Cynthia told me her last boyfriend was a warlock."

"*Wizard*, not warlock. Didn't you ever play Dungeons and Dragons?"

"No, I was a *normal* teenager," I said.

"I doubt that."

"So when's she coming back?"

"She is back. I sent her out for lighter fluid. Tell you what, since you enjoy your little conversations with Tabitha so much, from now on you can tell *her* your problems. I'm washing my hands of you."

I got the impression Viv was mad.

"Uh, can you put her on?"

"Would you mind clarifying that last answer for me, Mr. Dixon, sir? I'm a novice in these matters."

"Gladly," I said. "But you don't have to call me 'sir.' Here's how it works. At any given time, any given single guy probably has a couple of women in the picture. Two, three at the most. More is a pathology, sex-addict territory. Go down that road and you'll end up at a wellness center in Minnesota holding hands with Michael Douglas."

"Brilliant," Tabitha said. "Should I be writing that down, sir?"

"No, I'll fax it."

Viv had gone home. We'd been talking for half an hour about the new questions for next month's column.

"Nothing may be happening with any of these women, but they're in the picture," I rolled on. "You're thinking about them, comparing, computing odds."

" 'Paring, 'puting," Tabitha said. "Got it."

I liked the way Tabitha dropped first syllables, salted her speech with ironically juvenile slang—and called me "sir."

Viv needed to lighten up. It's not like I was asking her out or anything.

"One's got an 'up' arrow next to her name," I said. "The other has a 'down' or a sideways 'undecided' arrow."

"So who's the lucky girl with the 'up' arrow?"

I paused.

"This chick named Audrey," I said. "I just met her, but she's the top candidate for the Life Upgrade."

"Oh, *that*," Tabitha said. "Hey, can I call you right back, sir?"

Her other line was ringing. We hung up. I stayed at my desk.

In my circle, Audrey's name was invariably greeted by low whistles, audible gasps and forehead-slapping *wow*s. And that was from the women. Her résumé was impeccable. Associate editor at *Taste*, the thinking eater's food magazine. Short story published in the *Atlantic* when she was still in college. Supposedly the first person to get Lyme disease—being from Old Lyme, Connecticut.

The phone rang.

"Sorry about that," Tabitha said. "So, how did you meet this person?"

"At the New York Public Library."

"The library?"

"It was the opening of the Dead Sea Scrolls."

"Dude, you really make the scene."

She didn't know the half of it. There was no scene I *didn't* make in my new quest for quality. Audrey was with Nora, a chick I knew from around, so I grabbed a white wine from a passing mime and sallied forth. Audrey's face was flat and square, like an Easter Island statue, but with bangs. In heels, she was as tall as me. I couldn't see why no one had snapped her up.

"First Nora kisses me hello on the lips, which I always find disconcerting."

"*Word.* It's like moms kissing their little boy-children on the mouth."

"Then Nora says, 'Do you know Audrey?' and I say, 'Her reputation precedes her,' popping up on the balls of my feet and bowing like—"

"A headwaiter?"

"Mr. Darcy was more what I was going for, but you're right. Audrey says, 'Not as much as I've heard about you—'"

"Gag."

"*Then*, to get her interest, I spend the rest of the party talking to Nora. I may have blown it."

"*Du-ude.* You should *not* be intimidated by some Upper East Side, trust-fund . . . I mean, you're, like, a brilliant women's magazine columnist and all."

"Thanks. Actually, I think she lives in the Village. Anyway, next day Nora shows up at my apartment with sunflowers."

"Audrey, you mean."

"No, *Nora*. I didn't know what to do. I was only interested in

Nora to get to Audrey, though she is kind of sexy. I didn't totally trust myself alone with her. So I took her around the corner to El Quijote, this Spanish place in the Chelsea Hotel. Great sangria."

"Rico, suave."

"Don't mock my people. A pitcher of sangria later, Nora says, 'We're going to a party this weekend. You should come.'"

I left out that Nora acknowledged, by not acknowledging, the bold border crossing my hand had just made under her skirt line. And that I withdrew it as soon as she divulged the party coordinates.

"You got what you needed," Tabitha said.

"Basically."

"Don't worry, sir. I won't hold it against you. *Much.* Hey, I better go."

We hung up in unison.

Monday morning, I called again.

"Hi, sir. Do you need to talk to Viv? She's out for the week."

"Stop calling me 'sir.' You're like Marcie with Peppermint Patty. Where's Viv?"

"Vacation."

"Oh, yeah. I forgot. David's dermatologist convention?"

"In Hawaii, may I add."

I tried to think up a new excuse to be calling.

"How was the party?" Tabitha asked, reading my mind.

"Horrible. It was at this *Cosmo* editor's place. Her fiancé just landed a mil-a-year job on *The Simpsons*, so she's moving to L.A."

"An apartment-cooling, as it were?"

"Good one," I said. "Audrey was alone—Nora was sick—and I went up and said something lame like, 'Where's Nora?' and she just sort of *looked* at me."

"You really can't get it together with this one, can you?"

"She doesn't *respond* to anything," I said. "I start doing this whole shtick about the *Cosmo* ideas book. How I once had lunch with our hostess and she brought out this black binder with all the ideas *Cosmo* recycles year-in, year-out. It's their Ark of the Covenant, like hideous wraiths would fly out if the wrong person opened it. Or Helen Gurley Brown."

"Brilliant, sir."

"You wouldn't know it from Audrey's reaction. Without Nora, she's a mute. Smiling but silent. I began to think she was autistic, or mildly retarded. Did I mention she looks like an Easter Island statue?"

"Dot-dot-dot," Tabitha said.

"What?"

"Ellipses. I'm doing her side of the conversation."

I laughed.

"I try to tell myself, *Lacunae are sexy*. They make you want to fill them. But after fifteen minutes I'm, like, 'Hello! Is this thing on?'"

To illustrate my point, I made a tapping noise on the receiver like a microphone.

"Please don't do that," Tabitha said. "And did you just use the word *lacunae*?"

"Sorry. Then, out of nowhere, she says, 'So, I'm getting really into gourds.' Gourd farms, gourd recipes, gourdology. I ask, 'What exactly *is* the difference between a melon and a gourd?'"

"Because you really want to know," Tabitha said.

"I'm just relieved she's talking. I thought I was going to have to perform CPR."

Something told me not to tell Tabitha about how the crowd pushed our plastic drink cups together in erotic collision. Or how, after cabbing Audrey home, I made contact with those famed lips, on her Morton Street stoop.

"Did you hook up?"

"I . . . kissed her good night," I said, leaving out that I had walked, half run, home high on conquest and the hope that such first kisses have always given me.

My excuses for calling Tabitha got thinner and thinner. Like, "I've got some revisions on the third question." To which she would say, "You gave me those yesterday." And we'd be off and running.

"So I had a party," I said, about a week after the Audrey kiss.

"Really?"

"Yeah, I was overdue for a blowout and—"

"Don't tell me," she said, "I have it right here in last month's column. 'One surefire way for a guy to sort out a couple of top chick contenders, force a decision or just shuffle the dame deck, is to throw a party.'"

"Yesterday morning, I woke up in a boneyard of cigarette butts and empties—and that was just my bedroom. The living room was desecration on a much larger scale. Furniture not where it used to be. Sticky patches of booze and ash on the floor. The place looked like Captain Willard's hotel room in *Apocalypse Now*. Then I push open the door of my office and, to my amazement, see, bundled up in a coat on my Ikea pullout—"

"Not Audrey," Tabitha said.

"Audrey."

I allowed myself a pleasant memory of the strappy, high-heeled sentries guarding her slumber.

"Did you . . . ?"

"No! If we had, she wouldn't have been sleeping in the other room. And she was obviously still speaking to me."

"She spoke?"

"Yeah! She said, 'Somebody had to stay and take care of you.'"

"Triple gag," Tabitha said. "You don't just sleep at a boy's house. Not if you're not gonna *sleep* with him."

"She dosed me with Advil and, when I was ready to face food again, ordered Chinese."

It beat my usual hangovers, eating cold pizza in the company of my old friends, Guilt and Dread.

"Sorry, can you hold a sec?" Tabitha said.

"Sure."

I held, and allowed myself another pleasant memory of Audrey standing by my bed, asking if I liked root vegetables, saying she wanted to make me dinner. I showed up at her place at the appointed time that evening demanding to know the difference between a root vegetable and a tuber, watching her do complicated things with rutabagas. In her carefully antiqued environment, she loosened up and told me her father had money but she didn't really like . . . seeing him, so never . . . asked him for any. After dessert (radish ice cream), an after-dinner mint of *Taste*ful lovemaking was served. I succumbed, sated, to the sounds of her silence and the air purifier next to her bed. . . .

"I'm back," Tabitha said. "She *seemed* weird when I talked to her. But I can see why boys dig her."

"Who?"

"Audrey."

"When did you . . . ?"

"At your party," Tabitha said. "Briefly."

I stopped twirling the phone cord.

"You were *there*?"

"I crashed. Viv had to stay home for some wife reason, so I figured I'd come as her 'placement."

"I can't believe you were . . . I meant to invite you . . . I'm sorry I was such a bad host."

"I was gonna say hello, but you were busy shot-putting gourds out the window."

So that's how they got on the sidewalk.

"Nothing happened with her again, huh?" Tabitha asked, sounding a little less sure of herself than usual.

"Well, I did stay the night."

"*Du-u-ude.* You do *not* need to tell me that."

Maybe I'd gone too far.

"Sorry," I said. "I shouldn't have mentioned . . ."

"Was it at least hot?" Tabitha asked.

"I do *not* have to tell you that."

In Shakespeare—as everyone worth their Will Power T-shirt knows—the ear is the primary organ of seduction. Two weeks dating Audrey and I still couldn't wait to get on the phone with Tabitha. I called to tell her *Rolling Stone* had assigned me a Howard Stern cover—I wasn't working the margins anymore—and she confessed that she was glued to her radio every morning listening to his show. With Audrey I was the only man in New York who couldn't wait to see *The Piano*, because it meant three hours I wouldn't have to come up with material. Tabitha shared her dream of opening a breakfast bar called French Toast that served endless variations on her favorite food. When Audrey called, hysterical, because she'd seen a homeless man eating a mouse, all I could think was, *At last— something to talk about!*

"Eating a mouse—*gnarly*," Tabitha said. "I generally have too much to talk about. So my so-called friends complain. Which is why I'll be watching tonight's very special one-hour episode of *Blossom* alone."

Her taste ran to unabashed consumption of teen culture.

"Wanna come over?" I asked. "Watch *Blossom* on a big TV?"

It just came out. I hadn't planned it. She didn't think about it long.

"I'll bring the Pop Tarts."

Sometimes I wondered who was more attached to her youth: me or her. Tabitha wasn't "age-appropriate." But I'd tried that. Men get tired of one thing, they go for the opposite.

When I hung up, it occurred to me that I'd set *myself* up on a blind date. I'd gotten too busy to go in and give Viv massages but I plied her for a brief description. "She wears baggy hip-hop pants and clunky boots and crazy Japanese T-shirts. At her age, when you

look like her, you can wear anything." For a touch of adult entertainment after the teenybopper hour, I rented *Carnal Knowledge*.
Slightly naughty and I could impress her with some knowing patter
about Jack Nicholson and what men were like in 1971.

"I see you cleaned up since my last visit," she said, after giving
me a small circular wave and squeezing past me into my living room.

She was short, compact. A little older than I pictured, but not
much. A halo of tight dark curls framed a heart-shaped face. Some
baby fat went with the baby-sized teeth, whose slightly rotated inci-
sors struck me as a particularly sensual irregularity. Viv's wardrobe
description had been dead on.

That evening I made two discoveries. That even an hour of
Blossom was better than three hours of *The Piano,* and *Carnal
Knowledge* is not a great date movie. Tabitha pronounced it "way
dark," especially the ending.

"When Jack is lying in bed staring at home movies of Ann-
Margret?" I asked, thinking for a second about my Astrology Girl
in L.A.

"No, the fact that he could only get off with a prostitute."

I didn't even try for action. For one thing, I couldn't figure out
how, without it seeming like a violation of our phone friendship.
We went through two boxes of Pop Tarts.

The next night, at a stultifying *Taste* event, Audrey told me all
about a piece she was researching on charcoal. She also asked me to
get an AIDS test, so she could go on the pill.

My non-Audrey nights I starting spending with Tabitha, platon-
ically watching her tiny TV at her tiny studio on Twentieth Street,
innocently going to East Village dives. One night, after walking
back from a place called Babyland on Avenue A, she stopped in
front of her building and knitted her brow.

"Something the matter?" I asked.

"I have to tell you something."

I readied myself for "I had a really great time" or "I really like you."

"I'm seeing someone."

Impossible. The only person she saw was me.

"Who?"

"His name's Eric."

"What does he do?"

I needed information.

"He's in the accounting department."

She tried to say this in a caring, interested way.

"How long have you been . . . seeing him?"

"Five and a half months. I wanted to tell you, but I was worried you wouldn't want to be friends."

You worried correctly, I thought. I couldn't pin down the moment when Tabitha stopped being Viv's replacement as my female confessor and became something else. But I knew in a panicky rush I was past it now. Relax. Pretend like she hadn't said anything. Five and a *half*? I've got eight years on this chick and she's with some dweeb in accounting?

"My friend Mike Errico's playing at the Bitter End Thursday," I said. "Wanna come?"

"Oh," she said, excited, then remembering something, furrowed again. "I have plans."

She hugged me and went inside.

I started calling more than ever, sometimes twice a day. Doubly attentive, I still told her everything about Audrey.

"So she invited me to this foodie spa in Mexico," I said. "Some quasiwork thing, then a week later, *dis*invites me. What the hell is that about?"

"Those are some mixed signals, sir."

"She said, 'I just think I need to be alone.' This after the whole AIDS test request?"

I spared her the details of that gory medical procedure. My regular doc was in Israel, on vacation. I'd made an appointment with a urologist. Young guy, not much older than me. Seemed fine, until I found myself screaming, "I just wanted a blood test!" while he stuck a giant Q-tip where nothing should ever be stuck, swabbed it around, then pulled it out again. Pole-axed with pain on the examination table, I thought bitterly of Audrey on a south-of-the-border beach exfoliating with margarita salt and remembered Hyman Roth's line to Michael in *Godfather II*: "I'd give four million just to be able to piss without it hurting."

"She must have read an article that said the way to snag a boy is keep him guessing. Don't give away too much, until you've got the ring. I'm sure it's in the *Cosmo* ideas binder."

That explained the weird silences.

"I have stopped drafting the wedding page announcement," I admitted.

"Now that I've explained boys and girls, can we talk about something else?"

"Anything," I said.

The only call I got from Mexico was a weepy one on Audrey's last day, telling me her Saturday flight was canceled and she was going to have to take some bad-connection red-eye. I suppose I could have *talked* to her about my concerns about our relationship, such as it was after a little more than a month, expressed my feelings. But when it comes to women, men are conflict avoiders. We can't take "scenes." Easier and cleaner to wait until it's too late, then cut off. And I, being a lily-padder, was building a case for a jump.

Finding my evening unexpectedly free, I called Tabitha, who was freaking out over a "mega-gnarly water bug" that had crawled out from under her stove.

"Let me handle this," I said, when I arrived on the scene.

"Gro-*oss*!" she cried, as I strode into the tiny kitchen.

"There's a roach the size of a Buick in here!" I shouted, cracking the exoskeleton under my heel, and swaggered back out.

In reward for my heroism, or my *Annie Hall* reference, she hugged me closer than usual and said, "I have something to tell you."

"I know. You're seeing someone."

"We broke up."

My blood leapt.

"When? What did you tell him?"

Still hugging, we leaned our heads back to talk. She felt warm.

"That I met someone," she said. "But I want you to know I don't assume that makes you my boyfriend."

"Assume," I said, and kissed her.

"Good thing I'm a hedonist," she said, falling backwards onto the bed.

Sleeping over was a bit dicey, with Audrey coming in on the red-eye. What if she went straight to my place? I roused myself from Tabitha's at 7:30 and called Audrey from home. She'd just gotten in. I showered and made it to her place on Morton Street a little after 8:00.

"You didn't bring me flowers?" were her first words on opening the door.

No kiss.

"Was I supposed to?" I asked.

After *she* disinvited *me*? Maybe she'd been calling at night and hanging up when I wasn't home. Did she smell infidelity on me? As a cover, I put my arms around her. A content-free gesture, but she softened.

"Wanna see my bikini wax?"

I did.

A little while later, I told her to get some sleep and took off. Two in twenty-four hours. Not quite the coveted "hat trick," but I felt pretty pleased with myself. The flowers line, on top of the Q-tip torture, gave me all the ammo I needed. That night, I called Audrey and said we should stop seeing each other. She agreed and hurried off, then phoned back once, twice, three times.

"Is there someone else?" she asked.

"Yes," I said.

It seemed simpler than laying out a whole case.

"Are you sleeping with her?"

"Yes."

Honesty. Why not?

I expected hysteria. But each call was more conciliatory and apologetic than the last—a reverse Rabbit Boiler. "I do want to see you more than three times a week. I was acting stupid." She knew she'd kept me guessing too long. Tabitha called a couple of times in between, to suggest funny questions for my one-on-one with Howard Stern the next day. *That's what I'm talking about.* Tabitha may be just a woman-child, but conversation with her isn't like serving balls into an empty court.

I wasn't ready for that much honesty.

"Can I just come over?" she asked, not for the first time. "To get my gourd book?"

I said I didn't think now was a good time.

"Why not?" she asked

". . . ," I said.

"Say something!"

"That's my other line. I better take it."

WHY ARE YOU BEING SUCH A JERK?

Tabitha became my Sort-of Girlfriend. That was her joke—that she wasn't old enough to be a real girlfriend. "I'm your SOG," she'd say, rhyming it with *dog*. But to me, over the next six months, she seemed like exactly what I needed. Someone to go to the Central Park Zoo with, or roll around the Sheep Meadow with, replaying phone conversations, our first meeting— all the incantations of intimacy. Maybe take in the occasional experimental video-art exhibit, to kiss in the dimmed, flickering rooms. No Dead Sea Scrolls, no dead air. No *Cosmo* gameswoman-ship. A little mentoring maybe, a little hero worship. Was that so wrong? If retreating from the real world of grown-up women who were driving me crazy was a crime, then I pled guilty as charged.

When all else fails, go young.

"I'm hooked," Tabitha said, during one of our reveries.

I was hooked, too. *I could marry her*, I thought. I even said it out loud once, drunk on the adulation of my relationship intern as we lay in bed in the exposed-brick oven of her un-air-conditioned apartment.

"No way," she said, shoving me. "That would make me your SOW."

But I noticed she clung a little closer that night.

Then, in May of 1994, something happened—two things really—that changed everything.

Capouya, my *Times* editor, was going to *Newsweek* and needed a TV critic. Was I "innarested?" (John was a cultivated guy with a sort of mobbed-up demeanor.) Was I! I'd written a hundred free-lance pieces in the last year, broken six figures—but only by killing myself. I told him I'd gladly take a pay cut to write for a single pub-lication and not have to buy my own paper clips. I had also just made an offer, with the aid of a generous parental down payment, on a "loftlike" one-bedroom in the Flatiron District with a view straight up Madison Avenue. And a doorman. Well, security guard. Not a crackhead, anyway. As of June 1, I had both—job and apart-ment. I'd lucked into two elements of the Life Upgrade, but I was having doubts about the third.

The night before my first day at *Newsweek*, Tabitha came over to my new apartment. For reasons I couldn't grasp, she'd been avoiding the place. I cleaned up, not that there was anything to clean, and put some bubbly on ice. Around 6:00, the lobby inter-com buzzed.

"Jou got a joung fren' here," said Ramon the Inappropriate Doorman.

I'd started calling him that after he'd shown me the girly pic-tures he kept behind the security desk.

"Send her up."

I threw a couple of champagne glasses in the freezer.

"Why are you wearing a suit?" was Tabitha's first question. "You look like my brother."

"Just trying it on," I said. "Please, enter."

She threw off her jean jacket and stood in the middle of my gleaming maple floor, looking around suspiciously.

"When does your stuff get here?" she asked.

"It is here."

"Oh."

I was cultivating a not-yet-moved-in look, having bequeathed all remaining marital antiques to the friend who took over my place on Twenty-fifth Street. I sold my Conran's couch and the matching club chair and replaced them with an office-y, sixties sofa and a Saarinen womb chair from a cheap vintage place in the East Village called—aptly, for me—ReGeneration. I got into chrome and steel.

The surfaces of my life gleamed. Anything unsightly I put in storage.

"Well, whaddya think?" I asked.

"It's a little cold, sir," Tabitha said.

"You and Tad!"

"What did he say?"

" 'Share the warmth.' He said that should be my new personal slogan."

Tabitha moved over to the window.

"The view's fairly rad, I guess. Have you considered a rug?"

I couldn't believe she wasn't loving the place.

"It's minimalist. Hey, I want to show you something."

I led her into the bedroom. She froze in the doorway, pointing.

"Where did *that* come from?"

My new bed: a low, sleek platform number on wheels.

"Ikea. They delivered it today."

"Going somewhere?" she said, kicking the tires.

"Not until I get my license renewed," I said. "But look, dig the threads."

I waved to the array of suits laid out on the bed.

"Very *American Gigolo*," Tabitha said.

"No more Gap denim or upscale lumberjack shirts," I said.

I pulled some dress shirts and ties out of the closet and laid them on top of the suits. She sat on the only empty corner of the bed in her sneakers and elephantine pants.

"This is like three months rent for me," she said, flipping open one of my new jackets to inspect its label.

"I want that sixties sitcom look," I said. "Narrow lapels, flat-front pants. Like on *The Dick Van Dyke Show . . . Get Smart.* You know Marlo Thomas's boyfriend on *That Girl* worked at 'News-world' magazine."

"You forget, I wasn't born then."

I had bought a fistful of skinny ties. My favorite was a striped Dolce & Gabbana with a Varga-style pinup girl secreted away on the inside lining. I was about to show it to Tabitha, then put it back on the rack. No way she'd know what a Varga girl was.

"Shall we decant some bubbly?" I asked, putting my arms around her.

She scrunched up her face.

"Got any soda?"

Newsweek had just moved to 251 West Fifty-seventh Street. I knew the building well. Its side entrance, on Broadway, was where Tad and I had entered and exited our *Out There* offices. Returning through the front door was as satisfying as retaking the Pacific must have been for MacArthur. Possibly more so. My office was on the seventeenth floor, with a view across Eighth Avenue. No one had used it yet. Everything was new. I walked around my L-shaped desk, running my hands along the unscratched cherry veneer. I pulled the plastic off my state-of-the-art swivel chair. A Doctor of

Ergonomics came in and adjusted its hydraulic levers, making vigorous notes on his clipboard. I was being sized and fitted for service in the media machine—*and loving it.*

Capouya poked his head in and took me to meet the guy I was replacing. He was retiring, after thirty years at the magazine, and packing up an office down the hall.

"Why the hell are you wearing a suit?" my predecessor asked, once Capouya had left us alone.

"Job interview," I cracked.

His was the standard journalistic uniform: wrinkled chinos, striped button-down, probably Brooks Brothers, slightly frayed at the collar.

"I've always enjoyed your pieces," I said, truthfully.

He coughed and piled more dusty books and manila files into a cardboard box. "Where I live, all my neighbors are retired pilots— air force men. I look at them and I think, writing seventy-line TV reviews is no way for a man to spend his life."

"Yeah, well," I said, backing out. "I think they need me in human resources."

At five o'clock, the whistle blew and I took the N/R train home from "the office." How I loved those words. I loosened my tie, sank into my new couch. Because the cable hadn't been hooked up yet, I watched the view. Impressive by day, but at night! The Empire State Building glowed red, white and blue. The huge clock face on the Met Life building was lit up, too, and red taillights receded soothingly up Madison into the horizon. It was a view that said, like Sidney Falco in *Sweet Smell of Success*, "From now on, the best of everything is good enough for me."

Newsweek was one of the last cushy jobs in journalism. Not for the reporters and researchers, who worked their asses off, but for lucky writers like me, hired for their ability to condense long files of reportorial legwork into two or three columns of compact, know-it-all-y prose. This antiquated system was a holdover from the early days of newspapers, when scrappy reporters in the field called in breaking stories to the rewrite men on the desk.

As a congenital procrastinator, I adapted easily to the lifestyle of the Lifestyle section. Roll in at 11:00. Throw out a pile of mail. Go to lunch at "44," the high-powered media commissary in the Royalton, and table-hop with Capouya until 3:00. Our section closed on Friday night, but until Thursday, you never really knew if your piece was going to run or get bumped for some "harder" news story. There was no point doing any real work until then, so why not waste time in other ways?

I became obsessed with my apartment. To feed my Modernist fetish, I cruised the vintage shops, sometimes with Tabitha but more often alone. I went to a series of architecture lectures at Rockefeller University on a new book called *New York 1960*. Tom Wolfe gave one, a period scene-setter on the Electric Circus, the legendary protodisco where middle-aged Madison Avenue account execs in three-piece suits did the boogaloo and the Frug with go-go-booted secretaries half their age. A cautionary tale.

"What do you mean she's not your girlfriend?" Podhoretz demanded, over brunch at Pete's Place, my local Greek diner. "You've been together six months."

"She's my Sort-of Girlfriend," I said.

"You're still calling her that?"

"It's a running joke."

"I'm sure she finds it hilarious. Pleasant way to treat a girl who worships you."

"I don't want to be worshipped."

"I'm sure you don't."

"She's too young."

"How old is she now?"

"Twenty-three."

"*Oof.* It is great having someone who thinks you're a genius, but I don't want to have to listen to the first time a girl gets yelled at by her boss."

Let's see, since Viv hired Tabitha, how many times had she yelled at her? I could probably have described each one in detail.

"I keep thinking I should break up with her," I said.

"Does she know?"

"That I'm having breakup thoughts? She says, 'You hate me!' whenever she thinks I'm rushing her off the phone. That and, 'You're going to break my heart and make me cry.' Women should never say those things. They're self-fulfilling prophecies."

He blew out his cheeks. "What do you say back?"

I forked some strawberry slices onto my French toast.

"Something bad the other night."

"What?"

"'Cling much?'"

He swallowed his coffee.

"I was trying to sleep and she had her arms around me in a vise grip."

"You . . . are . . . the Devil."

"I should really break up with her."

"Yes, you should," Pod said, not kidding around.

"I can't."

"Of course you can. What do you mean *you can't*?"

"I need a place to shack up during the renovations."

"You know, you used to be a nice guy."

Gore Vidal said never pass up a chance to have sex or go on television. I started going on television. My *Newsweek* affiliation made me an officially credentialed talking head. *Entertainment Tonight, Extra!, Access Hollywood*, MSNBC, CNBC, movie reviews on CNN, the occasional *Charlie Rose*. All my life I had been terrified of any sort of public speaking. Wouldn't even make a toast at a wedding. TV cured me. Do it enough and, like anything, it's no big deal. And with TV came recognition. Even a byline in a national magazine with three million readers is nothing compared to a five-second sound bite on *E.T.* You start getting letters from women you haven't seen since high school:

> *I'm sure you have not had a thought about little old Bronwyn in the last fifteen years, but I was on the Lifecycle and* Entertainment Tonight *was on and an image of you as a very cool and confident teenager came into my mind.*

An early unrequited obsession, from a French-immersion course in Quebec when we were sixteen. Never got more than a kiss. Now here she was on engraved stationery.

Would I be interested in a drink, the letter asked, with a final provocative "Well?"

Was I reading in too much? I asked Capouya into my office.

"Check this out," I said, handing him the Bronwyn letter.

He stroked his beard.

"I might require some photographic evidence of this 'cool and confident' business. Was feathered hair involved?"

I leaned back in my swivel chair and propped my suede loafers on the desk.

"There's more where she came from," I said.

"I'm glad success isn't going to your head."

Temptation was everywhere. It seemed to come with the job. In the Fox News greenroom, of all places, I was accosted by the author of *X's and O's: The Gen-X Guide to Totally Orgasmic Sex.* Perhaps I'd like to "do" her, she offered, winking like Mae West, meaning write about her in *Newsweek.* In Vegas, at a syndicated TV convention, a Venezuelan publicist came on to me like Charo on Ecstasy—and she wasn't even in one of the porn-channel booths. My good fortune was taking on a garish, over-the-top quality. At a book party, a publishing ingenue asked me to take the PATH train to her place in Hoboken.

"Lord, lead me not into Penn Station," I said.

"Nice steal," she said. "I wrote my senior thesis on *Herzog*."

"Which was. . . ."

"Last year."

Even younger than Tabitha! But I wasn't a cheater.

Construction started on my apartment and I crammed my suits and ties into her studio. We were living together, sort of.

"Anniversaries are 'portant, sir," Tabitha said, standing in her kitchenette, scooping peanut butter out of the jar with her finger.

"You stop counting after a certain point," I said. "It's been— what? six—"

"Seven months."

"Don't you want to put that on a cracker or something?" I said, reaching into the drawer for a knife.

"You're not into interpersonal stuff," she said, screwing the lid back on and licking her finger.

"Interpersonal? We're together every night. How much more interpersonal can you get?"

Tad had a theory. When you spent more time talking about *It* than having *It*, the relationship is over. This was a corollary to his other theory that women were "*chi* burglars." When I asked if that was anything like a Hamburglar, he explained that women "steal your life force, your creative juices, your—" I begged him not to say mojo. The amazing thing was, his new girlfriend was right next to him when he laid all this out.

"Maybe we're 'motionally incompatible. Sometimes I feel like we're just buddies," Tabitha said. "I want you to be my boyfriend."

"I *am* your boyfriend."

"No, you're my Sort-of Boyfriend. My SOB."

"I believe that's pronounced *sob*," I said.

In her pullout futon that night, I flailed around until she woke up.

"What if it's all wrong?" I whined.

"What if what's all wrong?"

"The cabinets don't match the floor. The hardware on the kitchen sink looks wrong. All these decisions. Once you commit, you have to live with it. *Literally.*"

I got out of bed to look at the model. My architect had made a shoe box-size, balsa-wood replica of my apartment showing the proposed renovations. A floor-to-ceiling bookcase, low cabinets along the forty-foot length of wall, the new kitchen with its steel bar. A miniature bulb lit up the whole thing. I plugged it in and tried to picture myself inside.

"Do you see a miniature me in there?" Tabitha asked.

"It's not a dollhouse," I snapped.

I saw her worried look on the pillow. She was right. I wanted to live in that model. Alone.

The work dragged on. On Labor Day weekend, we took a break from cohabitation and got out of the city. Her older brother, Jeremy, an investment banker, had rented a big house in East Hampton. After dinner, on our first night, we settled down to a game of Celebrity. Me and Jeremy against Tabitha and his girlfriend, Lisa. Jeremy and I were not winning. Our turns went something like this:

"Actress. *Fatal Attraction.*"

Apologetic shrug from Jeremy.

"Rabbit Boiler?"

Nothing.

"Okay, *Dangerous Liaisons*. John Malkovich's—"

"Time," Tabitha said, pointing at the little hourglass on the table.

"How do you *not* get *Glenn Close*?" I said, throwing the scrap of paper back at the bowl like a twelve-year-old.

"Sorry, man."

Tabitha frowned. The next day, I was still paying for my outburst.

"You made him feel dumb," she said, as we lay basting on the beach.

"So you *told* me," I said. "And I told *you* I didn't *mean* to."

"He's not in the media. Why do you have to be so 'petitive?"

"Getting a little worked up over Celebrity is hardly a war crime. I was just trying to liven things up a little."

"I didn't say it was," Tabitha said. "Why are you being such a jerk?"

I knew why, but I couldn't tell her.

I was bored.

When the work on the apartment was finally done, I took Tabitha to dinner to thank her for putting me up and up with me through the renovation. Also to break up with her.

That was the plan, though I was having trouble getting to it.

Very politely, over dessert, she asked if she could have a key.

"Um, I don't know if that's really—"

"You have mine," she said.

"Yeah, but that's because I was *living* there."

I never asked for a key. I never wanted one. Because then I would have had to give you one, and. . . .

"Do you want to think about it?"

I nodded and changed the subject.

"How's work?" I asked.

"Sucky."

Silence.

"How's your brother?"

"Flying to Pittsburgh. Minneapolis. He may move to Jersey."

More silence.

When did we start having to *make* conversation? As easy and natural as everything seemed when things were going well was how awkward and loaded everything had become. Dinner was a tragedy of errors. Tabitha set her napkin on fire. I bumped the waiter and sent a tray flying. Afterwards, she wanted to go to her friends Zack and Leah's, who were having a "beach party." Their East Village apartment was half-assedly decorated with umbrellas, cheap sunglasses and tropical drinks. We were the only people not in Hawaiian shirts and bikinis.

"Isn't this a little . . . Spring Break?" I asked Tabitha.

"Don't be so mental."

"I'm not being mental."

"*Judg*mental. My cute way of dropping the first syllables off words, remember?"

I remember Howard Stern once saying that the thing you find most endearing about a woman at first is the thing you'll come to hate most. I think he was talking about his wife.

"Let's talk openly," Tabitha said, when we were back at her place, sitting on the edge of her futon.

"Okay," I said.

"Do you want to go out with other women?"

Well, yes, now that you mention it.

"No," I said.

"Do you want to be alone?"

No.

"Yes," I said.

No guy wants to be alone. We want to be with other women. Then when we're out with other women we want to be alone. *That* was the problem.

I didn't know what I wanted.

"Why are you just deciding this *now*?" she asked, and got up off the futon.

She walked over to her stereo and started flipping through CDs.

"I didn't know before," I said.

"You were just trying me out? I wish you'd figured this out, like, four months ago."

She opened her Marlo Thomas *Free to Be You and Me* CD a little too hard. It came apart in her hands.

"Why four months?"

"I don't know," she said.

She sat down on the futon and looked at her clear plastic sandals.

"Look, I just—"

"So now I'm your ESOG."

"What's that?" I asked, trying a smile.

"Ex-Sort of Girlfriend," Tabitha said, with no smile.

She was letting me out of it. I was free. All those temptations— I could take advantage of them. It wouldn't be cheating. I had a familiar end-of-something emptiness in my gut.

"Starting tonight, I guess," she said.

"How about tomorrow?" I suggested, my hand on the small of her back in a way she liked. "You're a hedonist, remember?"

KARMIC PAYBACK

Perhaps I had no talent for monogamy. I resigned myself to my fate with the sardonic self-pity of a Raymond Chandler antihero, glamorizing my loserdom in the noirish tones of a Bogie character on the lam from his past—hardened towards women and their ways. I was strictly business when it came to pleasure. I had cards made up that said, "Share the Warmth." No, I didn't. But I thought about it. I wanted to give off the air of a fellow who regards women as no more a part of his emotional life than going to the gym. I aimed myself exclusively at those with whom there was no danger of a relationship. When they marveled at the stark minimalism of my denuded digs, I told them I was going for a look that said, "Don't get too comfortable, you're not going to be here long."

To myself, I quoted A. E. Housman, the only four consecutive lines of poetry I've ever been able to remember:

> *When I was one and twenty*
> *I heard a wise man say,*
> *"Give crowns and pounds and guineas*
> *But not your heart away."*

My own words of wisdom were finding their place in the pantheon, too.

I was on the wall at Billy's.

The management had framed one of my *Mlle.* columns. The question was, "What is it with guys and strip clubs?" I answered with a defense of their harmless appeal and offered "my Cheers" as a shining example. They hung it in the back, by the ladies' room, next to another framed clipping, from the *New York Post.* A former Billy's dancer accusing Kelsey Grammer of fathering her love child. When I saw myself on that wall, I knew I had arrived in impolite society.

And just when I thought I couldn't go any lower, it turned out I could.

Martine, the sexologist from the Fox News greenroom, had been calling. Daily. Capouya was in my office when she hit me three times in the space of about ten minutes. Could we have lunch, dinner? Did I want to come over and watch her on *Hard Copy*? He kept getting up to go every time, but I waved him down. I read to him from her book jacket bio: " 'Being raised in both the African-American and Jewish traditions has given her a unique perspective on . . .' " What hair!

Our first night, I heard the words every man dreams of hearing: "Guess what? I have no gag reflex." Not long after that, I heard the words every man dreads hearing: "Now is not the time for sleeping. Now is the time for *talking*." Fingers tapping, prodding my shoulder. "What's an interesting thing that's happened to you? What are you thinking about? Are you thinking about me?" Sexologist, heal thyself.

"You don't act like other guys."

"How do they act?"

"Interested."

The frisson of free agency was all too fleeting.

"If you left now, we could both be asleep by midnight."

She was gone in time for *Beavis and Butt-head*.

An affair with a married woman seemed like a *new*, new low worth pursuing. I fished Bronwyn's letter out of my desk drawer and invited her to a party. "Jim—my husband—is dying to meet you," she said. "He loves people from my past. We'll have a drink at the apartment, then go." At their blandly tasteful classic six on the Upper East Side, we three had cocktails while a little boy and girl watched TV in the next room. I had no shame.

"So, Bron says you're on television," hubby said.

"I sometimes do—"

"Wish I had more time for TV. And books. I'm a numbers guy."

"Jim's very dull," Bron said.

"That's it," hubby said. "I'm dull. Now if you'll excuse me, I'm going to go and be dull with my son and daughter. Enjoy your dinner. I hope it's not dull."

Bron and I decamped to the Tenth Street Lounge to celebrate the publication of a novel I knew I was supposed to like but couldn't lift.

"I told my friend Anna I was seeing you," Bron said from her barstool perch. "She said, 'So are you gonna fuck him?'"

I straightened my tie. "What did you tell her?"

"I said, 'I didn't fuck him *then*, why should I fuck him *now*?'"

And I thought *I* was the emotional criminal. It seemed I wouldn't be having an affair with a married woman. Just as well. I embarked on a nobler pursuit.

Stewardesses. "Stews." No, *flight attendants*—they seemed to me the ultimate prize for a man with no final destination.

Buckling in for L.A., I spotted a fetchingly striped uniform perusing *Newsweek*.

"I have a piece in there," I said, having reached cruising altitude before we left the tarmac. "The one that says, 'Bad Boys: Men Are Rediscovering Their Inner Jerk.' "

Danielle, a Chicago-based blonde, kept coming back to my seat to talk after that. I gave her my card. You never knew.

Dispatched to report my first cover on a new medical drama called *E.R.*, I returned to New York the day my parents arrived. I looked forward to their visit, to bringing them up to *Newsweek* and showing them tangible evidence that their interest-free loans and patient parenting were paying off. But a first cover story was a hazing ritual of round-the-clock editing and second-guessing no *Newsweek* writer escaped. I didn't see how I was going to squeeze them in.

"I brought your *Twig*," my mother said, after I'd wowed them with a brief tour of the property they had so generously leveraged. *The Twig* was my high school yearbook. I'd taken it home for some reunion or other. "I enjoyed reading all the things people had written in there. Funny how they make you out to be this great ladies' man."

My father chuckled. I laughed, requesting examples.

Opening it on the back page, my mother inquired, "Who, for instance, is Stephanie?"

I said the name did not ring a bell. "What did she write?"

My mother put on her reading glasses and read: " 'I've spent the past, um, let's see, five months thinking of how to tell you that you're an asshole. But I lacked the guts—just like you, eh? You're not a bad guy. You've got so much charm it's not fair, but you use it wrong. I have never felt as used as I did after you. I really fell for it. I'm a sucker. Some of us are born that way. But I did like you, I probably still could, but I'm scared to risk it. Just wait till you're used. You'll understand. Love,' "—spelled l-u-v—" 'Stephanie.' "

It was coming back now. Shag carpeting may have been involved. In thirty-three years, I'd never heard my mother use the word she had just read aloud—to describe me. Bad enough my present was catching up with me. Now I had to worry about the past?

"That's really the only bad one," she said.

I said I'd better get to work.

I got them tickets to the Met. *The Marriage of Figaro.* Neither of them was crazy about opera, but Placido Domingo was in it and anything Spanish. . . . I met them for a quick dinner at Gabriel's, because it was only a few blocks from the office.

"I wish we were getting to see you more," my father said.

"I know, it's just work," I said, then, to change the subject: "So this is a big Hollywood East hangout. I saw Harrison Ford last week."

"What?" my mother said. "I can't hear anything. It's too loud in here."

Which it was.

"It's a pity you don't have time to write more book reviews, like you used to," my father said. "I feel so far removed from all this TV stuff." But he gave me two *New York Times* articles he'd clipped, on Neil Simon and George Lucas. "In case you didn't have time to read them. Of course it's wonderful to see you doing so well."

"Yes," my mother said.

Proud parents they were. My mother had a box overflowing with my clips. And I was giving them the bum's rush. I paid the check—they would have been horrified by the total—and rushed back to the office to close *E.R.* It was after midnight when I got home and heard the hissing from the hallway. When I unlocked the door, a hot, wet cloud hit me. I knew what had happened. The workmen had taken away the old cast-iron radiators—I was replacing them with sleeker baseboard heaters—and hadn't closed the valves. Steam must have been pouring out ever since the heat went on. I covered my hand in a towel, shut off the valves and opened all the windows. Everything was soaked. Paint peeled off the ceiling. I ran around mopping up pools of water with paper towels. My heart was racing. Who could I call? No need to freak out M&D. . . .

"I think this falls under the category of aiding and comforting the enemy, but all right," Tabitha said.

I ran to her place. She'd just come back from *Oleanna*, the David Mamet play.

"Hell hath no fury like a younger woman scorned," she said, making me tea.

My palpitations eased. She was watching me sip.

"You know my friends have a nickname for you."

"Sir?" I asked.

"No. You don't wanna know."

"Tell me," I said.

"The Fucker."

I couldn't help laughing. I'd been nailed, busted. No point arguing.

"Does that mean I can sleep over?"

Mario, the maintenance guy, promised to repaint the ruined ceiling "like new." With the *E.R.* cover on the newsstand and my parents safely home, I was starting to feel better. As I sliced through my mail with a *Chevy Chase Show* letter opener (my office was a warehouse of PR graft), I stopped at a stiff envelope addressed with familiar back-slanted handwriting. Inside was a birth announcement and more of the same handwriting.

Someday I hope we can sit down and
talk about your silence.

Thank-you notes for our wedding presents she hides under the bed, but birth announcements—*those* Elisabeth has no trouble mailing. I read the card again. *Talk about my silence?* That's going to be a fairly one-sided conversation, isn't it? *Because I'll be SILENT.* In my Week-at-a-Glance, I wrote,

THERE'S NO SUCH THING AS AN EX-WIFE.

Marriages end, but divorces don't. The damage is never really done being done. I had to tell someone about this, someone who knew Elisabeth. I made a lunch date with Pod.

"Why won't she leave me alone? She's got a husband—the guy she left me for, I might add—a kid, her own life—"

"So why should it piss you off so much?" Podhoretz asked behind a mountain of Carnegie Deli corned beef. "Does it bother you that she has a child?"

"No."

"Are you jealous?"

"No."

"Do you want her back?"

"No!"

The Pod chewed his corned beef philosophically.

I was angrier at her now, after, than during our marriage. Keeping me as a bit player in her puppet theater. Or maybe it was that she never said she was sorry for leaving me for another guy.

"You should stop blaming her for everything," he said.

"I don't."

"Yes, you do. You blame her for the fact that you're a thirty-four-year-old unmarried bastard."

"Well, yeah, but—"

"Weren't you like this *before*?" Pod asked, after a long swallow. "Like, in high school?"

He had a point.

"It's just . . . it's fucking annoying."

I noticed a dollop of mustard on my favorite Dolce tie and dabbed at it with a napkin dipped in Cel-Ray.

"I'm just saying," Podhoretz said. "Hey, are you gonna finish that?"

Nowhere was safe. Tad and I went to see Freedy Johnston at Tramps. Amid the mosh pit of balding guys, I spotted a full head of long, banged hair. I looked around for backup, but it was too late. As Freedy played "Bad Reputation," I felt myself being dragged back onto Easter Island.

"You've lost weight," Audrey said, booze on her breath. "You don't have AIDS, do you?"

It wasn't my week.

At the *Mlle.* Christmas party, I was cheerfully tanking up on eggnog when a thumb-ringed twenty-one-year-old intern Viv wanted to set me up with ruled me out as "too old."

"Sorry, big guy," Viv said, after relaying this stinging dismissal. "It's for the best."

"Thanks," I said, feeling more than a little nog on my face.

Fucker and *asshole* were bad enough, but *too old*? I scanned the bar for consolation prizes and spotted a chick I'd met at a Wavy Gravy benefit at Wetlands. I hadn't fully appreciated her under that tie-dyed T-shirt. I appreciated her now, bedecked in a sweater of festive green mohair and a tight plaid miniskirt.

I zeroed in.

"Maggi?"

She looked blankly at me. Wasn't that her name? With an *i*?

"Oh, hi!" she said, in a way that sounded like "Ahoy!"

Was that Long Island or New Jersey? I couldn't tell, but you could see the map of Ireland on her face.

"I'm in corporate imaging now," Maggi was saying.

"A woman of your talent and potential . . ." I was saying.

If anyone had asked me, I would have said she was lapping it up.

"Hey, I've never seen you with your glasses off."

The next morning, I rolled off the couch with a wicked nogover but on time for my 8:00 A.M. boxing session at Equinox. An hour later, I came back from a session on the heavy bag (and I don't mean my ex-wife) to Maggi passed out on my bed, still fully mohaired. The boots were off, but that was it. Total failure to close. She woke up, grunted good morning and reached for the phone. After a clipped exchange, she handed it to me.

"Romy wants to talk to you."

"Who's . . . hello?"

"*Don't* let her go anywhere."

"Why not? I'm late for work—"

"Just *don't*. I'm coming right over."

Romy hung up. Maggi came out of the bathroom.

"What was that all about?"

"She says don't leave. Wants you to wait for her here."

"Why would—"

"Look, I've gotta get to the office," I said.

The phone rang twice quickly, which meant the security desk downstairs. That was fast.

"Jou got another lady down here," said Ramon the Inappropriate Doorman. "Wan' I should get ridda her?"

"Send her up."

There were times I preferred Carlton.

Romy entered red-eyed and sniffling. I thought *I* was hungover. She said, "Your dad died last night."

Maggi collapsed to the floor, sobbing and gasping for air. I offered glasses of water, a handkerchief, clichés. This was no *E.R.* episode. Her father hadn't been sick. Just one of those awful, out-of-nowhere deaths that I had no business being privy to. I felt like an intruder in my own apartment. Romy took her home. I cleaned up and got ready for work in a cold sweat. At *Newsweek*, I closed my office door and wrote what I hoped would be my last Bachelor Hell letter to Dave Eddie. It had been a while. I finished it:

> *This is the Russian roulette you play chasing a different woman every week. Not that you'll get AIDS or some incurable boil on your dick, but that an impersonal, emotion-free encounter will suddenly turn deeply, dreadfully intimate.*

Then I called Viv.

"It's karmic payback," she said.

"For what?"

"You have to ask?"

THE ARRANGEMENT

I stopped drinking. Not that I had a problem. Alcohol is the necessary, if not sufficient, condition of single life. It's the ocean that floats all passing ships in the night, and sinks more than a few. But if I hadn't been wasted, maybe Maggi wouldn't have ended up at my place. . . .

"Sobriety '95," Tad labeled my New Year's resolution, with open hostility.

"Yeah, great," he berated me over his third pint at the Village Idiot, a dive on Fourteenth Street he'd started patronizing as a home away from Billy's. "You're just gonna sit there sipping your— what is that? Club soda? That's a lot of fun. What's the point of being in a *bar* if you're not gonna *drink*?"

True enough. I found myself leaving bars and parties early. I became aware of how much of going out was someone yelling in your ear the same thing they just told you two minutes ago. I became more interested in working my way through books than women.

A week turned into a month, a month into two, then three. I dropped ten pounds. I was superproductive. One Friday night, I was closing a cover on Carolyn Bessette Kennedy and, because there were always a couple of hours to kill while art and production people did the layouts, I escaped to a bar in the East Village where some friends were having a party for a 'zine called *Paris in the 20s*. Writers closing cover stories weren't really supposed to leave the building, much less take a car service to a party, but I took seriously Jake Barnes's remark about journalism in *The Sun Also Rises*, that "it is such an important part of the ethics that you should never seem to be working."

The first person I saw was Tabitha.

She was standing alone. I closed in on her reluctant smile.

"Hey, sir," she said.

"You don't have to call me sir now that you're not at *Mlle.*," I said.

She was working at an ad agency.

"Copy writing?" I asked.

"I sit in cigar bars drinking martinis, for the Hennessy account," she said. "Guys are supposed to ask what I'm drinking and then order one. My boss calls it guerilla marketing."

I felt jealous juices bubbling up. We exchanged searching looks.

"I better go save my friend," Tabitha said, directing my gaze to a tall girl slouching over a pencil-necked geek. "I think she's floundering."

"Yeah, I gotta go back to work," I said, heroically.

"Now?" Tabitha said, consulting a watch with a plastic bubble and small toys rattling around inside.

"I'm closing a cover on Carolyn Bessette."

"No . . . way. I am 'sessed with her hair."

"Buttery chunks," I said. "That's what her colorist says is his secret."

"You interviewed Carolyn Bessette's colorist? I so cannot wait to read your story."

We didn't kiss good-bye. But the next night, I dialed her number.

"This not calling has been killing me," I said.

We started up on the phone again, every other night, usually late.

"I feel like you're so much more . . . interpersonal," she said, during one of our split-screen sessions—her in her bed, me in mine.

"You know how different people bring out different sides of you?" I said. "I miss that side of myself."

I was laying it on thick. Now that all I wanted was to re-seduce her, I was Mr. Interpersonal. I waited until I heard sniffling, then pounced.

"Want me to come over?"

Long pause.

"You better not," she said.

"Sure?"

"I have to be the strong one," she said.

That night, the Arrangement began.

I should draw a distinction here between what I once called in a column "the Inevitable Reprise" and "the Arrangement." The Reprise is a one-off with an ex, or possibly sporadic recidivism. The Arrangement was a regular, reliable thing—mutual escape from dating despair. No dinner or movie preamble required (after Emma). Just a phone call, at 11:00 or midnight or 2:00 A.M. If I was already in bed, I'd change with Superman speed and sprint to her apartment. The understanding was that these get-togethers in no way implied getting back together. Like Same Time, Next Year, without Alan Alda.

A few months into this setup, I was lying on Tabitha's bed watching her casually undress, when she said, "You're not seeing anyone, right?"

My spine tensed. There *had* been some hot-tub hijinx in L.A. I couldn't resist a publicist named Shari covered head-to-toe in bronzer. I never should have started drinking again, but six months was enough.

"No," I lied.

"You haven't had sex with anyone?"

"No," I lied again.

"Good," she said, rubbing moisturizer into her arms.

She was a trusting person. I was a person who could be trusted.

"Have you?" I asked.

"You know *I* haven't. All I'm saying is when you do, tell me because then the 'Rangement will have to change."

"How do you know it'll be me?"

"I know," she said.

WANT TO SMELL MY NECK?

The first time I met Ilene, she ignored me. Registered such profound indifference to my presence that I backed away speechless into the party throng. I'm not even sure she spoke, just threw me a nod. Who *was* this chick? Entertainment editor at *Allure*. That much I knew. Something of a "bad girl," Viv, my Deep Throat, had informed me. Boyfriend situation unclear.

I'd put her out of my mind, until a panel on the oxymoronic subject of "Celebrity Journalism." I was on the panel, along with a few other oxymorons. Ilene was in the audience, a Reporter's Notebook balanced on fishnetted knee, scribbling away. I could only see the top of her head, a pair of sunglasses nesting in a tangle of blonde. I'd never seen anyone take such furious notes. *I* wasn't even listening to what I was saying. When it ended, I tried to time my exit to coincide with hers, but just as I got to the elevator bank, the doors shut. For all I knew, she'd pressed the close button.

So it was with some glee that I heard Ilene Rosenzweig on my machine pleading a "celebrity emergency" and begging for help.

"Is there any way you could fly to L.A. for an Andie MacDowell profile?" she asked, when I called. "You'd have to interview her and write it over the weekend."

"So I'd have to see the movie, interview her and write it all by. . . . ?"

"Monday," she said softly.

I heard a damsel in distress.

"Mmm." I pretended to think about it. "How long and how much?"

My standard freelance questions.

She told me.

I paused, savoring the moment.

"Sure," I said. "Why not?"

"You're . . . sure you can get it done that fast?" she asked, breathlessly. "Her PR firm can be a nightmare."

"Nightmare is my middle name," I said. "That and . . . Thomas."

She laughed. I quit while I was ahead and hung up without mentioning the party blow-off. I'd save that for later.

The movie was *Michael*, about an angel (John Travolta) who falls to earth and for an earth angel (Andie). Andie and the cast were appearing on *Oprah*, in L.A. Before the taping, the audience was to attend a special screening of the movie. A yellow school bus delivered them, like children or prisoners, to an old theater on La Brea. I stood outside thinking I should be getting some fan-in-the-street quotes, but I couldn't bring myself to ask a stranger,

"What do you think of Andie MacDowell?" So I filed in and watched the movie, thinking I'd get my quotes at the *Oprah* taping later.

One problem. Andie's "people" barred me from the taping, without explanation, and relegated me to forty-five minutes in the bar of the Peninsula Hotel.

Fine. I got what I needed in the time allotted. "You don't usually like the pieces about you?" I'd asked Andie at one point. To which she'd replied, "I read them and think, I'm so much more *complicated* than that." And why *should* she believe otherwise? All her life, men had doubtless been hanging on her every inanity.

I wondered, back in my suite at the Marquis, if I'd gotten over my famous-chick fantasy. Maybe I'd matured, moved beyond that sort of crude male superficiality. Maybe I was ready to embrace a real woman, my own earth angel.

Almost. I searched my Week-at-a-Glance for Astrology Girl's number. No luck. Good! I needed to go cold turkey. I locked myself in the room with room service and some porn-on-demand (my methadone), wrote and e-mailed the Andie piece, then flew back the next day.

When I got in to work Monday morning, Ilene was already on my voicemail with a message stamped 9:01 A.M., early for a supposed bad girl, cooing thanks for my "heroic performance." She'd read the piece, loved it and sent her assistant to *Newsweek* to pick up my notes for the fact checker. Could she take me to Michael's for lunch? Today, if I was free?

I was always free.

"You are the first to arrive," said the gazelle at the reservation lectern, escorting me to a table in the front room. I waited, conspicuously solitary, in this media fishbowl of magazine and book editors, agents, news anchors and the occasional celeb. It was eat or be eaten at Michael's, with everybody watching. The menu was like a giant tanning mirror. I hid behind it, sipping cranberry juice. You'd think a man of thirty-four could sit in a restaurant alone for a few minutes.

Salvation rushed in wearing a periwinkle dress. Blonder than I remembered, still with the sunglasses in her hair, and softer. A very pretty mess. I stood up.

"Hi!" she said, brushing my cheek hello and lingering in the vicinity for more than the usual amount of time.

"Hi."

She wiggled her eyebrows and gave me an expectant look. "What do you think of my perfume?"

"I didn't notice. I mean, very nice."

"I'm testing a different scent every day," she said, smoothing the napkin in her lap. "To see which is the sexiest. It's for an article. 'The Story of Eau.'"

"I thought you were an editor."

"Sometimes they let me be a cub reporter. Want to smell my neck again?"

I leaned over and inhaled.

"Fracas," she said. "The Venus flytrap of scents. Full of dirty notes."

"Daddy like," I said, with a dirty note.

She laughed, took a pen out of a miniature purse and jotted on a cocktail napkin.

"You didn't ask me to smell your neck the last time we met," I said.

"We've met?"

"At that party for *The Information*. You were with that TV chick. Laurie—"

"Laurie Pike?" Ilene looked stricken. "Gee, sorry. I'm the worst."

A waiter whisked over. Ilene ordered a glass of wine, and, without opening the tanning mirror, a plate of oysters.

"Half dozen or a dozen?" the waiter asked.

Ilene turned to me. "Will we be sharing?"

I nodded and requested wine, too. This didn't seem like a chick you drank cranberry juice with.

"I'm usually more memorable," I said, wishing I hadn't brought it up.

"I know," she said, smiling with her eyes. "You made quite an impression on Eleni."

"Your assistant?" I tried to remember our encounter that morning in the *Newsweek* lobby. "I just gave her my notes."

"After she met you, she came rushing into my office all flushed, saying, 'Who does that guy think he is? He really loves himself.' Then she went on about how your piece was all about how you wanted Andie MacDowell—and thought you could get her. She wanted us to add an editor's note saying, 'Ms. MacDowell would never date a guy like this.'"

My turn to look stricken.

"Well, uh, that was just a . . . conceit of the piece," I said, inhaling Pinot Grigio.

"Eleni's just young," Ilene said, in a calming tone. "I told her it's great for a guy to have that much confidence. She's always complaining about the weenies she dated at Harvard."

The oysters came. Ilene accessorized one from the mystery bowls and neatly up-ended it. I copied her.

"Thank you again for coming to my rescue," she said.

"It was nothing," I said, recovering from the Eleni fracas over our second glass of wine.

"I have this idea for an updated *Connecticut Yankee in King Arthur's Court*," Ilene was saying. "A big star, like a Sharon Stone, is sent back in time to a hundred years ago, when actors were considered one step up from prostitutes, and has to survive without limos and trainers and gurus."

"You should be a screenwriter," I said, wondering if this chick tossed off ideas like that every lunch hour.

"I couldn't cut it in Hollywood. My first job out of college was in development at Columbia Pictures. My boss had me carrying around her breast milk. She'd pump it out and I had to take it to her nanny. I was like a lactose mule."

"Got any on you now?" I asked.

She wrinkled her nose with amused disgust.

Maybe she hadn't made a great first impression, but she was making quite a second. I whipped off my glasses, did some pensive nibbling, and, apropos of nothing, said, "Yeah, I don't really like to talk about it. . . ."

Ilene covered her mouth to keep the wine in, swallowed hard and turned her head away laughing.

"That's great!" she said, catching her breath.

I stopped nibbling.

"What is?"

"That thing with your glasses. Austin Powers, right?"

I didn't know whether to feel mocked or flattered. Mike Myers was a hero of mine—and fellow Canadian.

"Come on! I have better teeth," I said.

She dabbed at her eyes with the napkin.

"I'm sorry. I didn't mean to interrupt. What were you saying?"

I put the glasses back on, refusing to be daunted, and launched into the Elisabeth material. Ilene went quiet. I wasn't sure it was going over. But when she started describing her parents' divorce, her hippie mom leaving her traditional-guy dad and how hard it was for him—I knew I had her.

"I think he saw it as an embarrassing failure," she said. "My mom going off and changing her name to Blue Jay."

"Blue Jay? How did he recover from that?"

Ilene laughed.

"He grew sideburns, started wearing turtlenecks and got a

bachelor pad on Central Park West, with rust wall-to-wall carpeting and lots of teak built-ins."

"Did it have a sunken living room?"

The waiter pointed to our empty wineglasses.

Ilene consulted an imaginary watch on her wrist and said, "Why not?"

"Elisabeth left me for another guy."

I'd never told anyone that before. Now it all came blurting out.

"This is such an intimate conversation, don't you think?" Ilene said. "For a first lunch?"

"Oh, I have these all the time," I said, feeling my cheeks burning, my eyes stinging.

"Hey, are you all right?"

"Allergies! Be right back."

In the men's room, I splashed cold water on my face and thought, *Misting up isn't part of the Señor Sensitivo act.* I dried my eyes and cleaned my glasses until they squeaked. When I ventured back out, Ilene was standing at the table, paying.

"Do you know it's quarter to four. I *totally* lost track of time. Linda's gonna *ki-ill* me."

Linda Wells. Her editor in chief.

"Just tell her who you were with," I said, as we stood blinking in the sunlight of Fifty-fifth Street. "She loves me."

Ilene laughed.

"I wish Eleni'd heard you say that," she said, kissed me and leapt into the oncoming traffic.

At the office, I told Capouya who I'd had lunch with.

"I met her a few times," he said. "With Malucci."

Her ex.

"What did you think?" I asked.

He leaned back in his chair and rubbed his beard.

"She seems like a real person."

PART THREE

"Love is consolation in desolation;
it is the sole medicine against death."

—MIGUEL DE UNAMUNO

I'M TOO OLD FOR YOU

Prostate cancer. I was sure of it. I couldn't sit through a movie without going to the bathroom. Snatched away in my prime! I wondered if I'd rate a Transition item—*Newsweek*'s narrow column of boldface deaths, births and divorces. I swiveled from the window to my keyboard and started typing:

> Likable TV critic and
> trends writer, 34. Penned
> many well-received TV
> reviews. Popularized the
> phrase "buttery chunks."
> Survived by his loving
> parents. No wife or children. . . .

"Drink less water," was my doctor's diagnosis, after a rubber-gloved physical. Damn her science! I was trying to have a pre-midlife crisis here.

I'd like to say that after my misty lunch with Ilene, the planets aligned, my mind cleared and I ascended to a Zenned plane of being whose sole intention was making this very special lady my wife. But it didn't quite work out that way. No, my endless cycle of girlfriend-bim-girlfriend-bim was a hamster wheel I had no idea how to get off. I was still cheating on the Arrangement, despite torturous late-night talks with Tabitha about "moving forward"—i.e., getting back together or breaking up for good.

If there was one direction I wasn't moving, it was forward.

Maybe I wasn't *literally* on the way out, but every time a wedding or birth announcement darkened my mailbox, I died a little. My friends were snapping up lifemates right and left, popping out heirs. I, too, longed for the pitter-patter of little feet—and for once I didn't mean the "Asian outcall" service on Channel 35.

That night, bouncing off the spare, white walls of my apartment, I did what I did when I had problems I couldn't bring to Billy's Topless. I called Viv.

"There's leftover Stroganoff," was all she needed to say.

I told her I'd be right down.

Viv and David had moved into my building. She'd left *Mlle.* to write mystery novels about a crime-solving magazine editor, and had become almost completely nocturnal. Up until 4:00 A.M., in bed past noon. Her shoulders had loosened up, though. She didn't need my massages anymore. And she'd given up smoking. I think they were trying to have a kid.

We sat on stools at the butcher-block table in her kitchen. Viv nuked the Stroganoff and dished it onto a plate for me, then popped some Nicorette gum out of its foil for herself.

"Your future wife is in New York," she said, cracking her gum.

"Ilene?"

"No. Too tough. You don't want to work that hard."

"I don't?"

"Forget her."

"I thought you weren't setting me up anymore, anyway." I speed-ate my first homecooked meal since . . . I was down here last night. "You said I'm too picky, I'm not ready for a relationship. . . . *Man*, this is hitting the spot."

Food: the passing lane to a man's heart. Viv had fed David into submission with a week of five-course repasts that, to hear her tell it, ended with him on his knees offering her a ring. Men will date all types of women, but they marry only a few: the High School Sweetheart (the jejune joint crush that never matures or gets old); the Trophy/Sexual Obsession (a possession he never truly possesses); the Organizer (or human Palm Pilot); the Audience (she flatters! she ego-boosts!); the Nurturer (three squares a day); and the Collaborator (the intellectual/creative rival and/or equal). Each man's priorities are different. Most of us don't know what we're looking for until we find it, then have to unlearn all the things we thought we wanted. But three squares goes a long way.

"You'd be *such* a good couple," Viv said, dishing me more Stroganoff. "She's ex-*quiz*-ite. I would kill for her ass. It's—"

"Not . . . *Solange*," I said.

"She split up with the French count," Viv said.

"And she totally blew me off last time," I said, sparks flying off my plate.

"So she's a little high-strung," Viv said. "She's like a prize filly. The man who tames her will be set for life."

My last, sad run at this tauntingly unavailable, olive-skinned temptress—this . . . *taunt*ress—was during Sobriety '95. She wore low-slung black hip-huggers and a gold bracelet around her bicep, like a slave girl or a Medici. Her "signature," according to Viv. With flashing eyes so green they were almost yellow, she hypnotized me with half confessions and dusky utterances. "I'm shattered. . . ."

"I'm a shell of my former self. . . ." Something to do with Le Comte de Eurotrash. All we had was one dinner and she evaporated into the night.

Viv cleared my plate, pushing up the sleeves of a stylishly cut gray shirt. Working at home, she dressed better than she ever had for an office. No more formless black T-shirts. Strictly skirts and loafers. She'd lost weight and blow-dried her hair every morning, to look nice when David came home from a hard day of dermatology.

Sexy domesticity—that was all it would take for me to feel "set for life."

"Firm as volleyballs!" Viv said, reminding me again of the flawless double convexity encased in Solange's ass-huggers.

But would a chick like that microwave me late-night snacks?

No way.

I wasn't calling.

Viv tossed a box of Fig Newtons on the table and poured me a glass of milk.

"Thanks," I said, tearing open the packaging. "In high school, I used to come home from soccer and eat an entire row of these with a quart of milk. Those were the days."

"I'm glad I could assist in your regression," Viv said. "Call her. What else have you got going on?"

Let's see. The Russian *mafiya* plaything I met in the revolving bar at the Marriott. (I was now a guy who had affairs at a Marriott.) The chubby speech therapist in L.A. who flopped around the Sunset Marquis hot tub like a manatee. The club kid from Ronkonkoma. . . .

"I've got the Arrangement," I said.

"Please," Viv said, popping another Nicorette. "I still don't see how you ever talked Tabitha into that. No woman ever said, 'You know what I need? To keep sleeping with a guy I have no future with.' "

"Not true! I just answered that question in the column: 'Is it okay to have sex with my ex?' In my answer, I said, 'Until one of you finds a meaningful replacement, there's no reason—' "

"Spare me. Your future wife is working at a gallery in Chelsea. I'll give you the number."

I poured myself more milk, admiring the shiny stainless-steel door of Viv's refrigerator.

"I wish I had a Sub-Zero," I said, thinking I'd never be able to shop for high-end kitchen appliances with a chick in an arm bracelet.

"Are you sure you're not gay?" Viv asked. "Solange'll fix that. I once walked in on her doing it standing up in a closet at a Christmas party."

"*Now* you tell me this?"

I stood outside a converted warehouse on West Twenty-second long enough to think I was being stood up when my future wife slid out of a cab and angled towards me. One shoulder forward, chin down, she looked like a celebrity squeezing through an invisible mob. Her small hand clutched a blue IT IS OUR PLEASURE TO SERVE YOU coffee cup—that New York-diner parody of a Grecian urn. She looked like she'd just woken up. It was 7:30—P.M. I called out her name.

"Oh . . . hi," she said, as if she hadn't expected to see me.

Those eyes were like a jungle cat's, or that Afghan girl on the cover of *National Geographic*.

An elevator man took us up to a room full of people making art-appreciation faces at large blurry photographs of ice floes. A "gallerist" friend had tipped me off to the opening. Solange wriggled out of her coat, revealing the signature bicep bangle. Did she sleep in it?

I got us some gallery Gallo.

"Don't say I never took you anywhere," I said, raising my plastic cup and sounding to myself like a used car salesman.

"I'm in such a weird mood," Solange replied, or rather didn't, draining hers in two long sips.

Conversation was a disaster of fits and false starts and mishearings, like a long-distance phone call with someone three time zones away. Then she'd grab my arm and come out with something tortured and intimate like: "Sometimes I want to just disappear. From all this. Do you know? Join Greenpeace. Do something *real*." I launched into an impassioned denunciation of Japanese whaling practices, but her distracted intensity was as impenetrable as the blurry ice floes.

At least she drank. We swam from party to party, bar to bar, and washed up at her Upper East Side studio sometime after 3:00. The hip-huggers came off, but not the black thong underneath.

"Count to five," she said, in the cruel arc light of morning.

Some kind of weird test, I figured, to be rewarded or punished. I counted.

No reaction. She slipped out of bed and stood in front of her armoire, trying to figure out what to wear. The volleyballs were in full effect.

"We're too different," she said, dropping a black dress down over her like a curtain, then angling off into the bathroom.

Punished.

I called that morning, left a message, waited two days, then called again.

No word for a week.

Women are like boomerangs. They always come back, but if you leave your place and chase after them, you'll be in the wrong spot when they do. I chased, my confidence crumbling with each passing day. I sat at my desk, ignoring work, composing casual messages and begging anyone who'd listen for an interpretation of

Solange's inscrutable behavior. Tad said: "I dated a chick like that. No sex for two years, then she moved to San Francisco." Pod referred me to a poem called "A Lover's Resolution" by George Wither (1588–1667):

> Shall I, wasting in despair,
> Die because a woman's fair?
> Or make pale my cheeks with care
> 'Cause another's rosy are?
> Be she fairer than the day,
> Or the flowery meads of May
>   If she not be so to me,
> What care I how fair she be?

But my whole identity as a soon-to-be-thirty-five-year-old guy seemed to depend on her caring.

She'd accept a date, then cancel, saying she felt weak, "like there's water in my veins." Or she'd agree to meet in a dark bar late at night to discuss giving up the art world for UNICEF. I nodded, entranced by her dreamy idealism, because *I* would never even consider running off to Africa to hurl sacks of flour at grateful children. And after a few hours of this, just when I'd think I was getting through, the ramshackle rope bridge of rapport would collapse and I was back to shouting across the gorge. Once she thrust her tongue in my ear and demanded I take her to bed, only to turn me back at her door. I went home and threw up.

I never throw up.

After one of her long, inexplicable evaporations, I got her out to a screening. *In the Company of Men*. Two hours of twisted misogyny from a Mormon weirdo. I ran to the bathroom three times, once just to stare at the mirror and ask myself, What was I *thinking*? Like many women born with more looks than personality, Solange was deeply suspicious of men. Desperate not to let her slip away yet again, I needed a stunt location, an irresistible venue for drinks. I suggested the Algonquin.

"Scene of the crime," I said as offhandedly as I could. "Haven't been since my . . . wedding."

I'd mentioned the marriage before, but it hadn't seemed to register.

"*Oh*," she said, her expression changing from lethal to lunar. "Let's *go* there."

The Algonquin! Where Elisabeth—a woman as unfathomable as this year's model—had "proposed" ten years ago. I felt like Jack Nicholson in *The Shining*. Any minute, the old white-jacketed bartender was going to tell me, portentously, that I'd been here before. "Your money's no good here, Mr. Torrance." Wait a second! Was that who I thought it was?

My Solange obsession had pushed Ilene out of my mind. Now she came rushing back in, literally, to the bar of the Algonquin— with four guys in tow. I let them settle into a corner booth, then went over to say hello.

"All right!" Ilene said, greeting us tipsily. "The gang's all here. The last guys in publishing who wear suits for a night on the town!"

Three of them were suited. One sported a black shirt and air tie and was smoking a cigar. Ilene made the introductions, heralding me as an illustrious newsman who sometimes slummed in the perfumed pages of women's magazines. Her consorts got similarly generous treatment. One was a wiry, hopped-up literary agent with horn-rims even denser than mine. The tall guy was a magazine writer I'd always admired for asking Rod Stewart if he'd really swallowed a quart of semen. ("The old belly-full-of-cum story!" Rod had replied, back when celebrities had a sense of humor.) There was a book editor whose mustache reminded me of my old G.I. Joe with the kung fu grip.

The air tie was Mr. Ex, whose cigar Ilene was now puffing.

I presented Solange, who shrunk like a teenager in the presence of unfamiliar grown-ups.

"His Andie MacDowell piece *saved* our April issue," Ilene informed her entourage. "The guy is a speed demon. And I didn't have to change a word."

I nodded modestly to Solange, who was inspecting the toe of one of her shoes.

"I don't really need a lot of time to extract the essence of a person," I said, with an air of semi-mock pomposity. "Andie and I had a . . . special rapport."

"I *thought* you slept with her," Ilene said.

The table went silent.

"No, I just meant . . ."

"Because she does have a thing for writers," Ilene said. "She famously fools around with journalists who interview her, right? I figured that's why you were mad you didn't get more time."

I checked for a wink. No wink.

"But she's . . . *married*," I said, hearing how feeble that sounded. "If I'd known she screwed around on her—"

Now Ilene was laughing.

"*Hee-hee.* Gotcha! You believed it for a second there, didn't you?"

The tall guy slammed his huge hand on the table. "You can't dangle something like that in front of a red-blooded male journalist," he said. "It's cruel and unusual!"

"Uh, I think my drink's getting cold. If you'll excuse us."

"No, wait!" Ilene said. "I shouldn't have teased. Don't *all* guys fantasize that actresses want to sleep with them? Please, stay."

"I'll give you a call," I muttered, beating my retreat.

At the bar again, Solange shot me a couple of Afghan daggers. "I can't believe that. You sounded like one of those *In the Company of Men* men."

"Saying I would have slept with Andie MacDowell? I was kidding!"

I could have done my taxes during the ensuing pause.

"I'm too old for you," she said, finally.

"You're twenty-five," I said.

And gotten a refund check.

"I'm really seventy," she said. "You need someone younger."

I couldn't even pretend to go along with that one.

At Ilene's booth, the tall guy was bellowing for another round. Ilene was waving her cocktail napkin at me like a white flag. My eye kept wandering in her direction, and not just because of her flurry of blonde and sequined halter top. Even with the leg pulling, I'd rather have been over there having wholesome alcoholic fun than hunched over the bar in *The Shining* with an old soul.

I waved to Ilene & Co. on the way out and dropped Solange off. After a pro forma attempt to come upstairs and the requisite blow-off, I took the cab to Tabitha's street for some Pop Tarts and ego massage. I buzzed her buzzer. No answer. I walked home, stopping at every payphone on the way. Back on the couch, staring up at my eleven-foot ceiling, I kept dialing. Every fifteen minutes.

"Just a quick pep talk," I said, my breath shallow, when she picked up a little after midnight. "That's all I need."

"Have you considered therapy?" Tabitha asked, evenly.

I pretended to consider it.

"I know," she said. "You don't want to mess with the formula. But I'm going to get you some numbers."

No shrinks. I would continue to search for the answers where I had always searched: in women.

"You could give them to me in person," I said.

HE JUST SEEMS LIKE A SWELL GUY

I had no reason to believe Ilene would say yes to a date. She was clearly unpredictable. Besides, I wasn't sure I had anything left to come at her with. Solange had sapped my charm, murdered my moves, cut my confidence off at the knees. I shuffled the stack of work-related invitations on my desk. Nothing good. An editor at Condé Nast was on all the same lists I was anyway. I needed something . . . spectacular. Then it hit me. I dived into my wastebasket and gingerly removed the banana peel from an invitation I'd rashly tossed earlier that morning. I hadn't spent six years—or a lifetime!—romancing the wrong women for nothing.

I placed the call.

"Hello, *Allure*," a female voice answered.

"Ilene?" I asked.

"Eleni."

The assistant.

"Oh, hi. It's—"

"I know who it is," Eleni said.

"Ah," I said. "So is Ilene—"

"She's busy. Can I help you with something?"

"No, I wanted to ask her—"

"For Andie MacDowell's phone number?"

"*Eleni!*" shouted Ilene's voice in the background.

"Was that her?" I asked.

"All right." Stage sigh. "I'll put you through."

"Sorry again about the Algonquin," Ilene said, once we'd been reluctantly connected. "Your date was very exotic. Is she your girlfriend?"

"Not exactly." I cleared my throat. "So the Museum of Television is showing this Rat Pack TV special. Frank, Dean, Sammy. From 1965. It's supposedly the only live TV concert recording of them all together. Johnny Carson is the emcee. It's called 'The Frank Sinatra Spectacular.'"

"*Wow.* You make me an offer I can't refuse."

That was easy.

In a new midnight blue Prada suit with a fantastic crepe texture— the most expensive article of clothing I'd ever bought—I stood outside the Museum of Television in the warming spring air. Just after 6:00, I saw Ilene making a mad stiletto dash towards me. Those fishnets again! And a short, white leather, belted trench coat.

She was panting slightly as she kissed me hello.

"New perfume?" I asked.

"Dolce and Gabbana," she said, thrusting her wrist under my nose. "It's a musky fragrance with a powdery luscious essence."

"I'll say."

"Hey, thanks so much for inviting me to this. How'd you know I'd be interested?"

"You just seemed like a Rat Pack kind of chick."

"*That* is the ultimate compliment."

I felt the old confidence coming back. We went in and settled into our seats.

Now, in truth, I wasn't even particularly into the Chairman or his Board. For all I knew, this was going to be like one of those old Dean Martin roasts—denturefests of stale gags and canned laughter where the highlight was Don Rickles calling Gene Kelly a "hockey puck." But the show swung like crazy from the opening bars. Quincy Jones leading the Count Basie Orchestra. Frank, Dean and Sammy all at the top of their games, their knife-edged tuxedoes glimmering on the old black-and-white Kinescope. Midway through "Luck Be a Lady," the camera zoomed in on Sinatra—an extreme close-up—blowing on a pair of imaginary dice. The corniest move in the book, but delivered with so much commanding intensity and emotion. I caught Ilene's eye and shook my head in disbelief. Grinning like a bobby-soxer, she put her hand on my arm and squeezed. This was a good date.

As the crowd swam around us on Fifty-second Street, Ilene was still shaking her head in awe.

"Can you believe Sammy Davis Jr.'s family was right in front of us?"

"I'm converted," I said.

"How could you not be into Frank? You've even got the Rat Pack threads."

Before I could ask her to the next stop on my itinerary, she said she ought to go home and transcribe her Ellen Barkin interview for the June issue.

"Did you sleep with her?" I asked.

"Very funny," she said, smiling with her eyes.

"I think . . . there's a book party at Elaine's," I said, as if I'd just remembered.

The old rehearsed spontaneity trick.

"What book?" she asked.

"An esteemed *New Yorker* writer's spanking memoir," I said.

Ilene made a face.

The book wasn't the draw. I knew Ilene's Pub Pack of slightly older media guys would probably be there and told her so. She stepped into the street to flag down a cab I hadn't even seen coming. We drove uptown through Central Park, with Ilene rhapsodizing about Frank.

"I never saw any performer who could be that sentimental and goofy and macho at the same time," she said. "It's like a lesson in true masculine sex appeal."

"What do you mean?" I asked.

"That the most seductive thing is to be totally vulnerable and yet at the same time so confident. It reminds me of 'The Song of Roland.' "

The French medieval poem? Her Reference Train was speeding ahead of me. I wondered what Tad would make of Ilene. Whatever she was, she was no "*chi* burglar."

"The only line I remember is '*Aiiieeeee*,' " I said.

"I *wish* I remembered any of the lines," Ilene said. "But the part about how the bravest warrior is the one who went into battle with no armor—that always impressed me. The most courageous lets himself be the most vulnerable and exposed. That's what I loved about that story."

"Doesn't Roland die in the end?" I asked.

"Oh, yeah," Ilene said. "I forgot about that part."

Her pallies were, as predicted, lined up at the bar.

"Twiggy! Come on over here, honey, and gimme a kiss," shouted the hepcat agent, with a faint southern accent. "Man, you smell good."

"Can I quote you?"

"Twiggy?" I asked, once we'd gotten our drinks.

Ilene wasn't *that* thin.

She told me "Ida Twigg" was a pseudonym she used to use, derived from some family names. I nodded, still trying to suss out her relationship to this retinue of admirers. When she excused herself to the ladies' room, the kung fu grip book editor scrutinized me again, as he had at the Algonquin. From behind his beer, he asked, "Are you Ilene's walker tonight?"

Walker? As in gay escort? In another era, I would have slapped him with my glove and demanded, "Pistols at dawn, sir!" Only that would have seemed *very* gay. Maybe these guys were content to be her walkers. Not me.

"Guess so," I said.

I went off in search of Ilene and hustled her out as fast as I could to another party I supposedly just remembered. By the door, I grabbed a signed copy of the spanking memoir.

"Here, I'll read you some," I said, as our cab fishtailed down Second Avenue, while I searched my pockets for the address of the party. " 'To put together a collection such as this for publication—to give it the time and attention it properly requires, so it appears to have some kind of shape, however imposed or arbitrary—is to . . .' "

I took a breath.

"May I?" Ilene asked, extending a neatly manicured hand for the book.

She opened it at random and began reciting: " 'And so it was that I found myself in the position I had been dreaming of for years: thrust over a man's knee, being soundly spanked for some concocted misdeed. . . .' "

Midsentence, she stopped reading and tossed the book out the window of the speeding cab.

I laughed out loud—as much at her deadpan delivery and timing as her wordless review.

"So where's the party?" she asked.

"Twenty-eighth Street and the West Side Highway!" I shouted at the driver, sounding perhaps a little too excited.

Over the next few weeks, I became . . . her walker. But her *number one* walker. Our dates were always press events, because then they didn't seem so much like real dates—platonic marathons fueled by oddball encounters. At an HBO dinner at Le Cirque, I was in the men's room, urinal-to-urinal with Regis Philbin, asking him to come back to my table because Ilene had a crush on him. "Sure, pal!" the great man exclaimed. "Always glad to be in service of young love." She swore she'd never wash that cheek again.

"As the spanker said to the spankee?" I asked.

"*Ew*," Ilene answered.

She was wearing Comptoir Sud Pacifique Vanille, which, as she said, "brought to mind golden butter cake." Really, I liked them all, and kept trying to come up with offers she couldn't refuse. We were so at ease in each other's company, people we'd just met were asking, "How long have you two been married?"

At some point, a man has to stop telling himself he's waiting for the right moment and plunge into the wrong one. Mine started at a party where some slick Hollywood suit was trying to get Ilene to go to VIP's—one of those high-end strip joints that gave Billy's a bad name.

"No, you don't," I said, steering her out of the party and onto Sixth Avenue, thinking if I didn't move now it would be too late.

A cab skidded up.

I blew on the dice and rolled.

"*Noooo*," Ilene said, smiling but dodging my lips for a cheek brush. "G'night!"

Denied.

I thrust my hands in my pockets and walked the two bleak blocks of Eighteenth Street home.

But lucky is the man blessed with the knack of suppressing unpleasant emotions with cold calculation. I'd made a plan to hang out with Ilene at an ABC party at Tavern on the Green a couple of nights later. I'd keep the plan—but add a twist. Solange.

Because I hadn't asked her out or even called in several weeks, or maybe because the fear was gone from my voice, she said yes. I think she sensed that she wasn't at the top of my To Do list anymore.

That didn't make it any easier. As soon as we got into the courtyard of Tavern on the Green, she started in on my *Mlle.* column, quoting it back at me like a prosecutor brandishing incriminating evidence.

"And what do you have against *cats*?"

"The musical?" I asked, craning my neck over the sea of suits in search of Ilene. "I've never actually seen it, but—"

"You wrote in your column this month that men hate women with cats."

"Did I?" I asked.

Out of the black shiny bag slung under her bangled arm she produced the current *Mlle.*

"You wrote, 'Men would rather date a woman with two kids than two cats. Cat ownership says something about a woman we'd rather not hear. Loneliness. Repressed sexual desire. A bedroom that smells like kitty litter.' Shall I go on?"

"Please," I said, still craning.

" 'One cat may be okay, but the second cat is usually the result of the bizarre belief that the first cat "needs company." ' " Solange made sarcastic rabbit ears with her free hand to mimic my sarcastic quotation marks and continued. " 'This turns the typical dating relationship into a full-blown "family" scenario.' "

More rabbit ears.

"Do you know how many cats I used to have?" she asked me.

"No, but you know those columns are *supposed* to be exaggerated a little—"

"Five."

"Oh. Well, not every—"

"They all died. It was a very rare—"

"Ilene!" I shouted.

Some guy had his arm around her waist at the buffet table. She wriggled free and came over holding a plate of hors d'oeuvres.

"I think you two know each other," I said. "From the Algonquin."

"I love your armlet," Ilene said, then, gesturing to the magazine, "Are you a fan of the Men column?"

"Yeah," Solange said, putting it back in her bag, and slipping off for a refill.

"Try one of these," Ilene said. "They're amazing."

I grabbed for a puffed something ball.

"I'm jealous," Ilene said, with a wink. "And flattered."

"What do you mean?" I asked.

"You *know*," she said, smiling. "It's so . . . transparent."

Foiled!

Ilene saw through my cheap jealousy ploy, yet seemed to find it—was this possible?—*endearing.*

"Who's the suit?" I asked, jerking my chin at the guy who'd been pawing her at the buffet table. "Another one of your agents?"

Now *I* was jealous. How did this happen?

"Who, 'Hands'? That's what I call him. I always see him at these things. Guess I'll just have to go back to fending him off. I had been hoping for dinner with you tonight."

"You could come with—"

"No," she said. "I don't want to horn in on your date. Here she comes. Good luck!"

Please, horn! I thought, suddenly and too late.

"Never let me go out with her again," I said.

"Ilene?" Viv asked, pouring me more milk.

"*Solange*," I said, working my way down a row of Fig Newtons.

"You slept with her on the first date and nothing since then?" she asked.

"Slept."

"I told her not to do that," Viv said. "I said the basic thing about guys is they want to have sex with you. The rest is ancillary. The good ones want more than that, because it's boring *just* to have sex. But *not* to have sex with him is setting up some kind of power thing that he's not gonna forget."

"You told her that, about me?"

"I thought it might help," Viv said.

"It didn't."

"And Ilene's not sleeping with you either."

"No," I said.

"People should just have sex on the first date," Viv said. "Because there's no way you can know if you really like someone or not until you've had sex."

I began to wonder, not for the first time, if Viv knew what she was talking about. For one thing, she'd been married five years. And she only ever set me up with wildly inappropriate women.

"Is Ilene coming to your birthday party?"

"I hope so."

"And Solange?"

"Dunno."

"Tabitha?"

"Probably."

"By the end of the night, you'll know who the right woman is," Viv said, and threw me a fresh package of Newtons.

Ilene stayed late, sneaking a KFC drumstick into her signature micropurse on her way out. Tabitha departed uncharacteristically looped, asking where the 'Rangement was going. Solange showed, very late, and vanished after giving me a card that said, "Now you're only half my age." I watched the sun rise alone, from my couch, and sleepwalked into the office around noon. My mother was on my voicemail.

"Your father had a minor stroke last night."

I didn't wait for the end of the message. He'd lost some feeling in his right side, but it was already coming back. The hospital had released him this morning. I talked to him. He sounded fine, told me the doctor said there was no reason to cancel the trip to Barcelona in June, where I was going to meet them for a week.

My hangover segued seamlessly into a day-long asthma-allergy attack. I couldn't breathe, couldn't see. My eyes poured pollinated tears, no matter how many times I doused them with drops. I was substance-abusing my inhaler, the unpleasant side effect of which was thumping heart palpitations.

In the middle of my allergy/heart attack, Ilene called, to thank me for the party, and throw out a "crazy idea." A summer share in the Hamptons. She knew about my Kay 2 experience, but promised this would be different. Fun. With fun people. She didn't have any of them lined up yet, just me.

"Isn't it a little late to start looking for a house in June?"

"That's when you get the good deals!" she said, sounding like a seven-year-old trying to convince her father to buy her a new bike, the one with the banana seat and high handlebars.

"Who can we get?" I asked.

"We'll find people. What about your friends? That TV guy—Ted? He must have money."

I tried to imagine Tad handing out his Mr. Loofah card at polo matches.

"We might be better off with your friends."

HE HASN'T CHANGED A BIT

Is it weird to vacation with your parents when you're thirty-five? I never thought so. They went to Spain every other year or so, and I joined them if I could. In Calzada de Calatrava, our ancestral village, I could bask in the hot La Manchan sun and the adoration of my Spanish aunts, even if I didn't understand half of what they were saying. I tagged along as my father called on ancient cousins or historic sites from his youth. Over here I got stuff he never seemed to talk about at home, as he loosened up around his sisters, ancient cousins and, especially, Tomàs Bartrolí, his oldest friend.

When I arrived in Barcelona, they were staying with Tomàs in La Floresta, a hilly northern suburb. The house was a pink stucco edifice emblazoned high on one wall with a symbol of his invention: a question mark with an infinity loop underneath:

?

∞

That was Tomàs. A character. Compact and wiry with a gaunt face, hawkish nose and gray-black hair, he was my father's age but his temperamental opposite. Tomàs could hardly walk by a compatriot without stopping to converse, cajole, shout, sing and run through all the emotions of tragedy and comedy in the time it took to ask directions. A historian by profession, he seemed more like an actor locked in a character role. His favorite exclamations in English were "*Dammit!*" and "*Wow!*" (sometimes extended to "*Wow-wow-wow!*"). Frequently, he broke into song. "I hate myself, but I am always singing," he said. "I have a difficult happiness!"

"He hasn't changed a bit in forty years," my mother said.

And in his company, my father was transported back even farther. At Monjuic, an old fort converted to a military museum, he pointed out one of the big guns he'd used as an artillery officer during the Spanish civil war. "Not actually manning," he said, "but supervising, doing all the trigonometric calculations." As we walked around the fort's windy battlements, he unloaded a barrage of memories.

"We were in the mountains, far from the action," he said. "Only once did we come under attack, from Franco's so-called Moors—his North African troops. The soldiers on our side were terrified. Many of them had never seen a black face in their lives. I was scared, too, but I had to keep their spirits up and persuade them to stay at their posts."

I saw Tomàs sitting on a bench with my mother, gesticulating wildly, and took the opportunity to ask about St. Cyprien. When the war was lost, many of the anti-Franco forces fled across the Pyrenees and the French, being the French, had interned them in concentration camps on the coast. "Transit camps," they called them. That was about as much as I knew. It was obviously not a pleasant memory, so I tried to craft a question that wouldn't put him off. I went for the most general.

"How did you survive?"

He shrugged. "My guardian angel, I suppose."

I assumed he'd stop there.

"It was no more than a barbed-wire pen on a desolate stretch of coastline. No protection from the elements." He looked down at the worn stone under our feet. "A small stream ran through the center of the camp into the ocean. That was the only source of water, for drinking, bathing, everything. Many of the men starved, or died of exposure. Some went mad. Eventually, the Red Cross was let in and built shelters."

As we kept walking, I pressed for more.

"How did you get out?"

"More luck, really. My English cousins. Because they were willing to vouch for me, I was permitted to leave."

That was 1939. It was hard to picture my father at that age, though I'd seen film of him then, on my trip here with Elisabeth. We went with my parents to Fuentevaqueros, the town outside Granada where Lorca's birthplace had been turned into a museum-shrine. My father had been in La Barraca, Lorca's traveling theater troupe, and on display were programs for Calderon's *La Vida es Sueño* (*Life Is a Dream*) with Lorca playing Death, and my father, under a long Jehovan prop beard, as God. An elderly tour group arrived and the curator screened footage of the troupe erecting stages in village squares to perform the dramas of Spain's Golden Age. And there was my father, at twenty-one, speeding across the screen in the coveralls they all wore, at the comically accelerated pace of an old silent movie, which this was.

Tomàs led our homage to Catalonia at a frenetic pace. My father could have kept up, but steadfastly held my mother's arm, helping her negotiate the cobbled streets. He would have retired here, I think, somewhere in Spain. But stayed in Canada for her. I wondered if good marriages had to mean sacrifice, or if it didn't feel like sacrifice if it was a good marriage.

At the end of the week, my parents left for Torrevieja, a seaside town near Alicante, to see Paca, the youngest of my Spanish aunts, and I went to the airport. Tomàs came with me and, in the café looking over the planes, asked me his six questions.

"Where would you prefer to be? With whom? Doing what? With whose money? What next? What about next month?"

Each query was put with full quiz-show drama. I didn't have any winning answers, so I quizzed him for more information about my father's first life, before my mother and me.

"So did you go to Venezuela together?" I asked.

I was trying to get him to cough up some bachelor escapades or angst from the years when he and my father were on the loose in Caracas, before he'd met my mother and settled down to a happy, productive domestic life in Canada.

"I went first, then he followed," Tomàs said. "We bought an old army jeep together and—*Goddammit!*—we were almost killed in it driving over a bridge. It rolled over into some mud. *Wow!* The first thing your father said was, 'Are you hurt?' Not, '*I* am hurt.' But 'Are *you* hurt?' His first marriage was not going so well. I don't know if I should be telling you these intimacies, but I suppose a son has a right to know."

Watching the planes take off one after the other, I listened to tales of my father's struggles with women—his own youthful, impetuous marriage, and episodes of what he himself had called "temporary madness." It amazed me that he could have had the same problems as I had, and survived them. And as his old friend railed and held forth, I realized another thing: Tomàs was his Tad.

"He has many books and great accomplishments to his name," Tomàs said. "A wonderful wife, a son. I have none of these things, *dammit*. But I have my freedom, you see? I have my freedom."

Iberia's 757 flight to JFK was full of semester-abroad students. Next to me, a Rutgers junior with a Power Ranger tattooed on her shoulder prattled away about how she couldn't eat the food her "*señora*" cooked for her because it was all *fried*. I congratulated myself for feeling not a twinge of desire for her. Well, maybe just a twinge. Pretending to sleep, I thought of Tomàs and my father as young bachelors. How one chose freedom, the other marriage, twice. His was my model. I was no eternal bachelor. But if I were to try again, I'd first have to answer the second of the six questions: *With whom?*

I'd narrowed it down. I was getting closer.

My *Mlle.* contract was up for renewal. Viv had warned me her replacement wanted to replace me with some-one more sensitive. All I needed to do was "work her a little." Go to lunch, drinks, and I'd be safe for another year. But the Men column now seemed as boring and juvenile to me as the idea of flirting with a female editor to keep it.

I quit.

Then I called Solange. I quit her, too. "You don't have to be all good-bye-y," she said. Yes, I did.

Next on my hit list was Elisabeth. Even after the "someday I hope we can sit down and talk about your silence" letter, she kept up a Chinese water torture of calls, messages and correspondence full of blithe bonhomie. Her last one said she and "the family" were all coming to New York for a few days. Did I want to have brunch?

Sliding into the smooth wooden booth at Pete's Place, I sipped my orange juice, knowing exactly what I wanted to say. When she pulled out more baby pictures, I handed them back and said I did not want to see baby pictures. I said it had been six years since we split up. There was no need for us to "keep in touch." She had her life and I had mine. I had never understood her desire to maintain the connection to me this long and I still didn't understand her disappointment now. We were together when we were very young. It didn't work out. How was that a lifelong bond? I suppose I may have sounded a little cold and vindictive, but that was a bit of an act. I didn't have it in me to be angry at her anymore. I thought coldness was the only way to get through. I gave her Michael's speech to Fredo in *Godfather II*: *I don't want to know you or what you do. I don't want to see you at the hotels, I don't want you near my house. When you see our mother, I want to know a day in advance, so I won't be there. You understand?*

Well, not the hotels and the mother part. But that week I got back from Spain, I was taking care of all family business.

Now, Tabitha. I rehearsed my script—*You're right, this Arrangement isn't fair to either of us*—and dialed.

"Sir!" she said. "Wanna come over?"

"Be there in two minutes."

Okay, maybe not *all* family business.

Keeping after Ilene made no sense. On hiatus from long-term involvement, she said she wasn't dating right now. Not me, not anyone. But the morning after Tabitha, I called to demand an explanation.

"What's happening with our house in the Hamptons?" I asked.

She'd recruited an English bird from *Marie Claire,* Michele Lavery, and *Allure*'s publisher, Alexandra "Sandy" Golinkin.

I told her she could count me in. Summer weekend access was the only way to advance my strategy of Maximum Exposure. The more time she spent with me, the less she'd be able to resist my charms. Or, I'd look like an even bigger walker than I did now.

The search kicked off that Saturday, in her parents' Mercedes. No twee inns. Day trips. The train to her parents' place for the car, then the Long Island Expressway. We covered a lot of ground on those commutes.

Biographical: Her mom had an entire room devoted to sprouts.

Religious: "You can't just have neurotic Jews marrying each other," Ilene said. "It's good to mix in a little Cossack blood."

Psychological: Ten years of analysis, neo-Freudian, four days a week—no mere mental manicure.

Her college boyfriend, a pitcher with a Yogi Berra streak, told her, "You're the first girl I dated not for her looks." I saw what he meant. She had a nice face, pretty, but more than that, it was an interesting face, with myriad expressions. I had plenty of time to study it from my shotgun seat, always wondering which one was going to turn up next.

There was her lady hot-rodder face, when she doubled over the wheel and floored the gas to "peel out." The hardball negotiator face she made when we checked out houses, which I tried to break up with juvenile clowning. "That thing looks like something out of *Papillon,*" I cracked, as some New Age eco-freaks showed off their homemade sauna. "Or the hot box in *Cool Hand Luke.*" And her sexy face, brown eyes lowered over a vodka gimlet at the bar of Bobby Van's.

Lazy June afternoons stretched before us. It was like high school again, hanging around with the cool girl I had a crush on. I was in full Eddie Haskell mode with her parents, flattering and praising whenever we picked up or dropped off the Mercedes. Sometimes we lingered at their suburban spread, to swim, watch some big-screen TV or get into trouble at the golf club. I don't play golf, but I hit such a long straight drive on the first tee that Ilene thought I was a hustler. Then I started with the mulligans. On the back nine, a Sansabelted retiree screeched his golf cart up to us, waving a stained Titleist in our faces.

"One of yours?" he snapped. "This isn't a practice course!"

A sympathetic caddy advised us to let this "Mr. Sapperstein" play through.

Ilene's eyes glinted mischievously. An hour later, we were at the 7-Eleven, cruising the aisles for weapons of juvenile destruction.

"Eggs?" she asked.

"Check," I said, throwing her a carton.

"Shaving cream?"

"Double check."

"Toilet paper?"

"Triple check."

We loaded our supplies into the Mercedes and patrolled the leafy suburban streets under cover of dusk, calling 411 for our enemy's address, ready to lay waste to his front yard. "Sapperstein!" we cursed, shaking our fists through the sunroof, and never did find the house. But it was fun.

We always had fun.

We still needed a fifth to fill the house. I'd run into Malucci at a party. He'd asked me to go in on a house he was trying to put together. I suggested he defect to ours.

"Whatttt?" Ilene said, throwing a lot of Long Island into the final consonant. "I didn't spend a hundred grand on therapy to share a summer house with my ex-boyfriend."

"You broke up three years ago," I argued. "Ancient history!"

"Phyllis is going to fire me," Ilene said, Phyllis being her shrink. "I can just hear her at our next session: 'I'm sorry, Ilene, I tried my best. . . .'"

I knew bringing in Malucci was a bad idea on many levels. Besides being the editor of a magazine called *Extreme Golf*, his reputation with women was even worse than mine. But better him in the house than no house at all.

I brokered a deal.

IT'S NO FUN WITHOUT YOU

The Pact, as it came to be known, stipulated that neither Malucci nor Ilene was allowed "sleepover guests." As long as they didn't bring their dalliances home, everything would work out just fine.

July Fourth was the first weekend at our small, revoltingly quaint nineteenth-century barn. I spent an hour throwing out twig garlands and potpourri. I would have dumped everything except the Sub-Zero, but I had more pressing design issues.

There were four bedrooms and five of us. Malucci and his golf clubs got the master, on the main floor, because he was paying a grand more than everyone else. Michele and Sandy took the small single rooms on the second floor. Ilene was in the attic, nicknamed Chucky's Room because of the creepy little rocking chair in the corner. I was on a futon in the living room.

That was fine for now. But I couldn't help noticing that Chucky's Room had two beds under its low, pitched roof. . . .

By Saturday, I'd finagled my way into one of them.

We'd spent the day at the beach, me chasing Ilene into the surf, pretending I loved semi-drowning in frigid eight-foot waves. As much as I'd planned to mock and revile this whole Hamptons scene, I found myself succumbing to its seductive surfaces. Especially our corner of it, whose flat farmland, wide-open sky and golden light were like a Dutch landscape, with bagel shops. But then, seduction was on my mind.

That night, we fireworks-gazed at the compound of a local restaurateur whose bald head and huge glasses were as impressive as his ocean view. Back at the barn, we were both punch-drunk and sun-stroked enough for me to follow her upstairs professing a dire need of an aloe application in hard-to-reach places. I declared myself "the Canadian Patient," moaning for Juliette Binoche and my morphine and flopping onto the unmade twin bed. Ilene had a giggling fit and fell out of hers.

"Perhaps you would be more comfortable over here," I croaked, in a lilting Indian accent now, keeping up my nothing-to-lose approach. "I assure you I can accommodate your slender bulk."

"That is a most pleasant idea," Ilene mimicked, adding in her native tongue, "but it's not gonna happen."

Just planting the seed. I drifted off contentedly on the bare mattress.

I was less contented in the morning when, shambling into the kitchen, I stopped in horror at the sight of Ilene bent over Malucci's foot, tending to some obscure golfing injury. "Come on," she was saying. "It doesn't hurt that much."

It seemed I wasn't the only one on her critical list. Maybe I'd been too blasé about letting the Golf Guido play through.

What did she see in this guy? I knew. He was about my height, dark hair, cocky, "emotionally unavailable"—he was me, before I met Ilene. And she lapped it up, making him eggs in the morning, fetching him drinks, driving him—in *our* Mercedes!—to the driving range. I reveled in any flare-ups of whatever had driven them apart three years ago. During one of our sunny picnic table lunches in the backyard, Sandy introduced the subject of how to get rid of a boyfriend.

"I just date them for three years," Ilene said, throwing some shade in Malucci's direction.

"Well, that's a surefire way of getting rid of them," Malucci said.

"Actually two years would have been enough."

Much as I delighted in these spats, they also troubled me. I saw live embers, a torch not fully extinguished—if not for him, then the player persona he represented. But a club-swinging, cigar-puffing Alpha male should never underestimate an extremely competitive Beta.

On our second weekend, I upped the ante from Platonic Pal to Overtly Enamored Friend. On the beach, I made sure we had adjacent towels. In the backyard, I sidled up to her recumbent, bikinied form and plied her with cheesy come-ons.

"Is this *chaise longue* taken?"

"Who are you, Pepe Le Pew?"

I might have been offended had not that suave Gallic skunk been one of my favorite Looney Toons—and an early role model. I made my intentions clear, but with a protective smoke screen of irony.

In the kitchen, I sat on the wicker sofa with a cocktail and a bemused expression, watching my favorite cooking show, *The Chaotic Chef*. Its host, in a tomato-print sundress, worked from no recipe, or discernible plan. She'd loot the local farm stand, sometimes the neighboring farmer's fields, then spin into crazed activity, covering all surfaces with bowls of abandoned sauces, fanning burnt breadcrumbs, searching for a lost piece of cheese. Her sidekick was a delightfully unruffleable English bird. The climax of the program was a creative crisis that could be resolved only by recruiting the audience of one to sample some Cuisinart-ed herb or crab puree and asking: "Do you think it would be better with basil or mint?" As if I knew, but it was flattering to be asked.

"You're a whiz in the kitchen," I said into the eye of the hurricane one afternoon of Weekend Three.

Ilene stopped concocting one of our al fresco feasts long enough to give me a quizzical squint. "I never know if you're making fun of me or if you mean it."

"*Of course* I mean it," I said. "I would *never* make fun of you. I'm just saying you have an intimate relationship with food."

She was also on speaking terms with liquid refreshments, and was the chief instigator and organizer of our sunset cocktail hours.

Ilene shook her head.

"Sometimes I feel like a big tuna and I'm watching you *reeling* me in," she said, then sent me off to fire up the grill.

Now she had me. My father never grilled, a vestige of his old-country view that cooking is done by women and indoors.

"I don't know how," I whined.

"Well, as my people say, this is the summer you become a man."

I went outside and began the manly business of frowning at dead coals. Just then, our next-door neighbor charged through a hole in the hedge. Alex Kuczynski was a tall, blonde dynamo from the *Observer*. Once I had explained my problem, she whipped off her white blouse and went to work in just her black bra and cutoffs.

"I've got what you need," she said.

I was inclined to agree.

She retrieved from her side of the hedge a giant can of lighter fluid.

"Thanks," I said, dodging the environmental disaster of flame and smoke roiling up from the old red Weber.

"Anytime."

At this tender moment, Ilene came out with an armful of corn.

"Uh," I said. "We were just—"

"See ya!" Alex waved, scramming.

"*Hmmm,*" Ilene said. "I never thought of wearing a black Wonderbra when helping neighbors light their briquettes."

I looked forward to dinner: chicken *jalouse.*

A reaction, any reaction, was good.

Idling in the backyard with the house copy of *You'll Never Make Love in This Town Again*, the Hollywood hooker memoir, we all took turns doing dramatic readings. I gloated gleefully over Ilene's grossed-out squirms and squeals as I recited its nastiest accounts of celebrity depravity.

I was always on the lookout for new properties to amuse her.

HBO had sent Malucci the screenplay of a new movie called *The Rat Pack* for a possible plug in *Extreme Golf*. He had no use for it, but I saw potential. In the mothy lamplight of Chucky's Room, I read to Ilene, doing all the voices. Frank, Dean, Sammy, Peter Lawford, a little JFK. Never more than half-awake, she cooed over each impersonation in my ham act. Her starstruck fan loosened up the performer in me. I was coming up with bits I didn't even know I had in our private nightclub.

And still, we remained chastely in our twin beds. Only now it was by design—*mine.*

The balance of power had shifted. The last few nights, Ilene had been parading around in a filmy nightie, showing off her sunburn. But I figured I only had one more chance to make a play. The timing wasn't *quite* right. There were still six weeks of summer to go—an eternity if I blew the moment.

So it was not without trepidation that I took myself out of the action for the next ten days. As far as I was concerned, I still had competition in the master bedroom. Not to mention that shirtless French guy at the tennis courts.

OH!

I thought of that bare-chested Parisian, who shouted *"jolie!"* every time he hit a winner, as my own doubles partner ran frantically around the deuce court at the Pasadena Ritz-Carlton, admonishing himself for each unforced error.

"Kato!" he'd exclaim good-naturedly. Or, "Kaelin!"

A likable fellow. He was after my friend A. J. Jacobs, on the other side of the court, to ghostwrite his autobiography, putatively titled *The Sixteenth Minute.*

A.J. worked at *Entertainment Weekly.* We were here because this hotel equivalent of a gated community was where the TV networks rolled out their new fall shows for the press every year. The hundred-odd members of the Television Critics Association (of which I was a lapsed member) cannot be bought, but we could be *rented* for a couple of weeks—as long as a fleet of stretch limos ferried us to free dinners at Spago with interviewable starlets. I'd bellied up to this trough before. In my *Washington Times* days, I had to crank out a piece a day. Now I only had to soak up the scene for a fall preview I didn't have to write until September, and gather tidbits to report back to Ilene in nightly dispatches.

My doubles with Kato. My interview with George Hamilton, the bronzed B actor and A-plus bon vivant, who at the opening of another of his cigar bars, was throwing out memorable moves left and right. Emptying flutes of Dom Perignon into the ice bucket because it was "bad luck to drink the first glass." Purring "That's not the Warren *I* knew" when his old pal tried to bag the party because of "family responsibilities." Beatty showed. My interview with Jenna Elfman, star of the new sitcom *Dharma and Greg*, who told me my glasses made me look like "one of those Beat poets, like Clifford Odets." To which Ilene asked, suspiciously, "Did you take them off?"

Holding her attention proved harder on the weekend.

"We miss you!" she shouted, over the clinking glasses and party racket. "It's no fun without you."

Was that French I heard in the background? I had to get back. I never should have let her out of my sight.

I flew in on Friday and on Saturday sat in my office counting the minutes until I was sprung. Every few weeks, a couple of writers had to work Saturday, in case a big story broke—which never happened. Car service voucher at the ready, I worried about how I would justify a three-hour ride to a party in the Hamptons. To a Canadian, that's grand theft auto. But I was willing to risk it. From three thousand miles away, my Chucky's Room romance was looking pretty shaky. From three hours away, it wasn't looking much better.

The driver inched along the Long Island "Distressway"—a bad joke of Ilene's that made me laugh, as it always did in horrendous traffic. It was a little like something Kay 2 might have said, but Ilene wasn't Kay 3. She had pieces of a lot of the other women I'd gone for. (A Pisces!) In some ways, she was like all of them, but none of them. And like me, but not like me. It made me think of a St. Exupéry line from Dave Eddie's wedding (even he was married): "Love does not consist in gazing deeply at each other, but in looking outward together in the same direction." I'd done enough deep gazing. Whatever Ilene had—I still wasn't sure—I needed. Now.

The party was a dinner Linda, Ilene's boss, was hosting at Sunset Beach, a trendified motel/restaurant on Shelter Island. I made it in time for the tail end of cocktail hour. A matched pair of sunkissed *Allure* assistants whose names were either Kristen or Kirsten greeted me at the stairs.

"G'wan *innnn*," one said, her voice a tinkling mint julep.

The fashion and beauty ranks of the magazine were filled almost entirely by southern belles and debutantes.

"She'll be tickled to see *yew*," said the other, batting sororitymixer eyelashes.

Bounding up two at a time, I scanned the restaurant's multileveled deck for Ilene. She was at the bar, in a white dress with an oval cutout below the breast, telling the bartender how to make a Hamilton.

"Can you believe he hasn't heard of it?" she asked, after a welcome back kiss that seemed to skirt the edge of my lips.

Same inscrutably friendly Ilene.

The so-called Hamilton was a concoction I'd seen George order—tequila and cranberry with lime—and told Ilene about. It was safe to say no one had heard of it.

"Shocking," I said. "Two please."

The bartender handed over our drinks, not looking as amused by the whole business as we were, and the evening was under way.

"Is that Matt Lauer over there?" I asked.

"Where?"

"With that hot chick."

"Lemme see," Ilene said, reaching for, and putting on, my glasses. "Wow! Heavy prescription. I feel like I'm high."

"Very intellectual," I said. "Sexy."

"Really?"

"Yeah, keep 'em on."

Leaning against the railing overlooking the water, she peeled them off and fixed me with some intense eye contact.

"I was married once, you know," she said.

"You *were*?" I said.

She waited, taking in my shocked expression.

"No, I'm doing *you*."

The corners of her eyes crinkled and glittered. A bell rang, instructing us to find our table, which was crowded with half a dozen *Allure*ing guests I barely noticed. The chairs were pushed close, almost touching.

"You know, Kristen and Kirsten think I should be going out with you," Ilene said.

"Maybe they're right," I said.

"I'm starting to see things more clearly now," she said, adjusting my glasses.

I slid the fallen spaghetti strap of her dress back onto her shoulder. Every time it slipped off, I eased it back up, letting my finger brush her arm a little longer than was absolutely necessary. During dessert, my hand wandered onto a warm knee.

"Oh!" Ilene said, seeming more pleased than surprised.

On the ferry back from Shelter Island, we were alone at last. Except for all the other cars full of people and the ticket guy rapping at our window. I slipped him a ten spot to get out of my face and opened the moonroof. With the mood just right, after three months of waiting, I leaned in. Ilene didn't pull back, or dodge or brush my cheek. She leaned in, too. And in broad ferry light, we necked in her parents' Mercedes all the way across the water.

———

"Let's go to the beach!" Ilene said, when we got back to the house.

"Wouldn't we be more . . . comfortable here?"

But Ilene was already running around for supplies. Go-cups of homemade Hamiltons and a blanket. Staring at the stars, we buried our feet in the cold sand. The wind coming off the ocean was cold, too. I forced myself not to shiver. *Born in an arctic tundra and I have no tolerance.* I slipped my hand under Ilene's sweater.

She sprang up with crossed eyebrows.

"Omigod! *One-handed?*" She refastened her bra. "How many women have you been with? *Thousands?*"

I laughed, nervously.

"That is the first time, honestly. I've only seen it done on *Happy Days.* You know, when Ritchie and Potsie had one on the men's room radiator at Arnold's and Fonzie came in and unsnapped it . . ."

"I'm off the boil," Ilene said, making her doe-eyed kvetcher face, and brushing the sand off her legs.

I'd blown the moment. If she was looking for an excuse not to get involved, I'd given it to her. Just as well. Under these extremely nippy conditions, I might not have been able to deliver the goods. And then I'd *really* have blown it. So I told myself as we fell asleep in our twin beds, affectionate and chaste as ever.

Sunday night, back from the Hamptons, I stayed home alone in my apartment breathing heavy city air and wondering whether Ilene had make-out moments with all her platonic pallies. The hep-cat agent? Kung Fu Grip? As I was thinking these unthinkables, Tabitha called. But instead of my usual Superman sprint over to her place, I said it was late, that I had to get up early to go to the gym. . . . Fine, she said. She was tired anyway.

In the morning, she called again.

"Something historic happened last night," she said.

"It did?"

"I offered, you declined."

"Oh."

"Did you meet someone?" she asked. "You sound like you have."

"Yes," I said, sounding more sure of it than I was.

Crickets chirped. She broke the silence.

"Remember when we talked about how the 'Rangement would end?"

"The consensus was that I would fuck it up," I said.

"And you did."

My options narrowed to one. Or zero. Ilene and I had uncorked the bottle, but I needed another weekend to know if it had gone flat or was still fizzing. Just one more Saturday night. But I had another plane to catch, to the anti-Hamptons.

YOU'RE TURNING
INTO HIM

Growing up, I spent most of every summer at our cottage on Georgian Bay, a couple of hours north of Toronto in what the locals call "cottage country." Here there are no hot restaurants, no frenzied social posturing, no polo. The point of cottage life is that there is *absolutely nothing to do* but read, swim, eat, drink and maybe pull out the backgammon board when it rains. My parents still spent the whole summer there, into the beginning of fall, and I always came for my mother's birthday.

John Daly met me at the airport in his mother's rusted '86 Cutlass Ciera, aka "the Pimpmobile," which was still loaded with guitars and amps from a Go! Bimbo Go! gig. By 5:30, we were piling beer into the old cottage refrigerator. I poured some gin-and-Frescas—my mother's summer cocktail of choice.

"Zippy little beverage," Daly said, smacking his lips.

We sat on the deck looking out at the water, which jumped and sparkled in the setting sun.

"It is refreshing," my mother agreed, happy to have us around.

"To August the eighth!" I toasted my mother. "A black day for the German army."

"What's that from?" Daly asked, laughing.

"Some World War Two documentary he saw once," she said. "Apparently my birthday was a black day for the German army, though I can't take the credit."

My father, who never drank gin-and-Frescas, said his hellos, then went back to throwing rocks from the water onto the wall he had been building as long as I could remember. It had started as a breakwater against erosion and grew year by year into a curving stone-and-concrete fortification protecting our cottage's entire frontage. Every summer, he built it up and every winter the waves and ice cracked and battered it—a Sisyphean endeavor he never seemed to mind.

The next morning, in the middle of reading a short story by Tomàs, he complained of blurred vision. I joked that maybe Tomàs's prose was the problem, but to be safe we drove him to the emergency room in Midland. He checked out okay, but the following morning I saw him come out of the bathroom, stagger and fall sideways onto a chair. More dizziness. He called his Toronto doctor, who told him to cut his pill dosage in half. Fine again, he went outside to do some weed-whacking.

Later that afternoon, Daly and I were at a roadhouse called the Maple Valley Club. For some reason, I called home. I think to see how much beer-and-horseshoes time we had left before dinner.

"Your father's had another dizzy spell," my mother said. "He's in bed. His speech is slurred. He keeps talking about lunch, because he was in the middle of making it when he fell."

He was in bed when I got there, facing the window, but his gaze was somewhere else.

"Have you had lunch?" he asked me, and I remembered what he had said to Tomàs when their jeep rolled over in Venezuela: not "I am hurt," but "Are *you* hurt?"

At the Midland ER, a lugubrious, gray-haired Eastern European with a Bela Lugosi accent did the examination.

"*Vot* is his prof-*ess*-ion?" the doctor asked my mother.

My father could no longer speak. Neither could I.

"Professor of Spanish literature," she said, adding, "retired."

"I recall a poem by *Pa*-blo Ner-*uda*," the doctor said, reciting a few lines.

No reaction.

"The stroke is serious," the doctor said. "Brain stem. I am *go*-ing to ad-*mit* him."

We stayed in the room as my father slept, unconscious, until a nurse said he was stable and we might as well go home and get some sleep. It was late, but I called Ilene and told her what had happened. She asked how I was doing, how my mother was doing. I played down the gravity of the situation, as much for myself as for her, explaining that he'd had a stroke before and was out of the hospital in a day. I didn't want to lay too much on her. I asked how she was.

"Me? I got too much sun this weekend. I'm turning into an overtanned blonde. My skin's like luggage . . . Louis Vuitton."

"You're funny," I said. "What did you do tonight?"

"Went on a horrible blind date."

That stopped me.

"I can't hear about that."

Maybe I'd played things down a little too much.

"*Agh*," Ilene said. "It was an old setup. From my parents. A bankruptcy lawyer. I shouldn't have said anything. I'm really sorry. I was just trying to amuse you."

"I should go," I said.

"It only made me miss you more," she said. "Call me tomorrow, please?"

I tried to sleep. Was she keeping her options open, when I wasn't? In the middle of the night, the phone rang—an old rotary with a bell like a fire alarm.

"Your father's condition has taken a turn for the worse," said a nurse named Cheryl.

In terrified silence, my mother and I drove as fast as I dared on the unlit country roads. At the hospital, the doctor said it was a coma and, with brain stem damage, it might be better if he didn't come to. In short, "The prog-*no*-sis is not good."

My uncle and aunt came up. Daly went back to the city. He'd already missed a day of work. My mother called Spain. Aunt Paca said my father had cried when they'd said good-bye and said he probably wouldn't see her again. I don't think my mother believed it. "I never saw him cry once in his life," she said.

I drove back to the cottage, sat on the rocks and cried. Ashamed that he wouldn't and I would, I pulled myself together and called the office, then Ilene again.

"Hello, *Allure*."

Eleni. I was in no mood for her third degree.

"Is Ilene there?" I asked quickly.

"Oh, hold on, please, okay? I'll go find her."

I held.

"Hi," Ilene said. "Any change?"

"Your assistant's gotten friendlier."

"You won her over with those six sunflowers you sent for the first six weekends at the house," she said. "But how are you? What's going on?"

I told her, not playing anything down.

"I was sad all day for you yesterday," Ilene said. "I didn't really work. That was my excuse. I guess I won't be able to today either."

That night, standing watch in the hospital room, I started a letter.

Huronia General Hospital
Midland, Ontario
12 August 97

(Tuesday night)

Ilene,

Everyone's gone home for the night and I'm in room 212 alone with my father and my thoughts, which keep turning to you.

He seems so normal lying there now. Breathing deeply and regularly. Blood pressure 140 over 70. Heart rate strong. (So says the Abbot/Shaw Lifecare Pump Model 5—this steel-and-cobalt sentinel, with its red-digital readout.) Like in a deep sleep—only one from which the doctors say he will not awake. I wonder what he is thinking or dreaming, if anything. For some reason I imagine him reliving scenes from his boyhood in the village in Spain, playing soccer in short pants and eating ants on a dare, as he told me he once did. How I wish he would open his eyes and look at me again! Ask me if I'm eating properly, if I'm very busy at work, if I've found a girl to marry.

Top of my long list of recriminations is that I didn't tell him about you. That you never got to know him, or even meet him. You might have had a little crush. You know how flattered I was when you said I seemed "European"? It all comes from him. Like the little cleft in my chin. Pronounced in him—mine you only see in the right light. Note for future TV appearances: adjust lighting to maximize cleft. . . .

In the morning, I drove back to the cottage, and found myself weeping over a set of car keys. I wasn't prepared for this level of waterworks. What would he do in this situation? Focus on the present, the practical. I phoned his doctor in the city, who said, "Your father was a tremendously fit individual."

Was.

Alone again in the room that night, I leaned close to my father and said, "I've met the girl I'm going to marry." Nothing. I went to the payphone in the lounge and called Ilene's apartment. Her machine picked up. Another blind date? If she was pulling back, who could blame her? This was no way to start a love affair. I continued the letter.

(Wednesday night)

Took a walk around the parking lot I call "the yard" because it is our only recreation zone. A vanity plate said, "B HPPY."

The sunshine on the trees makes my mother sad because he can't see it.

Went for a swim this afternoon. The water was choppy and just this side of ice. I thought, I'm numb, I won't feel it. I was wrong. I cold-footed it up to the deck and peeled off my bathing suit—one of his actually. For a moment I stood naked and shivering in the wind, feeling robbed of the ten more years I was sure I would have with him.

The days passed in a daze. The next night, I called Ilene again.

"Today I kept hearing this message over the PA system," I said. "'*Lobotomy,* call the desk.' Turned out to be *phleb*otomy, an office down the hall."

With my father dying, with me dying inside, I was on this hospital payphone trying to make *her* laugh.

She asked how I was.

"All right," I said. "We talked about pulling the IV. Or not putting in a new one when this vein is shot."

"What does the doctor say?"

"He says, 'Dehy-*dra*-tion is a eu-*pho*-ric state.'"

"You still have your sense of humor," Ilene said. "It's inspiring."

Jokes, if not grace, under pressure. That was the guy I wanted to be with her and that was the guy I became.

"The thing is," I said, "in the unlikely event that he were to come back, what kind of shape would he come back in? Paralyzed? Brain-damaged? My mother said, 'Imagine that brain not working.'"

Ilene went quiet.

"I'm sorry to be hitting you with all this heaviness," I said.

"Are you kidding? I'm just trying to picture it. You, and where you are."

"The cottage? It's a time capsule. Totally unmodernized. Getting a phone was a big deal. There are *Time* magazines from the seventies piled up on bookshelves with yellowed old paperbacks. Stuff like *More Stories in the Modern Manner from Partisan Review.* All the Snoopy birthday cards I used to make for my mother are still taped to the wall of their bedroom. So's my first poem."

"How does it go?" she asked.

"'Lightning is frightening / Through the night. / Lightning is frightening / And very bright.'"

"Genius. How old were you?"

"Seven," I said. "It's illustrated with a castle and ghosts. A young William Blake, I was. Or as you call him, 'Robert Blake.'"

"I'm seeing a whole new side of you," she said.

"Sarcastic and mocking?"

"Brave," she said.

"I'm not."

I was a basket case, and I was starting to hate this place. The long corridor, each open door a depressing tableau of some ancient soul frozen in bed or staring blankly at a TV. My friends had started calling, as did his stunned friends and colleagues. "We were just saying how well he always was," one said. With their Spanish accents, it was like talking to him.

Friday night. Ilene would be at the house. Why hadn't she called? That payphone had become my lifeline. I depended on her soothing elixir of comfort and levity.

The letter was losing steam, as was I.

(Friday)

Uncle Don reading a John Creasy mystery called Wait for Death.

Saturday night. Still no word from Ilene. Sunday morning, I woke up with swollen eyes. Allergies, not tears now. I put on his blue polo shirt. It fit perfectly.

"You're turning into him," my mother said.

That made me feel better.

In the hospital lounge, I watched Davis Love III win the PGA final and cry for *his* father. Later, I got through to Ilene and pressed her to tell me about her day at the beach and night at the demolition derby. I said it sounded fun.

"No, I'm just going through the motions."

But was she? Or just being kind?

I slept at the cottage that night, but with the phone in my room. Under the reading light nailed to the wall over my bed, I picked up the letter.

(early Monday morning)

This place is a minefield of memories. Little notes to himself in his hand, a hat on a hook. The books in Spanish and English, the tools and containers of old nails, screws, washers. Three decades of posters from the Spanish tourist office. The Mexi-

can serapes and the silver mask that scared me so much as a
child. The rocks of unusual shapes or smoothness (one like a
Brancusi) he mounted on blocks of wood and varnished to look
like they'd just been pulled out of the water. The little
makeshift table on a tree stump in the back where he'd sit and
read for hours and hours. . . .

The fire-alarm ring jolted me awake a few minutes before seven.

A nurse. "Your father has passed away."

No one ever wants to say "die."

I dressed—his blue polo shirt again—and brushed my teeth with detached calm. My mother came out of her bedroom in her nightgown.

"What was that call?" she asked me.

"He died fifteen minutes ago," I said.

She started crying. I, determined not to, hugged her. Don came out and hugged her, and ours is not a hugging family. She wanted to come to the hospital. I made her stay and eat breakfast.

The first shock was his smallness. The usual ruddiness was gone from his face. I touched his forehead. Still warm. As I slipped his watch from his wrist, it caught on the hospital name tag. I tugged it free with nervous impatience and put it on my wrist, where it hung loosely. I gathered up his slip-on shoes from the floor, the shirt and shorts that had been put in the closet a week ago and never worn again. I took the clothes to the car and waited in the early-morning sun for my family to come.

The water was calm. I went in, then drank a beer on the deck. I packed my things and folded up the letter to Ilene, unsigned and unsent, in case there wasn't an Ilene—as in the girl I was going to marry—when I got back.

I locked all the doors and turned off the electricity and water and closed the curtains, as we did at the end of every summer.

The Chevette seemed empty with just my mother and me. I tried to offer my own elixir of comfort and levity over Quarter Pounders at a sprawling highway service station.

"I once dropped acid in a McDonald's," I said, and proceeded to regale her with tales of my youthful malfeasance I hoped were shocking enough to take her mind off everything.

"I had no idea!"

"Oh, there's more," I said, and gave her all the material I had.

A tall, only slightly Dickensian man in a stiff green uniform suit handled the funeral arrangements. My mother and I picked out the music: a piano piece by Granados, Andrés Segovia playing "Recuerdos de la Alhambra." She wrote down a lyric from a flamenco lament she always liked: *Me duelen los ojos de mirar sin verte.* ("It hurts my eyes to look without seeing you.")

The service was—how can I put it?—awful. Well-intentioned, but with too much God for a man who'd given up Catholicism at something like thirteen. I wore his watch, an old wind-up with its original cloth band, and kept checking it to see when this hell would end. Afterwards, I dropped by Dave Eddie's, who'd leapfrogged me into adulthood with a pregnant wife and a published novel. He was sitting in the small yard of his new house drinking beer with his friend Scott Harper.

"My dad died when I was twenty-two," Scott said. "He was my hero. What can I say? It's a gaping hole that never really gets filled. You just learn to live with it."

"How?" I asked him.

The memorial was set for a month later. I flew back to New York early Saturday morning, changed at my apartment and took the first bus out. It pulled into Bridgehampton around 11:00. I saw Malucci standing in front of the Candy Kitchen—not the welcome committee I'd imagined.

"So, are you ever going back to work?" he said, once we were in his car and he was flooring it east on Highway 27 to Wainscott.

I looked at him.

"Not on a Saturday I'm not."

That was the extent of our small talk. When we got to the house, I saw why he'd been sent to pick me up. Ilene and Michele were in the kitchen, with aprons on. Sandy, who never cooked, stood up from the sofa and said "Nice tan!" and offered the words of condolence Malucci had been unable to find in his golf bag.

"I'm gonna get a little sun before lunch," he said, pushing the screen door to the backyard.

Michele gave me a warm hug. Ilene took off her apron, flushed and frizzy with excitement.

I tried to act like nothing had happened.

"Look what we made in honor of your return," she said, opening the oven door on their creation. "Spanish omelet. *Tortilla!*"

"Frittata, you mean." I put my hand around her waist and kissed her cheek. "You make tortilla in a pan."

"Darn it!"

"Oh *dear*," Michele said.

"You're still a whiz in the kitchen," I told Ilene.

"Let me take your bag," she said.

"I've got it."

"No-no." She tugged it from my hand. "I want to show you into your new room."

Ilene flip-flopped into the master bedroom. The bed was made. A vase on the dresser was filled with sunflowers. Not a golf club in sight. Now I saw why he was sulking.

We ate on the picnic table. Ilene and Michele entertained me with their tale of "nicking" the zucchini flowers from the farm down Wainscott Hollow Road, then barely making their getaway sharing one bad bicycle. I didn't even know you could eat zucchini flowers.

The wine bottles beaded in the August sun.

After lunch, I went inside for a shower. The master had its own bathroom. Under the hot water, woozy from the wine and still half in the waking dream of the last two weeks, I heard a knock.

"I brought you some fresh towels," Ilene said, from the other side of the half-closed door.

"Thanks!" I shouted.

"I'll just leave them right here," she said, and put the towels on the small wooden chair.

"Thanks," I said.

"Want me to bring them in?"

"Sure!" I said.

Now she was under the water, too, soaked in her tomato dress. We'd relocated to the bed when Malucci walked in.

"Anybody seen my golf clubs—oh my God."

Ilene buried her head in my shoulder.

"Close the door behind you," I said.

It wasn't that I didn't want to work. I just didn't want to go *to* work. I felt self-conscious, like showing up on the first day of school with braces or a bad haircut. But it was all right. Friends sent cards and notes. That was all I needed. I didn't need to "talk." I needed drugs. Sandy provided the Valium. When that didn't work, Ilene hummed me to sleep.

"You use me like a drug, too," she said, of those days and nights.

The house voted to extend our rental past Labor Day, though relations between Malucci and me had deteriorated to entire weekends of spaghetti Western stares. At an Indian-themed party where guests were encouraged to come in saris or paint dots or their foreheads, he and I wound up shoulder-to-shoulder at the bar.

"Nice dot," I said.

"You're not playing along," he said.

"Nope."

I wore neither dot nor sari.

"Just like you didn't play along with the Pact," he said.

"I brokered the Pact," I said. "I never signed it."

"Hey, I don't care, but there was a Pact."

"The Pact did not apply. I wasn't a sleepover guest."

The strain of her warring Latin lovers, former and current, Italian and Spanish, was wearing on Ilene.

"I'm not Miss Relationship, you know?" she told me one night when tensions were running high. "It's why I've been trying to avoid them for the last year."

We might not have made it under normal circumstances. But the stakes were higher now. *Did my father have to die for us to be together?* I wondered more than once.

Maybe this was my difficult happiness.

Tomàs flew in from Barcelona for the memorial and accosted me in his usual state of apoplexy.

"*Dammit.* I prepared my speech in English and read it in Spanish! I am a flop!"

I reassured him that it was a fine speech, relieved to find myself not feeling like a flop as I took my mother's arm and accepted condolences and you-look-so-much-like-hims.

Julia came. The wild pre-Raphaelite hair I'd fallen in love with in college had been tamed to a length appropriate for the host of a home-decorating show. Now a bona fide Canadian celebrity, she glowed with cable-TV fame.

"I'm so sorry," she said. "I always really liked your dad."

I thanked her, touched that she'd come, and we stood in silence in the crowded, noisy room.

"Still married?" I asked, giving her one of the old looks.

"Yes, thank you very much," Julia said, giving me one back. "Still divorced?"

"Yes—"

A hand brushed mine.

"But he doesn't like to talk about it."

Ilene. It seemed she'd been witnessing our little exchange. As I introduced them, I noticed the black lace on the hem of her skirt looked sort of Spanish.

"I come to New York all the time," Julia said. "We should keep in touch. Do you have a card?"

"Uh," I said slowly, going through the motions of a man frisking himself.

"Here," Ilene said, producing my *Newsweek* card from her tiny black purse and handing it to Julia with a smile.

I laughed. She had my number now.